T0055090

New to this edition

- A thorough general update of the text.
- Consideration of the legal background to the UK's departure from the EU, the legal process through which the UK left the EU and the key provisions of the European **Union (Withdrawal Agreement) Act 2020**, and the foundation of the new relationship between the European Union and the UK contained in the **Trade and Cooperation Agreement 2020** as implemented by the **European Union (Future Relationship) Act 2020**.
- Consideration of the impact of the **Human Rights Act 1998** on parliamentary sovereignty and proposals for reform in the current political climate.
- Explanation of the key principle in the Supreme Court decision in *R (on the application of Miller) v the Prime Minister* [2019] 3 WLR 589, [2020] AC 373.
- The use of secondary legislation under the **Coronavirus Act 2020** and the **Public Health (Control of Disease) Act 1984**.
- The implications of the Covid-19 pandemic on the operation of Parliament.

Acknowledgements

I owe a debt of gratitude to the Law School at the University of West London, which is committed to a practical and interactive approach to law teaching as well as the implementation of online learning. I wish to acknowledge the kindness of Ms Nina Scott who initially gave me the opportunity to teach Public Law in 1989 and encouraged me in my early years of teaching, and the help and support of Ms Scott's successor, the late Mr William Brown. I also wish to acknowledge the contributions made by Toufik Meddah LLB Hons, a former student, to the development of the pedagogic features and current debates sections, and to the research and writing of the new chapters on grounds for judicial review. Finally, I wish to thank all my colleagues at the University of West London, past and present, without whose kindness, help, and support this book could never have been contemplated, let alone written.

CONCENTRATE
PUBLIC LAW

Colin Faragher

Formerly Senior Lecturer in Law, University of West London

7TH EDITION

OXFORD
UNIVERSITY PRESS

Great Clarendon Street, Oxford, OX2 6DP,
United Kingdom

Oxford University Press is a department of the University of Oxford.
It furthers the University's objective of excellence in research, scholarship,
and education by publishing worldwide. Oxford is a registered trade mark of
Oxford University Press in the UK and in certain other countries

© Oxford University Press 2021

The moral rights of the author have been asserted

Fourth edition 2015
Fifth edition 2017
Sixth edition 2019

Impression: 1

Public sector information reproduced under Open Government Licence v3.0
(http://www.nationalarchives.gov.uk/doc/open-government-licence/open-government-licence.htm)

Published in the United States of America by Oxford University Press
198 Madison Avenue, New York, NY 10016, United States of America

British Library Cataloguing in Publication Data

Data available

Library of Congress Control Number: 2021932618

ISBN 978–0–19–289725–1

Printed in Great Britain by
Bell & Bain Ltd., Glasgow

Contents

Table of cases

Note—All judicial review cases of the form R (Respondent) v Appellant are tabled as R (on the application of Respondent) v Appellant

Table of UK, European and international legislation

Table of UK secondary legislation and non-statutory codes

Introduction to constitutional law

1

KEY FACTS

- Constitutional law in the wide sense is a body of legal and political rules which concern the government of a country.

- A constitution in the narrow sense is a document or set of documents intentionally drafted to form the fundamental law of a country.

- Constitutions may be classified as written or unwritten, flexible or rigid, monarchical or republican, federal or unitary, supreme or subordinate to the legislature, or based on the separation of powers.

- The British Constitution is unwritten, flexible, monarchical, unitary, subordinate to the legislature, and based on a partial or a limited degree of separation of powers.

REVISION TIP

Essay questions, focusing on current debates about the nature and development of UK constitutional law, are common. To begin with, make sure you can define or identify and explain basic concepts accurately.

What is constitutional law?

There are wide and narrow definitions of constitutional law. In the wide sense, constitutional law is simply a set of rules concerning the set up and government of a country. In the narrow sense, constitutional law is a set of rules contained in a document or set of documents intentionally drafted to be the fundamental or basic law which establishes a country and sets up its government. Such documents are often called the 'Constitution' of a country. Definitions of constitutional law in both the wide and narrow sense are discussed at length by Sir Ivor Jennings in the *Law and the Constitution* (1959), KC Wheare in *Modern Constitutions*, 2nd edn (1966), and Colin Munro in *Studies in Constitutional Law*, 2nd edn (1999). They are also considered in standard textbooks written by commentators like Bradley, Ewing, and Knight in *Constitutional & Administrative Law*, 17th edn (2018) and Hilaire Barnett in *Constitutional & Administrative Law*, 13th edn (2019). Whether defined widely or narrowly, constitutional law puts a country and its government together on a legal basis and contains the ground rules which regulate it.

LOOKING FOR EXTRA MARKS?

Essay questions in examinations may focus on the different ways constitutional law is defined and its perceived role within a country's legal system. You should adopt an analytical and critical approach which shows the examiner that you have an enquiring mind capable of drawing conclusions from independent research. Read, compare, and contrast the definitions given by leading authorities and contained in standard textbooks. Make up your own mind about them.

Thomas Paine, in *The Rights of Man* (1791), describes a constitution as an antecedent act of the people which creates the government, defines its powers, and grants it the right to exercise them. This has three implications.

1. Constitutions are antecedent. The word 'antecedent' means that constitutions are made before a country's ordinary laws are made when a country comes into existence, or when the people want a fresh start as far as their government and legal system are concerned. This can happen following independence from colonial rule, revolutions, wars, and fundamental political crises.

2. Constitutions are an act of the people. In this context, 'the people' means everyone legally entitled to participate in the political life of the country and/or their elected representatives. They have to agree on matters like the name of the country, its territory, what legal form it

will take, its flag, national anthem, religion, and capital city. They also have to agree on how the country will be run and by whom and identify and state fundamental human rights.

3. The constitution gives a country legal legitimacy, sets up its governmental institutions, grants them their powers, regulates them, defines the relationship between the citizen and the state, and describes fundamental human rights.

Why do countries have constitutions?

There is a widely held assumption in the modern world that constitutions are necessary. They are assumed necessary to ensure that laws are made in a way which serves the relationship between the citizen and the state positively, by benefiting the country as a whole, and protecting fundamental human rights. They are assumed necessary to make sure that the administrative functions of government are carried out properly within well-defined legal limits only by those empowered to do so. They are assumed to be useful to ensure the efficient administration of justice by setting out the structure and jurisdiction of courts and tribunals. All this may, of course, be very difficult to achieve in practice.

The classification of constitutions

KC Wheare, in *Modern Constitutions*, 2nd edn (1966), expresses the opinion that constitutions can be classified as written and unwritten, flexible and rigid, unitary and federal, monarchical and republican, constitutions in which the legislature or the constitution is supreme, and constitutions based or not based on the separation of powers.

Written and unwritten constitutions

Constitutions in the narrow sense are also called written constitutions. In the decision of the United States Supreme Court in **Marbury v Madison** (1803) Chief Justice Marshall said that those who draft written constitutions intend them to be the fundamental law of the state. This means that they have special legal status. When discussing so-called written constitutions KC Wheare, Colin Munro, and Bradley, Ewing, and Knight also emphasize the point that a written constitution has special legal status. This implies that all laws must be compatible with the constitution and that the organs of government are subject to it as they carry out their functions. Constitutions in the wide sense are also called unwritten constitutions. When discussing unwritten constitutions most legal commentators stress the point that constitutional law has no special legal status.

An example of this is the constitutional law of the UK, the development of which, as Lord Birkenhead observed in **McCawley v The King** (1920) is largely based on historic development with no special legal status. These principles were explained further by the UK Supreme Court in **R (on the application of Miller) v Secretary of State for Exiting the EU** (2017). The Supreme Court held that, unlike most countries, the UK does not have a constitution in the sense of a single coherent code of fundamental law which prevails over all other sources of law. Our constitutional arrangements have developed over time in a pragmatic as much as in a principled way, through a combination of statutes, events, conventions, academic writings, and judicial decisions. In coming to this conclusion, the Supreme Court supported the view expressed by AV Dicey in *Introduction to the Study of the Law of the Constitution*, 8th edn (1915), p 87 that British constitutional law is 'the most flexible polity in existence'.

REVISION TIP

Think how you would define, describe, or explain these terms as legal principles. This highlights the necessity of understanding the historical, political, and social context when reading standard constitutional law textbooks.

Written constitutions may not contain all the rules which govern the constitutional law of a country. This is illustrated by the decision of the United States Supreme Court in **Marbury v Madison** (1803) in which the key constitutional principle, stated by Chief Justice Marshall, is that 'an act of the legislature repugnant to the constitution is void'. This is not expressly written in the Constitution of the United States. Unwritten constitutions, on the other hand, are never solely based on oral customs and traditions. Colin Munro in *Studies in Constitutional Law* (1999) supports this view. The distinction between written and unwritten constitutions, therefore, does not focus on whether or not constitutional law is contained in a document or set of documents. It focuses on the type of legal document used and the legal status of its contents.

Flexible and rigid constitutions

In **McCawley v The King** (1920) Lord Birkenhead observed that the constitutions of some countries contain clauses requiring a special procedure and, in some cases, a special legislative assembly to amend them, while other countries like the UK have no special procedure for making, amending, and repealing constitutional law. He called constitutions which required a special procedure 'controlled constitutions'. Those which did not require a special procedure he called 'uncontrolled constitutions'. KC Wheare recognizes the same distinction referring to flexible and rigid constitutions. A rigid constitution requires a special procedure to make and amend it. A flexible constitution does not.

Federal and unitary constitutions

In a federal constitution the governmental powers are divided between a central government, which may be called the federal government, and state, regional, or provincial governments. Each state, region, or province has its own government. One important feature of a federal constitution is that the member states retain their sovereignty, freedom, and independence. Every power, jurisdiction, and right not expressly delegated to the federal government is retained by the states. It follows that the federal government exercises its powers separately in its own sphere according to the powers delegated to it by the states.

The key feature of a unitary state is that all governmental powers originate from the central or national government. The central or national government can transfer powers to regional and local authorities but these remain subordinate to the central or national government and can be overridden by it. In the context of the UK this means that the Westminster Parliament and the departments of state headed by the Prime Minister, Secretaries of State, and other ministers, run the country as a whole. This is subject to the process of devolution. The Westminster Parliament has transferred some of its law-making powers to the Scottish Parliament, the Northern Ireland Assembly, and the National Assembly for Wales. Some of the work done by central government departments of state for the whole UK has been transferred to the Scottish and Welsh Governments as well as to the Northern Ireland Executive. In London, powers have been given to the Greater London Authority, consisting of the Mayor and the London Assembly. Powers are also granted to local authorities including, under the **Localism Act 2011**, a general power of competence. This means that local authorities have the right to do anything an individual person over the age of 18 can do unless it is forbidden by law.

Republican and monarchical constitutions

A republic has an elected president as head of state who may or may not exercise executive functions within the process of government. France and the United States of America are republics in which the elected president exercises executive powers and is involved in the political process. The Federal Republic of Germany has a non-executive elected president who does not exercise political power. The duties of the German President include the protection and promotion of the well-being of the German people, safeguarding the Basic Law, signing international treaties, and signing off the documents appointing diplomats and civil servants. Political power is exercised by the German Chancellor and the other members of the federal government. A monarchy has a king or queen as head of state who is appointed according to the hereditary principle. The British Constitution is monarchical in this sense.

Constitutions in which the legislature or the constitution is supreme

When looking at the distinction between written and unwritten constitutions, rigid and flexible constitutions, and federal and unitary states, KC Wheare observes that some federal states in particular, which have written and rigid constitutions, require the legislature to make laws which are compatible with the constitution. These constitutions may also stipulate the procedure which must be followed when making different types of laws. An example of this is the Federal Constitution of the United States. Chief Justice Marshall in the US Supreme Court decision in **Marbury v Madison** (1803) said that an act of the legislature which is repugnant to the constitution is void. This means that the constitution is supreme and that the legislature must act in a way which is consistent with the constitution. The UK system of government, which is a unitary state with an unwritten and flexible constitution, is based on the sovereignty of Parliament.

Constitutions based or not based on the separation of powers

The separation of powers presupposes that a system of government is divided up into three functions with three corresponding organs. The functions of government are legislative, executive, and judicial, and the corresponding organs of government are the legislature, the executive, and the judiciary. In such a system the legislature, the executive, and the judiciary should check and balance each other as they each exercise their powers independently. No one person should be able to exercise power over all the organs and functions of government.

Although it is practically impossible to find a system of government completely based on the separation of powers it is equally difficult to find a country which does not at least pay lip service to it. The real value of the separation of powers lies in its potential to prevent tyranny. In this context tyranny means government subject to the personal interests and ambitions of an individual or small group which exercises wide discretionary and arbitrary powers. The separation of powers promotes government which serves the people as a whole and not the political and economic interests of a self-serving and self-perpetuating elite.

 REVISION TIP

Go online and look up a selection of constitutions which illustrate the classification of constitutions. Think about how each constitution fits into the appropriate classification.

 KEY CASES

CASE	FACTS	PRINCIPLE
Marbury v Madison (1803) 5 US 137	Among other things the US Supreme Court had to decide whether it had jurisdiction to review acts of Congress and determine whether they are unconstitutional and therefore void.	Those who draft written constitutions intend them to be the fundamental law of the state. Any act of the legislature which is repugnant to the constitution is void. The US Supreme Court has the jurisdiction to review acts of Congress and determine whether they are unconstitutional and therefore void.
McCawley v The King [1920] AC 691	The Privy Council had to decide whether or not the Legislature of Queensland Australia had power, under s 5 **Colonial Laws Validity Act 1865** to authorize the appointment of a judge of the Supreme Court for a limited period.	There are constitutions which contain clauses requiring a special procedure and, in some cases, a special legislative assembly to amend them. Countries like the UK have no special procedure for making, amending, and repealing constitutional law. Constitutions which require a special procedure are controlled constitutions. Those which do not require a special procedure are uncontrolled constitutions. The appointments were valid.

KEY DEBATES

Topic	'What is a Political Constitution?'
Author/Academic	Graham Gee
Viewpoint	Analyses the notion of a 'political constitution' as it purports to describe the constitution in a jurisdiction, such as the UK, which lacks a legal constitution. Compares the accounts of the UK Constitution by JAG Griffith, Adam Tomkins, and Richard Bellamy.
Source	(2010) 30(2) Oxford Journal of Legal Studies 273–299

Topic	'Emotions in Constitutional Design'
Author/Academic	András Sajó
Viewpoint	Examines the role of emotions in developing the culture of constitutionalism out of which formal constitutions are devised or interpreted. Discusses how emotions operate at a social level, and how regulation may be conceived as emotional restraint.
Source	(2010) 8(3) International Journal of Constitutional Law 354–384

Topic	'Two Doctrines of the Unwritten Constitution'
Author/Academic	Pavlos Eleftheriadis
Viewpoint	This article analyses the parties' arguments in *R (on the application of Miller) v Secretary of State for Exiting the European Union* (2017), on whether parliamentary authorization was required for the UK to give notice of its intention to withdraw from the EU, to examine the nature of the clash between two rival views of the unwritten constitution, pertaining to 'simple sovereignty' and the 'legal constitution'.
Source	(2017) 13(3) European Constitutional Law Review 525–550

Topic	'Reforming an Unwritten Constitution'
Author/Academic	Jack Beatson
Viewpoint	Discusses constitutional reform in the UK since 1997, looking at government initiatives and the roles of parliamentary committees such as the Joint House of Lords and House of Commons Committee. Summarizes developments since 1997, subdivided into the periods 1998–2003, 2003–7, July 2007–March 2008, and March 2008–present. Provides an assessment of the process of reform.

Topic	'Reforming an Unwritten Constitution'
Source	(2010) 126 Law Quarterly Review 48–71

Topic	'Classification of Constitutions'
Author/Academic	Neil Walker
Viewpoint	Argues that unitary conception of constitution is very flexible. Fundamental limits set by unitary conception are not great. Competition between state and other authorities militates against transformation of unitary conception.
Source	[2000] Public Law 384–404

EXAM QUESTION

Essay question

Explain what is meant by 'constitution' and how constitutions might be classified.

Online Resources

For an outline answer to this essay question, as well as interactive key cases and multiple-choice questions, please visit the online resources.
www.oup.com/he/faragher-concentrate7e

Concentrate Q&As

For more questions and answers on public law, see the *Concentrate Q&A: Public Law* by Richard Clements.

Go to the end of this book to view **sample pages**.

Sources of constitutional law and constitutional conventions

2

- The primary sources of constitutional law are the common law, statutes, European Union (EU) law, decisions of the European Court of Human Rights, and the law and custom of Parliament.

- These legal rules play an important role in the process of government.

- Vitally important parts of the process of government in the UK are regulated by binding political rules and practices called 'constitutional conventions'.

- There is an identifiable distinction between binding constitutional conventions and non-binding 'practices'.

- Some writers suggest that they can be recognized and stated with precision by applying the appropriate test.

- The courts have no jurisdiction to grant a remedy where the sole basis of the claim is that a constitutional convention has been breached.

- The only way a constitutional convention can become law is by statute.

Sources of constitutional law

The sources of constitutional law in the UK are:

- the common law;
- Acts of Parliament;
- retained EU law;
- the jurisprudence of the European Court of Human Rights which must be taken into account by the UK courts in cases involving the **European Convention on Human Rights and Fundamental Freedoms**.

See Fig 2.1.

The common law

The binding rules formulated and applied by judges in decided cases in the senior courts have made a vital contribution to the development of constitutional law. Examples of areas heavily influenced by judicial decision-making include the use of the Royal Prerogative by the executive, the rule of law, the separation of powers, and parliamentary sovereignty.

Figure 2.1 The sources of constitutional law

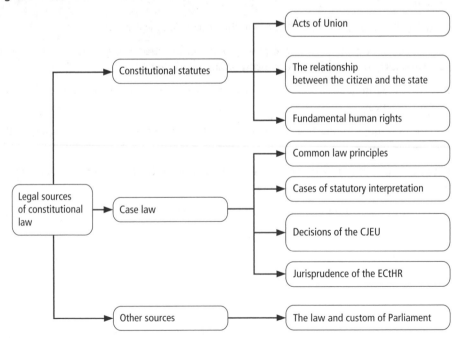

The constitutional role of the courts, when interpreting statutes, was explained by Lord Nicholls in *R (on the application of Spath Holme Ltd) v Secretary of State for the Environment, Transport and the Regions* (2001). The court must ascertain the intention of Parliament. Under normal circumstances the courts will not look at what was said or done in Parliament itself. The judges give the words in a statute their ordinary and natural meaning. The approach is an objective one. The question is whether it is reasonable for a statute to be interpreted in a particular way.

Acts of Parliament

In *Thoburn v Sunderland City Council* (2003) Laws LJ defined constitutional statutes as those which condition the legal relationship between the citizen and state in some general, overarching manner; or which enlarge or diminish the scope of fundamental constitutional rights. Laws LJ concluded that the special status of constitutional statutes follows the special status of constitutional rights. He went on to say that constitutional statutes included **Magna Carta 1297**, the **Bill of Rights 1689**, the **Union with Scotland Act 1706**, the **Reform Acts** which distributed and enlarged the franchise (**Representation of the People Acts 1832, 1867**, and **1884**), the **Human Rights Act 1998**, the **Scotland Act 1998**, and the **Government of Wales Act 1998**. Finally, he said that the **European Communities Act 1972**, is also a constitutional statute because it incorporated into UK law the whole body of substantive Community rights and obligations, and gave overriding domestic effect to the judicial and administrative machinery of Community law.

Retained EU law

EU law was incorporated into UK law by **ss 2** and **3 European Communities Act 1972** ('the 1972 Act'). Its legal status was stated in the following way by Laws LJ in *Thoburn v Sunderland City Council* (2003). Rights given to people under EU law prevailed over the express terms of UK law, including Acts of Parliament made or passed after the coming into force of the 1972 Act, even in the face of plain inconsistency between the two. **Section 18 European Union Act 2011** subsequently made it clear that EU law took effect subject to the will of Parliament. **Section 1 European Union (Withdrawal) Act 2018** repealed the **European Communities Act 1972** on the day set for the UK to exit the EU in accordance with **s 20(1) European Union (Withdrawal) Act 2018**, as amended by subsequent regulations made by the government under **s 20(4)** or by primary legislation.

Rules made by the European Court of Human Rights

Under **s 2 Human Rights Act 1998** the UK courts are obliged to take into account all the rules laid down by the European Court of Human Rights when considering a claim involving the rights contained in **s 1** and **Sch 1 Human Rights Act 1998**. This has meant that new rules, such as those on proportionality, have found their way into UK constitutional and administrative law. This remains unaffected by the UK's exit from the EU.

Constitutional conventions

REVISION TIP

Essay questions on this topic are common. Make sure you understand the arguments dealing with the basis and validity of the distinction between laws and conventions.

Constitutional conventions are binding political rules many of which may be stated with the same precision as laws. AV Dicey, in *Introduction to the Study of the Law of the Constitution* (1885), distinguished between laws and conventions. Laws are enforceable in the courts. Conventions are not: there are no judicial remedies or penalties if conventions are violated.

REVISION TIP

After being able to define constitutional conventions and explain how they are different from laws, you should be prepared to identify the elements of the most important constitutional conventions.

Examples of constitutional conventions

Constitutional conventions are of fundamental practical importance in many vital areas of government. These include the granting of the Royal Assent, the appointment of the Prime Minister, the appointment and dismissal of ministers, the formation and membership of the Cabinet, opening and closing Parliament, government formation in hung Parliaments, and judicial constitutional conventions. They apply to Parliament, the executive, and the judiciary. Table 2.1 gives examples of constitutional conventions which enable the government to run smoothly.

LOOKING FOR EXTRA MARKS?

The constitutional conventions outlined in Table 2.1 are a selection. To gain a fuller knowledge of the true extent and significance of constitutional conventions you should read your recommended standard textbook.

Table 2.1 Constitutional conventions

LAW	CONVENTION
Royal Assent Every bill must receive a Royal Assent after it has passed its necessary parliamentary stages.	The monarch will give the Royal Assent to every bill which has passed successfully through Parliament when advised to do so by ministers.
The appointment of the Prime Minister At common law under the Royal Prerogative, the monarch has unlimited power to appoint ministers including the Prime Minister.	The government must have the confidence of a majority in the House of Commons. This means that the Prime Minister is appointed from the membership of the House of Commons. The Prime Minister is normally the leader of the political party with a majority of seats in the House of Commons. If the party of which the Prime Minister is a member loses its majority in the House of Commons, they, and the other members of the government, will normally resign before the first meeting of the new Parliament.
The appointment of ministers There are no legal rules governing the appointment of ministers beyond the Royal Prerogative at common law and those contained in statutes like the **House of Commons (Disqualification) Act 1975**, the **Parliamentary and other Pensions Act 1972**, and the **Ministerial and other Pensions and Salaries Act 1991**.	The monarch appoints ministers upon the advice of the Prime Minister and ministers are individually responsible to Parliament. This means that ministers are appointed from the membership of the House of Commons and the House of Lords.
The Cabinet The Cabinet is recognized in statutes concerning ministerial salaries and pensions.	The most important constitutional convention governing the Cabinet is collective Cabinet responsibility. This means that members of the Cabinet do not voice dissent on government policy once a decision is taken. A Cabinet minister who cannot sustain a Cabinet decision should resign.
Opening and closing Parliament, hung Parliaments, and government formation The monarch is the only person who has the legal power to open and close Parliament. The life of a Parliament is governed by statutes like the **Parliament Act 1911** and the **Fixed Term Parliaments Act 2011**. The rules governing the conduct of elections are statutory.	In the event of a hung Parliament the incumbent Prime Minister has the first opportunity to continue in office and form an administration. If they are unable to do so (and resigns, or is defeated on the Address or in a no confidence motion at the meeting of the new Parliament) then the Leader of the Opposition is appointed Prime Minister. It is for the political parties to negotiate any inter-party agreement for government among themselves without royal involvement.
The judiciary High Court judges in England and Wales hold their offices by statute during good behaviour, subject to a power of removal by the monarch on an address presented to her by both Houses; by statute they are disqualified from membership of the Commons.	Because the judge's primary task and responsibility is to discharge the duties of office, it follows that a judge should, so far as is reasonable, avoid extrajudicial activities that are likely to cause the judge to have to refrain from sitting on a case because of a reasonable apprehension of bias or because of a conflict of interest that would arise from the activity. A specific application of that principle is that a judge must forego any kind of political activity and on appointment sever all ties with political parties.

LOOKING FOR EXTRA MARKS?

Robert Blackburn's article gives a valuable insight into how the constitutional conventions concerning hung parliaments are determined, interpreted, and applied in the factual context of the formation of the Conservative Liberal Democrat Coalition Government. It also shows how new conventions might be developed. You should read his article.

Enforceability and the distinction between laws and conventions

Although Sir Ivor Jennings, in *Cabinet Government* (1969), said that constitutional conventions are outside the law and not recognized by it, he used cases like ***Watt v Kesteven County Council*** (1955) to claim that not all legal provisions confer directly enforceable rights on the individual. The Court of Appeal had to decide whether a local education authority was in breach of statutory duty because it had failed to provide education for pupils in accordance with the wishes of their parents as required by **s 76 Education Act 1944**. Denning LJ held that the duty to make schools available could be enforced only by the minister and that **s 76** did not create a cause of action entitling an individual to a remedy in the civil courts.

Munro's response to this is that the court refused to recognize an actionable statutory duty because the law said that the duty should not be enforced in this way. The law was enforced. The courts obeyed the law and put it into effect.

REVISION TIP

Views expressed in the standard textbooks are important in constitutional law. In essay questions on this topic you should be able to compare and contrast the arguments advanced by leading authorities. This will make your answer stand out.

Are laws and conventions different in kind?

In *Cabinet Government* (1969), Sir Ivor Jennings said that laws and conventions work in similar ways and that both are obeyed by those to whom they apply. Some conventions were as fixed as laws and could be stated with as much precision. JDB Mitchell, in *Constitutional Law*, 2nd edn (1968), said that it may be wrong to distinguish between laws and conventions because both were based on precedent and can overlap. Munro, in *Studies in Constitutional Law* (1999), says that nothing in Mitchell's argument demonstrates conclusively that distinguishing between laws and conventions will fail. Munro concludes that conventions and laws appear to be similar because they are both rules operating in society. They are not necessarily the same because they look similar.

Are there different categories of constitutional conventions?

Dicey focuses on the purpose of law and the jurisdiction of the courts. He was aware that there are different classes of rules. Some conventions are as important as laws. As political rules they are obeyed to a greater or lesser degree. Maitland, in *The Constitutional History of England* (1961), also recognized that such rules differed in stringency and definiteness. Munro, in *Studies in Constitutional Law* (1999), agreed with Maitland. Munro concluded that it was sensible to have a two-class approach where it is clear that groups of uniform non-legal rules of a high degree of stringency and definiteness exist. Where such uniformity does not exist a two-class approach is not so easily achieved.

Are all constitutional conventions binding?

Constitutional conventions are, generally speaking, binding political rules. Some authorities, however, distinguish between binding and non-binding political rules. For instance KC Wheare, in *The Statute of Westminster and Dominion Status*, 5th edn (1953), said that there were usages and conventions. According to Wheare, a constitutional convention is binding. A usage is a non-binding rule of political practice. A usage may become a convention from a single precedent or by agreement. Many authorities have adopted a similar approach. Hood, Phillips and Jackson, in *Constitutional and Administrative Law* (2001), for instance, incorporate the distinction between usages and conventions into their definition of constitutional conventions. JDB Mitchell, in *Constitutional Law*, 2nd edn (1968), also stressed the need to distinguish between non-binding political practices and binding constitutional conventions. De Smith and Brazier, in *Constitutional and Administrative Law* (1998), said that conventions were forms of political behaviour regarded as binding, and as such were distinguishable from non-binding usage. G Marshall and GC Moodie in *Some Problems of the Constitution* (1971) draw a distinction between obligatory and non-obligatory rules. A rule must prescribe something if it is to guide action or state obligations. The true basis for a rule is prescription not description: description is not a weak form of prescription.

 REVISION TIP

To obtain top marks you must be aware of current debates and critical thinking.

What is the jurisdiction of the court over constitutional conventions?

Dicey's answer is that constitutional conventions are not legal rules because the courts have no power (jurisdiction) to enforce them.

> ### *Madzimbamuto v Lardner-Burke* [1969] 1 AC 645
>
> After the unlawful declaration of independence by the Government of the Crown Colony of Southern Rhodesia in 1965, the UK Parliament passed the **Southern Rhodesia Act 1965** to deal with the circumstances arising from this unconstitutional action. In this case, the question was whether or not Parliament could properly legislate for Southern Rhodesia.
>
> The relevant constitutional convention was that the Parliament at Westminster would not legislate for Southern Rhodesia on matters within the competence of the Legislative Assembly of Southern Rhodesia except with the agreement of the Southern Rhodesia Government.

The key principle is that a constitutional convention has no legal effect in limiting the legislative power of Parliament.

The Privy Council held, by majority, that Parliament could properly legislate for Southern Rhodesia.

In **Attorney General v Jonathan Cape Ltd** (1976) the Attorney General sought permanent injunctions restraining the publishers Jonathan Cape Ltd as well as a newspaper from publishing the diaries or extracts from the diaries of former Cabinet Minister Richard Crossman. The diaries contained accounts of disagreements on matters of policy and details of discussions concerning the appointment of senior civil servants. The Attorney General argued that all Cabinet papers, discussions, and proceedings were confidential and the court should restrain any disclosure if the public interest in concealment outweighed the public interest in the right to free publication.

The following key principles were stated by Lord Widgery CJ. The court must have power to deal with publications which threaten national security. The Attorney General must show (1) that such publication would be a breach of confidence; (2) that the public interest requires that the publication be restrained; and (3) that there are no other facts of the public interest contradictory of and more compelling than that relied upon. Moreover, the court, when asked to restrain such a publication, must closely examine the extent to which relief is necessary to ensure that restrictions are not imposed beyond the strict requirement of public need and there must be a limit in time after which the confidential character of the information, and the duty of the court to restrain publication, will lapse.

This case involved detailed consideration of the constitutional convention of collective cabinet responsibility. Lord Widgery CJ said that there is a specific interest in maintaining the confidentiality of ministerial communications arising from the convention of collective responsibility of Ministers of the Crown, which is that once a policy decision has been reached by the government it has to be supported by all ministers, whether they approve of it or not, unless they resign: that convention and the free discussion between ministers may be prejudiced by the 'premature disclosure' of the views of individual ministers.

Applying theses key principles, Lord Widgery CJ decided to refuse to grant the injunctions. The contents of the first volume of the *Crossman Diaries* were such that their publication, after the lapse of nearly ten years, could not inhibit free discussion in the existing Cabinet and would not, therefore, prejudice the maintenance of the doctrine of joint Cabinet responsibility.

The possible legal enforceability of a constitutional convention which is recognized by a statute was considered by the Supreme Court in *R (on the application of Miller) v Secretary of State for Exiting the European Union* (2017). The Sewel Convention, which is recognised in **s 2 Scotland Act 2016** and **s 2 Wales Act 2017**, states that the Parliament of the UK will not normally legislate with regard to devolved matters without the consent of the Scottish Parliament/Welsh Assembly. Because the legislation concerning the withdrawal of the UK from the EU alters the powers of devolved bodies, it was generally accepted that the Sewel Convention required the legislative consent of the Scottish Parliament and the Welsh Assembly. The UK Supreme Court decided that the courts can recognize the operation of a political convention when deciding a legal question, but they cannot give legal rulings on its operation or scope. The validity of conventions cannot be the subject of proceedings in a court of law. This means that the devolved governments cannot enforce the Sewel Convention against the UK Government or Parliament in the courts. It also gives them no legal right to veto a bill.

Can the courts do anything with a constitutional convention?

Although the courts do not grant remedies for breach of constitutional conventions, they do sometimes look at them, at least indirectly, in the course of legal proceedings. There are two principles:

- the courts may be prepared to take constitutional conventions into account and give an opinion as to their existence and extent; and
- the courts can take constitutional conventions into account to interpret the statutes or Commonwealth constitutions.

The first principle is supported by *Liversidge v Anderson* (1942). **Regulation 18B Defence (General) Regulations 1939** gave the Secretary of State for the Home Department the power to make orders to detain people if he had reasonable cause to believe that they were of hostile association. One such person brought an action against the Secretary of State for false imprisonment, which failed. In coming to its decision, the majority in the House of Lords took notice of the convention that the Secretary of State is answerable to Parliament under the doctrine of ministerial responsibility.

Sir Ivor Jennings, in *Cabinet Government* (1969), said that the existence of a constitutional convention can be determined by asking what are the precedents, do the actors in the precedents believe that they are bound by a rule, and is there a reason for the rule.

This test was accepted and applied by the Supreme Court of Canada in *Reference re Amendment to the Constitution of Canada* (1982). Until the **Canada Act 1982** came into force any amendments to the constitutional statutes of Canada had to be approved by legislation in the UK Parliament. In this case the Supreme Court of Canada had to decide whether the Canadian Federal Government was obliged to consult the provinces and obtain their agreement before requesting an amendment which would affect the relationship between the

Federal Government and the provinces. After applying the Jennings' test, a majority of the Supreme Court concluded that the alleged constitutional convention existed and that it would be unconstitutional for the proposals to go forward. The court did not enforce the convention. This was beyond the constitutional role of the judges.

In *R (on the application of Southall) v Secretary of State for Foreign and Commonwealth Affairs* (2003) the claimant said that the British Government was bound by constitutional convention that it would not introduce legislation making substantial constitutional changes without the approval of the electorate in a referendum unless the proposal was included in its election manifesto. The Court of Appeal held that there was no evidence to support the existence of such a convention.

The second principle is supported by the Privy Council decision in *Ibralebbe v R* (1964). This case arose out of certain criminal appeals from Ceylon (now Sri Lanka). Basnayake CJ, in the Court of Criminal Appeal of Ceylon, held that, in effect, when Ceylon ceased to be a colony and became an independent sovereign state within the Commonwealth, the right of the Crown to hear criminal appeals ceased. The Judicial Committee of the Privy Council took jurisdiction and in so doing took into account the constitutional convention that the Order in Council accepting the Report of the Privy Council turns its report into the equivalent of a judgment of a court.

REVISION TIP

When answering examination questions, the most important thing is the general legal principle which forms the basis of the decision in each case. Essay questions may ask you to explore contextual issues or the significance of the rule.

Can constitutional conventions become law?

REVISION TIP

When considering the essential difference between law and convention, it is vital to distinguish them from customs which can be adopted as common law rules, and conventions, which can only become law through the legislative process.

A constitutional convention can become law by statute. An example of this is contained in **s 20(1) Constitutional Reform and Governance Act 2010**. This provides that a treaty cannot be ratified unless a minister of the Crown has laid a published copy of it before Parliament which has 21 sitting days to object to its ratification by resolution. This is a codification of the Ponsonby Rule.

Parliament may recognize a constitutional convention in legislation. The UK Supreme Court, in *R (on the application of Miller) v Secretary of State for Exiting the European Union* (2017) held that the UK Parliament, in recognizing the Sewel Convention in **s 2 Scotland Act 2016** did not intend it to become law.

Conventions cannot become part of the common law in the same way that customs are capable of doing. This was determined by the Court of Appeal in *Manuel v Attorney General* (1983). This was an attempt to question the legality of the **Canada Act 1982** in the British courts by a minority group within Canada. It was suggested that the constitutional convention that the UK Parliament should not legislate for Canada, except with its consent, might have crystallized into a law by formal recognition or by long acceptance. Slade LJ, giving the judgment of the court, rejected this argument saying that it was 'quite unsustainable in the courts of this country'.

NW Barber in 'Laws and Constitutional Conventions' (2009) LQR 294 at 309 suggests that conventions can become more formalized over time as political actors create authoritative statements of their content and mechanisms which can create, modify, and adjudicate upon, these rules. His comments are particularly based on the publication of the Ministerial Code which contains many constitutional conventions governing the conduct of ministers.

KEY CASES

CASE	FACTS	PRINCIPLE
Attorney General v Jonathan Cape Ltd [1976] 1 QB 752	The Attorney General sought injunctions to restrain the publication of the diaries of a former Cabinet minister.	A court can restrain publication of Cabinet material only where there is breach of confidence or it is in the public interest to do so to protect collective Cabinet responsibility. But this lapses with time according to the circumstances of each case. Applying this principle, sufficient time had lapsed to allow publication.
Madzimbamuto v Lardner Burke [1969] 1 AC 645	The Privy Council had to decide whether the UK Parliament could legislate for Southern Rhodesia, following the Unilateral Declaration of Independence.	A constitutional convention, however important, can have no legal effect to limit the legislative supremacy of Parliament.
Manuel v Attorney General [1983] Ch 77	This was an attempt to question the legality of the **Canada Act 1982** in the British courts by a minority group within Canada. It was suggested that the convention that the UK Parliament should not legislate for Canada except with its consent might by formal recognition or by long acceptance have crystallized into a law.	Conventions cannot become part of the common law in the same way that customs are capable of doing.

CASE	FACTS	PRINCIPLE
R (on the application of Southall) v Secretary of State for Foreign and Commonwealth Affairs [2003] CMLR 18	This was an appeal from the Administrative Court which had refused permission to proceed with judicial review. One of the issues was whether it is a convention of the constitution of the UK that a substantial constitutional change cannot be made (and therefore cannot be adopted) unless such a proposal has been approved by the electorate either as a result of the proposal being included in the manifesto of the party returned to government or in a referendum.	There is no seriously arguable case that a court will determine that an Act of Parliament passed without first having been the subject of a referendum or being included in a party manifesto will for that reason be unenforceable as a matter of law. There is nothing to substantiate that such a convention has the force of law.
Reference re Amendment to the Constitution of Canada (1982) 125 DLR (3rd) 385	In 1980 the Canadian Federal Government devised a package of constitutional reforms which were opposed by a majority of the provinces. The Supreme Court of Canada was asked to decide whether the Federal Government could go ahead with the scheme without the consent of the provinces.	The courts have jurisdiction to determine whether a constitutional convention exists by asking: 1. what are the precedents; 2. do the actors in the precedents believe that they are bound by the rule; and is there a good reason for the rule.

KEY DEBATES

Topic	'The Proper Roles for Constitutional Conventions'
Author/Academic	Joseph Jaconelli
Viewpoint	This article identifies six possible criteria for determining the circumstances when an aspect of governance might be better suited to regulation by constitutional convention than by law, with reference to the UK context. It also examines the distinction between constitutional laws and conventions and compares the operation of constitutional conventions with that of equity in its relation to the common law.
Source	(2015) 38(2) Dublin University Law Journal 363–385

Topic	'Conventional Constraints'
Author/Academic	Julien Sterck
Viewpoint	This article considers how the challenges of defining constitutional conventions can result in uncertainty over the legitimacy of their judicial recognition and enforcement. It goes on to discuss the problems arising from the conceptualization of constitutional conventions as rules or as being analogous to customary law. The article concludes with an assessment of the value of viewing them instead as descriptions of the constraints produced by the relationships between constitutional rules.
Source	(2015) 38(2) Dublin University Law Journal 465–476

Topic	'Laws and Constitutional Conventions'
Author/Academic	NW Barber
Viewpoint	Examines the jurisdiction of the court in relation to constitutional conventions and the extent to which the courts are prepared to recognize them.
Source	(2009) 125 Law Quarterly Review 294–309

Topic	'Statutory Conventions: Conceptual Confusion or Sound Constitutional Development?'
Author/Academic	Conor Crummey and Eugenio Velasco Ibarra
Viewpoint	This article reviews the implications of *R (on the application of Miller) v Secretary of State for Exiting the European Union* (SC), which held that the UK Parliament was not under a legal duty to seek the Scottish Parliament's consent before passing legislation to leave the EU. It goes on to discuss the finding that **s 28(8) Scotland Act 1998** is a political norm not a legal rule, and whether this creates a new constitutional category of the statutory convention.
Source	[2018] Public Law 687–707

Topic	'The Brexit Case and Constitutional Conventions'
Author/Academic	Tom Mullen
Viewpoint	Discusses the implications for the court's future treatment of constitutional conventions of *R (on the application of Miller) v Secretary of State for Exiting the European Union* on whether the UK Government could rely on prerogative power to give notice under **Art 50 Treaty on European Union** of the intention to withdraw from the EU, or whether statutory approval was required.
Source	(2017) 21(3) Edinburgh Law Review 442–447

EXAM QUESTIONS

Problem question

Assume that the government loses a vote of no confidence following a debate in the House of Commons. The reason for this is that a large number of MPs were unable to attend the House of Commons because of exceptionally bad weather.

The Prime Minister refuses to resign. His argument is that the government has a clear majority in the House of Commons and that had the MPs affected by the weather been able to get to Westminster, the government would have won the vote of no confidence. The Leader of the Opposition argues that this is nonsense and that the Prime Minister and the government should resign.

Advise the Queen's Private Secretary on the constitutional issues involved and the Leader of the Opposition as to whether he may take legal action to force the Prime Minister and the government to resign.

See the Outline Answers section in the end matter for help with this question.

Essay question

Explain how and to what extent legal rules are enforceable in the courts and constitutional conventions are not.

 Online Resources

For an outline answer to this essay question, as well as interactive key cases and multiple-choice questions, please visit the online resources.
www.oup.com/he/faragher-concentrate7e

 Concentrate Q&As

For more questions and answers on public law, see the *Concentrate Q&A: Public Law* by Richard Clements.

Go to the end of this book to view **sample pages**.

The rule of law

3

- AV Dicey's conception of the **rule of law** is widely accepted.

- AV Dicey formulated the rule of law around the supremacy of law over arbitrary and wide discretionary power, equal subjection to the law, and origins of constitutional law in private law.

- Dicey's views were based on the constitutional principles in *Entick v Carrington* (1765).

- Government according to law is an important principle connected with Dicey's conception of the rule of law.

- Jennings and others have put forward different views about what the rule of law means.

- Government according to law is a principle connected with the rule of law.

- There are examples of wide discretionary powers within the law of the UK which appear to run contrary to Dicey.

- There are other recognizable limitations and threats to the rule of law.

What is the rule of law?

AV Dicey in *Introduction to the Study of the Law of the Constitution* (1885) said that the rule of law means three things:

- the predominance of law in preference to the influence of wide discretionary arbitrary prerogative power which means that a person may be liable or punished for a breach of the law but nothing else;
- everyone is equally subject to the law; and
- the principles of British constitutional law do not, as in other countries, originate in a higher constitutional code but from the ordinary law dealing with the rights and obligations of private individuals.

Dicey's views are still highly influential and are supported by judges in decided cases. In *R v Rimmington* (2006), for instance, Lord Bingham said that conduct forbidden by law should be clearly indicated so that a person is capable of knowing that it is wrong before they do it and that nobody should be punished for doing something which was not a criminal offence when it was done. Moreover, both Lord Bingham and Lord Walker in the Privy Council decision in *Sharma v Brown-Antoine* (2007) said that the rule of law requires that, subject to any legal immunity or exemption, the law should be even-handed and apply to all alike.

Other views about what the rule of law means

Since Dicey, many other views have emerged concerning the meaning and nature of the rule of law.

Von Hayeck: The Road to Serfdom *(1944)*

Von Hayek was one of the leading academic critics of collectivism in the twentieth century. Collectivism embraces a number of political and economic philosophies which make the rights of the individual subject to rights of society as a whole. In constitutional terms it means totalitarian regimes. which could be either socialist or fascist Examples include the Soviet Union, the Peoples' Republic of China, and Nazi Germany. Hayek expressly drew on political repression in the Soviet Union under Joseph Stalin and argued that all forms of collectivism (even those theoretically based on voluntary cooperation) could only be maintained by a central authority of some kind. In Hayek's view, the central role of the state should be to maintain the rule of law with as little arbitrary intervention as possible. The followers of Hayeck, for instance, would argue that it is wrong for the government to nationalize industries, or regulate the banks and other businesses. In *The Road to Serfdom* (1944) and in subsequent academic works, Hayek argued that socialism required central economic planning and that such planning in turn leads towards totalitarianism. Hayek said that a central planning authority would have to be endowed with powers that would impact and ultimately control social life, because the knowledge required for centrally planning an economy is inherently decentralized, and would need to be brought under control.

Sir Ivor Jennings: The Law and the Constitution, *5th edn (1959)*

Sir Ivor Jennings, in *The Law and the Constitution*, 5th edn (1959), critically reviewed Dicey's conception of the rule of law. Jennings's main criticism of Dicey's views is that his preference for liberty, certainty, and the limitation of discretionary powers was inconsistent with twentieth-century ideas of social justice which involved the extension of discretionary powers. This assertion is based on the distinction between civil and political rights on the one hand and social and economic rights on the other. We have already referred to this distinction in the introductory section of this book and we will be looking at it again in greater detail in Chapter 14 on human rights in the UK. This implies that, when Dicey delivered his lectures on the rule of law in the 1880s, there was a greater emphasis on civil and political rights like the right to life, personal liberty, and the right to own property than on social and economic rights. In the twentieth century, social and economic rights—like the rights to health, welfare, education, and housing—were thought to be as important as civil and political rights. Accordingly, the work and discretionary powers of the executive expanded to provide health and welfare services, education, and housing. Utilities such as water, gas, electricity, and transport services were, in the 1950s and 1960s, under state control. Jennings believed that the legal concept of the rule of law should have some key features. The state as a whole must be regulated by law. There must be an implicit separation of powers. Police powers must be clearly defined. There must be clear general rules interpreted and applied by the courts. Criminal statutes should be interpreted strictly. Equality and liberty are also essential features of the rule of law.

LL Fuller: The Morality of Law *(1969)*

In *The Morality of Law* (1969) LL Fuller identifies eight requirements of a legal system based on the rule of law.

1. There must be a body of precise rules of law which can be identified and stated clearly.

2. These rules of law must be published so that people know where they stand.

3. Legislation must be written in clear language so that people can understand it and it must be freely available to the public.

4. Legislation must not be retroactive so as to outlaw something done in the past which was not against the law when it was done.

5. The law must be consistent both in substance and application so that there is nothing contradictory in it.

6. Laws must be capable of being obeyed without undue hardship. This takes into account the cost and practicality of implementing and enforcing the law. It also focuses on the likely economic impact of bringing in new regulations. For instance, in the 1980s new regulations were brought in designed to protect consumers against damage caused by defective products. This was done by the **Consumer Protection Act 1987**. Opponents of the new law argued that it would cause undue hardship to manufacturers because of the time, complexity, and cost of testing products for defects before they were put on the

market. It would discourage investment and lead to industries moving their operations away from the UK.

7. Legislation must be stable and not subject to over-frequent revision.

8. There must be no divergence between adjudication/administration and legislation.

Fuller applies these principles to a theoretical scenario in which a king attempts to rule but finds he is unable to do so in any meaningful way when any of these conditions are not met. Fuller contends that the purpose of law is to 'subject human conduct to the governance of rules'. If any of these eight principles are not present in a system of governance, a system will not be a legal one. The more closely a system is able to adhere to them, the nearer it will be to the ideal, though in reality all systems must make compromises. These principles, Fuller argues, represent the 'internal morality of law', and he argues that compliance with them leads to substantively just laws and away from evil ones.

HLA Hart's criticism of LL Fuller

Fuller's idea of legal morality was criticized by HLA Hart, on the basis that Fuller's requirements concern the efficiency of a legal system rather than its underlying morality expressed in terms of whether it is good or bad. Hart's views were also supported by commentators like Professor Matthew Kramer. He says that both good and evil systems of government could make equally good claims to have a legal system based on the rule of law applying Fuller's criteria. Other writers, like Dr Nigel Simmonds, contend that adhering to the rule of law has value in and of itself, giving citizens a liberty to act as they please and conform their conduct to the rules and know that, if they do so, force beyond that which is prescribed will not be used against them by the state. Evil regimes would have every reason to operate outside the rule of law to 'chill' the population into compliance, rather than to use the rule of law for their own ends as Kramer suggests.

Joseph Raz: 'The Rule of Law and its Virtue' (1977) and The Authority of Law (1979)

Joseph Raz in 'The Rule of Law and its Virtue' (1977) 93 LQR 195 identified several principles which may be associated with the rule of law in some (but not all) societies. His principles focus on guiding an individual's behaviour and minimalizing the dangers associated with the exercise of arbitrary and discretionary power.

Some of Raz's principles are as follows:

- That laws should be prospective rather than retroactive.
- Laws should be stable and not changed too frequently, as lack of awareness of the law prevents one from being guided by it.
- There should be clear rules and procedures for making laws.
- The independence of the judiciary has to be guaranteed.
- The principles of natural justice should be observed, particularly those concerning the right to a fair hearing.

- The courts should have the power of judicial review over the way in which the other principles are implemented.
- The courts should be accessible; no man may be denied justice.
- The discretion of law enforcement and crime prevention agencies should not be allowed to pervert the law.

According to Raz, the validity of these principles depends upon the particular circumstances of different societies, whereas the rule of law generally 'is not to be confused with democracy, justice, equality (before the law or otherwise), human rights of any kind or respect for persons or for the dignity of man'.

In *The Authority of Law* (1979) Raz advances the view that the rule of law can be formulated as any political ideal to be realized in legal terms. This means that even a totalitarian regime may claim to have a 'Rule of Law'.

Lord Bingham

Lord Bingham in 'The Rule of Law' (2007) 66 CLJ 67 said that at the heart of the rule of law is the principle that '. . . all persons and authorities within the state, whether public or private, should be bound by and entitled to the benefit of laws publicly and prospectively published and publicly administered in the courts'.

He went on to identify and state eight key principles or sub-rules which characterize the rule of law. The first is that the law must be accessible and so far as possible intelligible, clear, and predictable. The second is that questions of legal right and liability should ordinarily be resolved by application of the law and not the exercise of discretion. The third is that the laws of the land should apply equally to all, save to the extent that objective differences justify differentiation. The fourth is that the law must afford adequate protection of fundamental human rights. The fifth is that means must be provided for resolving, without prohibitive cost or inordinate delay, bona fide civil disputes which the parties themselves are unable to resolve. The sixth is that ministers and public officers at all levels must exercise the powers conferred on them reasonably, in good faith, for the purpose for which the powers were conferred, and without exceeding the limits of such powers. The seventh is that adjudicative procedures provided by the state should be fair. The eighth is that the existing principle of the rule of law requires compliance by the state with its obligations in international law, the law which whether deriving from treaty or international custom and practice governs the conduct of nations.

LOOKING FOR EXTRA MARKS?

Some essay-type questions will ask you to compare and contrast different views about what the rule of law means. You should read your recommended standard textbook. Hilaire Barnett's textbook, *Constitutional and Administrative Law* (2006), contains a particularly good chapter on the rule of law and you should read this.

The key features of a legal system based on the rule of law: government according to law

REVISION TIP

You should be able to identify and state the key features of a legal system based on Dicey's conception of the rule of law and in particular the key features of the principle forming the basis of Dicey's conception that government must be conducted according to law.

Judges have also identified guiding principles. One of these is the constitutional principle in **Entick v Carrington** (1765) that the executive can do nothing without legal authority. Furthermore, the decision of the Irish courts in **Wolfe Tone** (1798) supports the principle that the supremacy of law means that governments must act in a way which is consistent with the law and required procedure.

LOOKING FOR EXTRA MARKS?

Some examination questions ask students to explain how the rule of law has been applied in English law in practice. You should be able to compare and contrast the views of senior members of the judiciary.

Government according to law

The executive must follow procedural requirements when carrying out statutory duties. This was held by Lord Goddard CJ in **Stroud v Bradbury** (1952). **Sections 36** and **290(6) Public Health Act 1936** said that if a householder failed to maintain their drains properly the local authority could enter their premises and do what was necessary to make sure they did work properly. They had to give 24 hours' notice to the householder before entering their premises. Because they failed to do so the householder was entitled to deny entry to their premises.

Another key principle is that the courts are duty-bound to correct any abuse of power by the executive and the judges are free to exercise this jurisdiction independently. This was determined by the Court of Appeal decision in **Congreve v Home Office** (1976). The Court of Appeal held that although the Home Secretary had discretion to revoke TV licences under **s 1(4) Wireless Telegraphy Act 1949**, the discretion was limited to the extent that the courts would intervene if it were exercised arbitrarily or improperly. It was an improper exercise of the minister's discretionary power to revoke a validly obtained licence as a way of raising money which Parliament had given the executive no authority to demand.

Judges commonly use the idea of government according to law or the rule of law to explain the role of the courts and what the judiciary can and cannot do. Lord Templeman, in the House of Lords' decision in *M v Home Office* (1994) said that the judiciary enforces the law against individuals, institutions, and the executive. Judges cannot enforce the law against the monarch because the monarch can do no wrong but judges enforce the law against the executive and against the individuals who from time to time represent the executive. A litigant complaining of a breach of the law by the executive can sue the Crown as executive bringing their action against the minister who is responsible for the department of state involved. To enforce the law the courts have power to grant remedies against a minister in their official capacity. If a minister has personally broken the law, the litigant can sue the minister in their personal capacity. For the purpose of enforcing the law against all persons and institutions, including ministers in their official capacity, the courts also have coercive powers such as the power to imprison people for contempt of court.

Lord Mustill, in his dissenting speech in the House of Lords' decision in *R v Secretary of State for the Home Department, ex p Fire Brigades Union* (1995) said that, 'the role of the courts is to make sure that powers are lawfully exercised by those to whom they are entrusted, not to take powers into their own hands and exercise them afresh'. He concluded that, in order to be challenged, a decision has to be 'so obviously and grossly wrong as to be irrational, in the lawyer's sense of the word, and hence a symptom that there must have been some failure in the decision-making process'.

Other key features of a legal system based on the rule of law

Further key features of a legal system based on the rule of law have been identified by the judiciary. In *R (on the application of Anderson) v Secretary of State for the Home Department* (2003) Lord Steyn said that in a system based on the rule of law 'only a court or an independent tribunal may decide on the guilt or otherwise of an accused person. The executive have no role to play in the determination of guilt. Secondly only a court or independent tribunal may decide on the punishment of a convicted person. Again the executive have no role to play in the determination of punishment.'

Another important case is the House of Lords' decision in *Matthews v Ministry of Defence* (2003). One of the issues the House of Lords had to consider was whether the claimant had been unjustly deprived of the civil right to sue. Lord Hoffmann stated the key principle that where a litigant claims on arguable grounds to have a civil right then they have the right to have that question determined by an independent and impartial court. Furthermore, the executive should not arbitrarily be able to instruct the court to dismiss a claimant's action either by saying that there is no cause of action without the government's consent or by issuing a certificate that the action is not to proceed. He went on to conclude that 'A right to the independence and impartiality of the judicial branch of government would not be worth much if the executive branch could stop you from getting to the court in the first place. The executive would in effect be deciding the case against you. That would contravene the rule of law and the principle of the separation of powers.'

In *R (G) v Immigration Appeal Tribunal; R(M) v Immigration Appeal Tribunal* (2005) Lord Phillips MR said that 'it is the role of the judges to preserve the rule of law' and that it is 'a "constitutional norm" to protect the independence of the judiciary'. This, according to Lord Phillips MR, is exemplified by the provisions of **ss 11, 12,** and **15 Senior Courts Act 1981** which define the jurisdiction of the judges. It is also recognized by a large number of statutes which confer rights of appeal. Lord Phillips MR goes on to say that these rights are additional to the common law right of the citizen to have access to the courts. He concludes that judicial review is the cornerstone of the rule of law and that if Parliament attempts by legislation to remove or limit judicial review the rule of law is threatened. The courts will not readily accept that legislation achieves that end.

The Human Rights Act 1998 and the rule of law

The impact of the **Human Rights Act 1998** was discussed in the Court of Appeal decision in *R (Al Rawi) v Secretary of State for Foreign and Commonwealth Affairs* (2008). Concerning the rule of law, Laws LJ begins by agreeing with Lord Hoffmann's point in *R (ProLife) v British Broadcasting Corporation* (2004) that 'In a society based upon the rule of law and the separation of powers, it is necessary to decide which branch of government has in any particular instance the decision-making power and what the legal limits of that power are.' Laws LJ then observed that since the **Human Rights Act 1998** the rule of law has ceased to be a purely formal and procedural matter. It is now a more substantive principle. The rule of law requires not only that a public decision should be legally authorized but also that it be reasonable and (generally in human rights cases) proportionate to a legitimate aim. In reaching this conclusion, Laws LJ recognized that reasonableness and proportionality are substantive virtues rather than formal legal standards.

REVISION TIP

You may be asked in an examination question to assess the continuing value or even the true existence of the rule of law today. You should acquaint yourself with current debates.

Is arbitrary and wide discretionary power ever justified?

Judges appear, at least in principle, to see some value in the rule of law. Hence Lord Hoffmann's assertion in *R (Alconbury Developments Ltd) v Secretary of State for the Environment, Transport and the Regions* (2003) that judicial review gives effect to the rule law. Similarly, Lord Hope in *R (Jackson) v Attorney General* (2006) affirmed that the rule of law enforced by the courts is the ultimate controlling factor on which our constitution is based and Moses LJ, delivering the Court of Appeal's judgment in *R (Corner House Research) v Director of the Serious*

Fraud Office (2009) said that at the heart of the obligations of the courts and of the judges lies the duty to protect the rule of law. Statutory provisions like **s 1 Constitutional Reform Act 2005** also stress the importance of maintaining the rule of law.

All these assertions, however, must be viewed against the background of a continuing debate about what the rule of law actually means. The rule of law is not absolute. National security, as well as other public interest considerations, can outweigh the Dicean injunction forbidding wide discretionary and arbitrary powers. Again, we will be looking more deeply into these issues when we consider the law concerning police powers, public order, and terrorism.

A statutory provision that a public body may do something if/as it sees fit or if it reasonably believes something, is a subjective discretionary power. Such discretion can be wide and arbitrary. Can the courts intervene, and if so how far? In *Liversidge v Anderson* (1942) the House of Lords said that under normal circumstances, the judges are 'no respecters of persons'. They stand between the citizen and any attempted encroachments on their liberty. But in times of emergency, arbitrary and wide subjective discretionary powers are permitted. Even in times of peace subjective discretion can be given to the executive. **Section 3(5) (a) Immigration Act 1971** provides that a person may be deported if the Secretary of State 'deems' their deportation to be conducive to the public good. **Section 21(1) Anti-Terrorism Crime and Security Act 2001** provides that a person could be deported if the Secretary of State reasonably believes that the person's presence in the UK is a risk to national security, and suspects that person to be a terrorist.

The provisions of the **Immigration Act 1971** as amended by the **British Nationality Act 1981** were considered by the House of Lords in *Secretary of State for the Home Department v Rehman* (2003). The House of Lords made four essential points. The first is that what is conducive to the public good is a matter for the executive discretion of the Secretary of State. Second, the Secretary of State is entitled to take an overall view which means that they can look at anything they think is relevant without legal restriction. Third, the interests of national security can be threatened not only by action against the UK but also indirectly by activities directed against other states. Fourth, while any specific facts on which the Secretary of State relies must be proved on the ordinary civil balance of probabilities, no particular standard of proof is appropriate to the formation of their executive discretion or assessment as to whether it is conducive to the public good that a person be deported, which is a matter of reasonable and proportionate judgement.

Nevertheless the courts retain some jurisdiction. Lord Nicholls in *A and Others v Secretary of State for the Home Department* (2005) spelt out the court's role when scrutinizing wide discretionary power. This case concerned **s 23 Anti-Terrorism Crime and Security Act 2001** which provided for the detention of non-nationals if the Home Secretary believed that their presence in the UK was a risk to national security and they suspected that they were terrorists who, for the time being, could not be deported because of fears for their safety or other practical considerations. A number of fundamentally important principles, relevant to the rule of law, were set out in the speech of Lord Nicholls. He begins by asserting that indefinite imprisonment without charge or trial is anathema in any country which observes the rule of law. It deprives the detained person of the protection a criminal trial is intended to afford. Wholly exceptional circumstances must exist before this extreme step can be justified. He went on to make the following points. First, all courts are very much aware of the heavy burden, resting on the elected government and not the judiciary, to protect national security. Second, all courts are acutely conscious that the government alone is able to evaluate and decide what counter-terrorism steps are needed and what steps will suffice. Courts are not equipped to make such decisions, nor are they charged with that responsibility. Third, the duty of the courts is to check that legislation and ministerial decisions do not overlook the human rights of persons adversely affected. In enacting legislation and reaching decisions, Parliament and ministers must give due weight to fundamental rights and freedoms. Fourth, when carrying out their assigned task the courts will accord to Parliament and ministers, as the primary decision-makers, an appropriate degree of latitude. Fifth, the latitude will vary according to the subject matter under consideration, the importance of the human right in question, and the extent of the encroachment upon that right. Finally, the courts will intervene only when it is apparent that, in balancing the various considerations involved, the primary decision-maker must have given insufficient weight to the human rights factor.

Subsequently in *R (Al Rawi) v Secretary of State for Foreign and Commonwealth Affairs* (2008) Laws LJ emphasized that judicial non-intervention is justified where the executive has access to special information and expertise and a decision, because of its nature and consequences, requires such legitimacy that it can be made only by a person accountable to Parliament and the electorate.

See Table 3.1 for a summary of the role of the executive and the role of the judiciary in the rule of law.

Table 3.1 The executive and judiciary's role within the rule of law

THE EXECUTIVE	THE JUDICIARY
Takes primary responsibility for enacting legislation and decision-making.	Makes sure that legislation and ministerial decisions do not overlook legal formalities and the human rights of those adversely affected.
May evaluate and decide upon appropriate measures.	Gives both Parliament and the executive a degree of latitude.
	The degree of latitude depends on the nature of the matter being considered, the importance of the human rights in question, and the extent of the encroachment.
	The courts will intervene only when it is apparent that, in balancing the various considerations involved, the primary decision-maker must have given insufficient weight to the human rights factor.

Are privileges and immunities consistent with the rule of law?

Both Lord Bingham and Lord Walker in the Privy Council decision in *Sharma v Brown-Antoine* (2007) recognized that the requirement that the criminal law should apply to all alike in an even-handed way is subject to immunities and exemptions provided by law. Special powers, privileges, and immunities from the ordinary law have been granted by Parliament, so that it is possible to argue that the principle of equal subjection to the law is not absolute. An example of this is the absolute immunity of MPs from actions in the tort of defamation arising out of anything said or done in the course of a parliamentary debate or parliamentary proceeding given by **Art 9 Bill of Rights 1689**. The **International Organisations Act 2005** enables the UK to fulfil international commitments to confer legal capacity and privileges and immunities on a number of international organizations and bodies, and certain categories of individuals connected with them. Trade unions enjoy some immunities under the **Trade Union and Labour Relations (Consolidation) Act 1992**. The **Diplomatic Privileges Act 1964** is another example.

Is the extension of the criminal law by the judiciary consistent with the rule of law?

Dicey said that a person may be punished for a breach of the law, but they can be punished for nothing else. As a result, the courts should not be able to create or extend criminal offences. This issue was addressed by the House of Lords in *Shaw v DPP* (1962). Shaw published a Ladies Directory containing the names of prostitutes. He was charged, among other things, with conspiracy to corrupt public morals in that he conspired with the advertisers and other persons by means of the Ladies Directory and the advertisements to corrupt public morals. He was convicted. He appealed on the ground that there was no such offence as conspiracy to corrupt public morals. The case reached the House of Lords. Speaking for the majority Lord Simonds claimed that there was a residual judicial power to enforce the supreme and fundamental purpose of the law. The purpose of the law, according to Lord Simonds, was to protect the safety, order, and moral welfare of the state. He concluded that the courts had a duty to protect the state against novel and unexpected attacks. In the House of Lords' decision in *R v Rimmington* (2006) Lord Bingham said that if the ambit of a common law offence is to be enlarged, it must be done step by step on a case–by-case basis and not with one large leap. The cases discussed above seem to indicate that the courts do follow Dicey in the sense that they do not now create completely new offences but instead restrict themselves to extending the scope of offences which already exist.

 KEY CASES

CASE	FACTS	PRINCIPLE
A and Others v Secretary of State for the Home Department [2005] 2 AC 68	The House of Lords had to decide on the legality of certain anti-terrorist measures.	Indefinite imprisonment without charge is contrary to the rule of law because it deprives the detained person of the protection given to them by the process of criminal trial. The role of the judiciary, in a legal system based on the rule of law, is to make sure that legislation and ministerial decisions do not overlook the human rights of those adversely affected. In carrying out its role, the judiciary will give both Parliament and the executive an appropriate degree of latitude, which will depend upon: the nature of the matter being considered; the importance of the human right in question; and the extent of the encroachment upon the right. The courts will intervene only when it is apparent that, in balancing the various considerations involved, the primary decision-maker must have given insufficient weight to the human rights factor.
Entick v Carrington (1765) St Tr 1029	The Court of King's Bench had to decide whether national security could be raised as a defence to an action in trespass to land and property.	The executive can do nothing without legal authority. Where a public authority claims to have the power to do something it must be able to identify the precise legal source of its powers.
M v Home Office [1993] 3 WLR 433	Proceedings were brought against the Home Secretary for contempt of court. The House of Lords determined that the courts had jurisdiction.	The judiciary enforces the law against individuals, institutions, the executive, and against the individuals who from time to time represent the executive. A litigant complaining of a breach of the law by the executive can sue the Crown as executive bringing their action against the minister who is responsible for the department of state involved. The courts have power to grant remedies against a minister in their official capacity. If a minister has personally broken the law, the litigant can sue the minister in their personal capacity. The courts are armed with coercive powers exercisable in proceedings for contempt of court.

CASE	FACTS	PRINCIPLE
R v Secretary of State for the Home Department, ex p the Fire Brigades Union [1995] All ER 244	The House of Lords had to decide whether the Home Secretary had acted lawfully in the way he had dealt with the implementation of a scheme to provide compensation to the victims of violent crime.	The courts ensure that powers are lawfully exercised by those to whom they are entrusted, not to take those powers into their own hands and exercise them afresh. A claim that a decision under challenge is wrong leads nowhere, except in the rare cases where it can be characterized as so obviously and grossly wrong as to be irrational, in the lawyer's sense of the word, and hence a symptom that there must have been some failure in the decision-making process.
Secretary of State for the Home Department v Rehman [2001] 3 WLR 877	The applicant, a Pakistani, arrived in the UK in 1993 after being granted entry clearance to work as a minister of religion. In December 1998 the Secretary of State refused his application for indefinite leave to remain in the UK and gave notice that, because of his association with an organization involved in terrorist activities in India, he had decided to make a deportation order under **s 3(5)(b) Immigration Act 1971** on the ground that it would be conducive to the public good and in the interests of national security.	What is conducive to the public good is a matter for the executive discretion of the Secretary of State. The Secretary of State is entitled to take an overall view. The interests of national security can be threatened not only by action against the UK but also indirectly by activities directed against other states. While any specific facts on which the Secretary of State relies must be proved on the ordinary civil balance of probability, no particular standard of proof is appropriate to the formation of their executive judgement or assessment as to whether it is conducive to the public good that a person be deported, which is a matter of reasonable and proportionate judgement.

KEY DEBATES

Topic	'The Rule of Law in UK Public Law Textbooks: From Critique to Acceptance?'
Author/Academic	Brian Christopher Jones
Viewpoint	The author reflects on the expanded coverage which contemporary public law textbooks are giving to the rule of law. He goes on to discuss the justifications for the limited treatment of the topic by many twentieth-century textbooks, the factors responsible for the greater coverage in the subsequent period, the implications of studying the subject in such depth, and the range of perspectives from which it is viewed.
Source	[2018] Public Law 594–604

Topic	'Compassion and the Rule of Law'
Author/Academic	Susan A Bandes
Viewpoint	This article considers whether compassion in legal reasoning is compatible with the rule of law, distinguishing between its possible uses as a guide to substantive decision-making on who should prevail in a legal dispute and as a way of understanding the issues at stake for the disputants.
Source	(2017) 13(2) International Journal of Law in Context 184–196

Topic	'The Contribution of Legislative Drafting to the Rule of Law'
Author/Academic	Philip Sales
Viewpoint	This article discusses how good quality legal drafting contributes to the rule of law, understood both in terms of the law's clarity and predictability and its consistency with constitutional principles and values. It also considers how drafters perform their rule of law role from their first receipt of instructions.
Source	(2018) 77 Cambridge Law Journal 630–635

Topic	'"The Judges versus the People?": Brexit, Populism and the Rule of Law'
Author/Academic	Christopher Clement-Davies
Viewpoint	This article condemns the personal attacks, in some national newspapers, on the judges in *R (on the application of Miller) v Secretary of State for Exiting the European Union* (2017). It outlines the constitutional issue to be determined regarding how **Art 50 Treaty on European Union** should be invoked and then expresses concern at the rise of populism and what this could mean for Western societies. The article concludes by noting the continuing uncertainty affecting the energy sector as to the timing and terms of Brexit.
Source	[2016] 7 International Energy Law Review 279–281

Topic	'The Contested Constitution: An Analysis of the Competing Models of British Constitutionalism'
Author/Academic	Robert Brett Taylor
Viewpoint	This article examines the debate over the meaning of British constitutionalism, and analyses key features of its three competing models. It goes on to review the elements of legal constitutionalism, common law constitutionalism, and political constitutionalism, and suggests why an appropriate view of such constitutionalism requires a combination of elements from all three theories.
Source	[2018] Public Law 500–522

EXAM QUESTIONS

Essay question 1

Explain Dicey's conception of the rule of law.

Essay question 2

Explain the extent to which, if at all, Dicey's conception of the rule of law is of value today.

 Online Resources

For outline answers to these essay questions, as well as interactive key cases and multiple-choice questions, please visit the online resources.
www.oup.com/he/faragher-concentrate7e

 Concentrate Q&As

 For more questions and answers on public law, see the *Concentrate Q&A: Public Law* by Richard Clements.

Go to the end of this book to view **sample pages**.

4 The separation of powers

KEY FACTS

- There are three functions of government, namely, the legislative function, the executive function, and the judicial function.

- There are three corresponding organs of government, namely, the legislature, the executive, and the judiciary.

- In its present form, 'separation of powers' was first formulated by Montesquieu, and was partly based on the writings of John Locke.

- The same persons should not form part of more than one of the three organs of government.

- One organ of government should not exercise the functions of another.

- Each organ of government should act as a check against the other and should be able to do this independently without any undue threat of preventative control or interference.

- The separation of powers is mentioned in the opinions of judges in decided cases and is supported by statutes like the **Constitutional Reform Act 2005**.

- A detailed analysis of the structure of and interrelationship between the functions and organs of the UK Government reveals that the 'British Constitution' departs from the principle of 'separation of powers' in many vital respects especially at the higher levels.

What is the separation of powers?

REVISION TIP

It is important to understand how the separation of powers is formulated as both a political and a legal principle.

The separation of powers means three things:

- the same persons should not form part of more than one of the organs of government;
- one organ of government should not exercise the functions of another; and
- each organ of government should act as a check against the others and should be able to do this independently without any undue threat of preventative control or interference.

This was first developed by John Locke in his *Second Treatise of Civil Government* (1690). It was developed further by Montesquieu in his book, *De l'Esprit des Lois* (1748).

REVISION TIP

The separation of powers assumes that government is based on three recognized functions. When examining the legal concept of the separation of powers you should have a clear idea of the nature and extent of the functions of government. See Chapters 6, 7, and 8.

These writers assumed that government can be broken down into legislative, executive (or administrative), and judicial functions and organs.

- The legislative function involves the drafting, making, and publication of new laws as well as the amendment of existing laws and, in the UK, consists of the monarch, the House of Lords, and the House of Commons.
- The executive or administrative function enforces the law. This is done through the formulation of policy and discretionary decision-making and action. It consists of the reigning

monarch who is legally the head of state, the Prime Minister, Cabinet, Secretaries of State, Ministers of the Crown, departments of state, non-departmental public bodies, devolved administrative organizations like the Scottish Government, the Welsh Government, the Northern Ireland Executive, and the Greater London Authority, local authorities, the police, and the armed forces.

- The judicial function involves the interpretation and application of the law, and also covers the resolution of disputes, provides remedies, and determines punishments when the law is breached. It consists of all the judges who preside in the senior or lower courts and tribunals within the UK.

The purpose and practical use of the separation of powers

The separation of powers is meant to act as a safeguard against arbitrary and discretionary power, prevent tyranny, and protect individual liberty. John Locke, in the *Second Treatise of Civil Government* (1690), defined tyranny as the exercise of wide discretionary and arbitrary power by those in government for their own private advantage. Baron de Montesquieu in *De l'Esprit des Lois* (1748) said that loss of individual liberty is inevitable where there is no separation of powers. The government could make tyrannical laws and execute them in a tyrannical manner. The danger, according to Montesquieu, is that laws would be applied in an arbitrary way which undermines personal liberty if judges were also legislators and members of the executive. They might also apply the law in a way which was violent or oppressive.

The practical usage of the separation of powers to prevent tyranny and preserve liberty can be seen in the written constitutions of other English-speaking jurisdictions. It is explicitly evident in the **Constitution of the United States** (1787) which uses a form of the separation of powers in order to prevent an individual or small group of people gaining absolute power. The separation of powers has played an influential role in the development and interpretation of the written constitutions of British Commonwealth countries. An example of this is the Privy Council decision in *R v Liyanage* (1967). In this case the Privy Council had to decide whether measures passed under the Criminal Law (Special Provisions) Act, No 1 of 1962 by the Parliament of Ceylon (now Sri Lanka) were inconsistent with the written constitution of Ceylon. The Privy Council held that the Act was inconsistent with the constitution because the legislature had unlawfully exercised a function which belonged to the judiciary. Although the constitution itself did not say so expressly there was an implied adherence to the separation of powers in the form of an intention to secure the freedom of the judiciary from political, legislative, and executive control.

What do judges say about the separation of powers in the UK?

REVISION TIP

As with the rule of law you should be able to compare, contrast, and assess the judicial appreciation of the separation of powers.

Senior judges often refer to the separation of powers when deciding cases. They do so when discussing the relationship between the organs and functions of government and the role of the judiciary.

- Lord Steyn in *R (on the application of Anderson) v Secretary of State for the Home Department* (2003) used the separation of powers to assert that a decision to punish an offender with a term of imprisonment should be made by the courts.
- Lord Hoffmann in *Matthews v Ministry of Defence* (2003) used the separation of powers to say that the executive must never be able to order a court to dismiss a case or decide it in a particular way. Decisions about people's civil rights should be made by the judicial branch of government.
- Lord Diplock in *Duport Steels Ltd v Sirs* (1980) points out that the role of Parliament is to make laws. The role of the judiciary is to interpret them.

Lord Templeman in the House of Lords decision in *M v Home Office* (1993) made the following additional points.

- In the seventeenth century, Parliament established its supremacy over the Crown as monarch, over the executive, and over the judiciary.
- The judiciary enforce the law against individuals, against institutions, and against the executive.
- The judges cannot enforce the law against the Crown as monarch because the Crown as monarch can do no wrong, but judges enforce the law against the Crown as executive and against the individuals who from time to time represent the Crown.
- A litigant complaining of a breach of the law by the executive can sue the Crown as executive, bringing their action against the minister who is responsible for the department of state involved.
- To enforce the law the courts have power to grant remedies including injunctions against a minister in their official capacity. If the minister has personally broken the law, the litigant can sue the minister in their personal capacity.

- For the purpose of enforcing the law against all persons and institutions, including ministers in their official capacity and in their personal capacity, the courts are armed with coercive powers exercisable in proceedings for contempt of court.

Lord Mustill in *R v Secretary of State for the Home Department, ex p Fire Brigades Union* (1995) said that the role of the judiciary in relation to the executive was to verify that the powers asserted accord with the substantive law created by Parliament, and also to ensure that the manner in which they are exercised conforms to the standards of fairness which Parliament must have intended.

What do statutes say about the separation of powers in the UK?

There is no statutory definition of the separation of powers in the UK. Acts of Parliament never mention it explicitly. There are, however, statutes which impliedly support the separation of powers. One example is the **House of Commons (Disqualification) Act 1975** which aims to limit the power of the executive to control the legislature. Under **s 2 House of Commons (Disqualification) Act 1975** not more than 95 holders of ministerial offices are entitled to sit and vote in the House of Commons at any one time. The result, as far as the separation of powers is concerned, is that it is impossible for the House of Commons to be completely composed of members of the executive.

The **Constitutional Reform Act 2005** makes a number of important adjustments to the legal system in order to create a greater separation between the judiciary, the legislature, and the executive. The judicial functions of the Lord Chancellor were transferred to the President of the Courts of England and Wales also known as the Lord Chief Justice. They now represent the views of the judiciary to the executive and take responsibility for the training, guidance, and deployment of judges. The executive functions of the Lord Chancellor are presently carried out by the Lord Chancellor and Secretary of State for Justice. They are now a member of the House of Commons and heads the Ministry of Justice. The parliamentary functions of the Lord Chancellor are carried out by the Lord Speaker of the House of Lords. The significance of these changes lies in the popular perception, prior to 2005, that the office and functions of the Lord Chancellor violated the separation of powers. The **Constitutional Reform Act 2005** imposes a duty on the Lord Chancellor and Secretary of State for Justice, as well as other government ministers, to uphold the independence of the judiciary. They must not seek to influence particular judicial decisions through any special access to the judiciary.

The **Constitutional Reform Act 2005** also strengthens the separation of powers by establishing the Supreme Court of the United Kingdom, which took over the work of the Appellate Committee of the House of Lords in October 2009. Prior to 2009, the House of Lords had legislative and judicial functions. The UK Supreme Court is completely separate from Parliament and its current members have no right to sit and vote in the House of Lords. The jurisdiction of the Judicial Committee of the Privy Council was also devolved to the UK Supreme Court.

Another area covered by the **Constitutional Reform Act 2005** is judicial appointments. The Act created the Judicial Appointments Commission which is responsible for selecting candidates to recommend for judicial appointment on merit and in an open and transparent manner. It also created the Judicial Appointments and Conduct Ombudsman, responsible for investigating and making recommendations concerning complaints about the judicial appointments process, and the handling of judicial conduct complaints.

On the other hand, there are some statutes which seem to undermine the separation of powers. These include the **Regulatory Reform Act 2001**, as amended by the **Legislative and Regulatory Reform Act 2006**, which enable a Minister of the Crown to make orders for the purpose of amending certain categories of provisions in statutes. Other statutes allow ministers and local authorities—that is, the executive—to make laws. These may take the form of Orders in Council, Statutory Instruments, Regulations, Rules, Orders, Schemes, Warrants, Bylaws, and Directions. Acts of Parliament which create such powers are called primary legislation. The regulations created under them are called **delegated legislation**. **Section 10 Human Rights Act (HRA) 1998** enables Ministers of the Crown to make remedial orders amending legislation which is incompatible with human rights incorporated by the 1998 Act. The possibility of remedial orders has been criticized by some as too drastic a power and contrary to the separation of powers because it allows the executive to change the law contained in Acts of Parliament bypassing the full legislative process.

Is the government of the UK based on the separation of powers?

In the House of Lords decision in *R (Anderson) v Secretary of State for the Home Department* (2003) Lord Steyn said that the UK Constitution has never embraced a rigid doctrine of separation of powers. In terms of legal formality the monarch, as the head of state, is the head of the executive, the legislature, and the judiciary. The Prime Minister, the members of the Cabinet, and all the other Ministers of the Crown are members of the executive. They are also Members of Parliament. If the organs and functions of government within the UK were organized strictly according to the doctrine of separation of powers the Prime Minister, the members of the Cabinet, and all the other Ministers of the Crown would not be permitted to be Members of Parliament. The monarch too would not be permitted to be part of the legislature or have any part to play in the appointment of judges. See Table 4.1.

 REVISION TIP

This is a very commonly examined aspect of the separation of powers and you should be prepared to follow up this topic in the standard textbooks. This part of the topic links up with human rights and sovereignty of Parliament and should be revised in conjunction with those topics. When you revise the topics set out in Chapters 5, 6, 7, 8, and 14 you should bear in mind the separation of powers implications.

Table 4.1

No separation of powers	
The monarch	Titular head of the executive, legislative, and judicial functions and organs of government.
The Privy Council and Cabinet	Exercises executive, legislative, and judicial powers and contains members of each organ of government.
Partial separation of powers	
Legislature	Contains members of the judiciary and the executive but the executive's hold limited by statute.
Executive	Under the supervision of the legislature and the judiciary but can exercise considerable power over the legislature through the whip system. See Lord Hailsham's views on the elective dictatorship.
Judiciary	Organizationally independent but subject to parliamentary sovereignty.

The relationship between the executive and Parliament: checks and balances

Walter Bagehot, in *The English Constitution* (1876), said that there was a close union or fusion of the executive and legislative powers in the British system of government. He did not see this as a bad thing: it actually made the government work better. LS Amery in *Thoughts on the Constitution*, 2nd edn (1953), on the other hand, suggests that, 'Government and Parliament, however closely intertwined and harmonized, are still separate and independent entities, fulfilling the two distinct functions of leadership, direction and command on the one hand, and of critical discussion and examination on the other. They start from separate historical origins and each is perpetuated in accordance with its own methods and has its own continuity.' This implies that although the relationship between the executive and the legislature is close, the undesirable consequences of a complete fusion are avoided by a system of checks and balances. A system of checks and balances works by making each branch of government accountable to the other. In the UK, for instance, government ministers who are members of the executive are accountable to the courts and Parliament.

The relationship between the executive and the legislature during the process of exiting the EU

The critical debate and examination function of Parliament, referred to by LS Amery in *Thoughts on the Constitution*, 2nd edn (1953), was enhanced, by **s 13 European Union (Withdrawal) Act 2018**. **Section 13** concerns the process of negotiating and making the

UK's withdrawal agreement from the EU. This would normally be carried out by the executive without parliamentary input subject to the requirements of **s 20(1) Constitutional Reform and Governance Act 2010**. **Section 13(1)–(12)** provides for a series of ministerial statements addressed to the House of Commons, made in writing and published in an appropriate way, neutral motions in the House of Commons and motions tabled in the House of Lords if, before the end of 21 January 2019 the Prime Minister makes a statement that no agreement in principle can be reached in negotiations under **Art 50(2) Treaty on European Union (TEU)** on the substance of the arrangements for the UK's withdrawal from the EU and the framework for the future relationship between the EU and the UK after withdrawal.

The use of Henry VIII clauses in the European Union (Withdrawal) Act 2018

Henry VIII clauses are provisions in statutes which enable the government to amend primary legislation by using secondary legislation thereby avoiding the full legislative procedure of parliament. Parliamentary scrutiny is still possible but not necessary if a minister believes they have the expertise to make the right amendments without parliamentary scrutiny.

Sections **8**, **9**, and **23 European Union (Withdrawal) Act 2018** contain examples of Henry VIII clauses. **Section 8(1)** gives Ministers of the Crown a power to make secondary legislation to deal with deficiencies that would arise on exit in retained EU law. This includes the law which is preserved and converted by **ss 2, 3, and 4** (ie both domestic law and directly applicable EU law). **Section 9** gives Ministers of the Crown a power to make secondary legislation to implement the withdrawal agreement (as defined in **s 20(1)**) agreed between the UK and the EU under **Art 50(2) TEU** (or that Article as applied by the **Euratom Treaty**). **Section 23** deals with consequential and transitional provisions.

The whip system

The dangers of combining the legislative and executive branches of government were explored by Lord Hailsham, in the *Dilemma of Democracy: Diagnosis and Prescription* (1978). He called the British system of government an elective dictatorship. He begins by considering the doctrine which gives Parliament absolute and unlimited legislative powers. The question is whether this doctrine ought to be modified because of changes in the way Parliament is structured and operates. The basis of his argument is that there has been a continuous enlargement of executive power and a corresponding decline of parliamentary influence. All effective powers are placed in the hands of the executive and the checks and balances, which in practice used to prevent abuse, have now disappeared. Another major factor is the development of the **whip system**. Whips are MPs or Lords appointed by each party in Parliament to help organize their party's contribution to parliamentary business. One of their responsibilities is making sure the maximum number of their party members vote, and vote the way their party wants. In Lord Hailsham's opinion this gives the whips, party leaders, and the executive the power to control Parliament and suppress the debate and argument which once dominated the parliamentary scene. He concludes that elective dictatorship is a fact and not just a lawyer's theory.

Backbench revolts

There are circumstances in which the whip system described by Lord Hailsham in *Dilemma of Democracy: Diagnosis and Prescription* (1978) does not operate successfully especially when the party in government does not have an overall majority in the House of Commons. **Section 13 European Union (Withdrawal) Act 2018**, for instance, was inserted because the Chief Whip had no choice but to advise the government that it did not have an assured majority in the House of Commons and there was a real possibility of a backbench revolt. On 12 March 2019, in spite of a government three-line whip against it, the House of Commons passed a motion that it would never under any circumstances agree to the UK's withdrawal from the EU without an acceptable negotiated withdrawal agreement. Under normal circumstances, defying a three-line whip is very serious, and has occasionally resulted in the whip being withdrawn from an MP or Lord. This means that the Member is effectively expelled from their party (but keeps their seat) and must sit as an independent until the whip is restored.

The relationship between the executive and the judiciary

This was explained fully by Lord Mustill in *R v Secretary of State for the Home Department, ex p Fire Brigades Union* (1995). He said that the role of the judiciary in relation to the executive was to verify that the powers asserted accord with the substantive law created by Parliament, and also to ensure that the manner in which they are exercised conforms with the standards of fairness which Parliament must have intended.

The judiciary and the executive: is the judiciary really independent?

REVISION TIP

Again, this should be revised in conjunction with human rights and sovereignty of Parliament.

An independent judiciary is essential to the separation of powers. This is illustrated by two decisions of the House of Lords. The first case is *R (on the application of Anderson) v Secretary of State for the Home Department* (2003). Here, Lord Steyn restated the principle, linked to both the rule of law and the separation of powers, that a decision to punish an offender with a term of imprisonment should be made by the courts. The only recognized exception is the ancient power of Parliament to imprison those who are held to be in contempt of Parliament. This is based on the medieval principle that Parliament may act as a court of justice. The second case is **Matthews v Ministry of Defence** (2003). Here, the House said that the executive must never be put in a position where it effectively decides a case in the sense that it could order a court to dismiss a case. What matters is whether the effect of a legal provision is to give the executive a right to make decisions about people's rights which should be made by the judicial branch of government.

Section 3(1) Constitutional Reform Act 2005 provides that the Lord Chancellor, other Ministers of the Crown, and all those with responsibility for matters relating to the judiciary or otherwise to the administration of justice must uphold the continued independence of the judiciary.

The appointment of judges

Judges are legally appointed by the monarch on the advice of ministers. The question is whether the judiciary can be really independent if the judges are all appointed by the executive. Following the **Constitutional Reform Act 2005** two important developments in the way judges are appointed have separation of powers implications. First, the **Constitutional Reform Act 2005** created a new appointments process for Justices of the UK Supreme Court. New Justices are selected by a selection commission, the members of which include the President and Deputy President of the Supreme Court, a member of the Judicial Appointments Commission of England and Wales, the Judicial Appointments Board for Scotland, and the Northern Ireland Judicial Appointments Commission. Second, the 2005 Act created the Judicial Appointments Commission which selects new judges in the senior courts. Both these measures were designed to reinforce the independence of the judiciary.

The dismissal of judges

Judges cannot be dismissed summarily by the executive. The **Act of Settlement 1700** and the **Senior Courts Act 1981** provide that judges hold office 'during good behaviour' and cannot be removed from office without the permission of both Houses of Parliament. This takes the form of a petition to the reigning monarch.

The Civil Procedure Rule Committee

The Civil Procedure Rule Committee is an advisory non-departmental public body set up under the **Civil Procedure Act 1997** to make rules of court for the Civil Division of the Court of Appeal, the High Court, and the county courts. As such, it is part of the executive and provides the executive with a role in the development of civil procedure. The issue here is whether the executive could influence the development of civil procedure in its favour. On the other hand, the committee is largely staffed by members of the judiciary and the legal profession, which alleviates the problem to a large extent.

The Sentencing Council for England and Wales

The Sentencing Council for England and Wales is an independent, non-departmental public body of the Ministry of Justice. It was set up by **Pt 4 Coroners and Justice Act 2009** to promote greater transparency and consistency in sentencing, whilst maintaining the independence of the judiciary. In particular the Sentencing Council promotes a clear, fair, and consistent approach to sentencing; produces analysis and research on sentencing; and works to improve public confidence in sentencing. The Sentencing Council fulfils the following functions contained in the **Coroners and Justice Act 2009**:

- preparation of sentencing guidelines;
- publication of the resource implications in respect of the guidelines it drafts and issues;
- monitoring of the operation and effect of its sentencing guidelines and the drawing of conclusions;
- preparation of resource assessments to accompany new guidelines;
- promotion of awareness of sentencing and sentencing practice; and
- publication of annual reports which include the effect of sentencing and non-sentencing practices.

The primary role of the Council is to issue guidelines on sentencing which the courts must follow unless it is in the interest of justice not to do so. In addition, the Sentencing Council considers the impact of sentencing decisions on victims, monitors the application of the guidelines, and seeks to promote greater understanding of and increasing public confidence in sentencing and the criminal justice system. Because the Sentencing Council is part of the executive, could it be said that this is one way in which the executive could influence the way judges pass sentence in its favour? It should be noted, however, that the problem is alleviated to a large extent because many of its members are drawn from the judiciary and legal profession.

The relationship between the courts and Parliament

The *sub judice* 'rule' prevents the discussion of ongoing cases in Parliament but, subject to that, the decisions and conduct of individual judges may be mentioned in debates in either House of Parliament. This does not, however, mean that judges are accountable to Parliament for their decisions in particular cases.

Parliament may legislate to reverse the effect of a decision or change the law as established or interpreted by a judicial decision. An example of this is the **War Damage Act 1965** which immediately followed the decision of the House of Lords' judgment in *Burmah Oil Co Ltd v Lord Advocate* (1965) and took effect retrospectively to reverse the House of Lords' decision that Burmah Oil Co Ltd was entitled to compensation for war damage suffered in 1942. Another example is the **Terrorist Asset Freezing (Temporary Provisions) Act 2010**. This Act, which was repealed by the **Terrorist Asset Freezing Act 2010**, was rapidly passed following the decision of the UK Supreme Court in *HM Treasury v Ahmed* (2010) not to suspend orders to quash two Orders in Council because they were incompatible with the **United Nations Act 1946**. The Act said that the orders in question were validly adopted according to the provisions of the **United Nations Act 1946**. It retained in force all the directions made under those Orders.

The Independent Human Rights Act Review 2021 and the impact of the HRA 1998 on the relationship between the judiciary, the executive, and the legislature

The Independent Human Rights Act Review 2021 will consider the way the **HRA 1998** balances the roles of the judiciary, the executive, and the legislature. It will examine whether the current approach risks 'over-judicialising' the executive while requiring the judiciary to consider matters of policy best left to the executive.

The review will also consider the following questions:

- Should any change be made to the framework established by **ss 3** and **4 HRA 1998**?

- Are there instances where, as a consequence of domestic courts and tribunals seeking to read and give effect to the compatibly of legislation with the Convention rights (as required by **s 3**), legislation has been interpreted in a manner inconsistent with the intention of the UK Parliament in enacting it? If yes, should **s 3** be amended (or repealed)?

- If **s 3** should be amended or repealed, should that change be applied to the interpretation of legislation enacted before the amendment/repeal takes effect? If yes, what should be done about previous **s 3** interpretations adopted by the courts?

- Should declarations of incompatibility (under **s 4**) be considered as part of the initial process of interpretation rather than as a matter of last resort, so as to enhance the role of Parliament in determining how any incompatibility should be addressed?

- What remedies should be available to domestic courts when considering challenges to designated derogation orders made under **s 14(1)**?

- Under the current framework, how have courts and tribunals dealt with the provisions of subordinate legislation that are incompatible with the Convention rights? Is any change required?

- In what circumstances does the **HRA 1998** apply to acts of public authorities taking place outside the territory of the UK? What are the implications of the current position? Is there a case for change?

- Should the remedial order process, as set out in **s 10** and **Sch 2 HRA 1998**, be modified, for example by enhancing the role of Parliament?

CASE	FACTS	PRINCIPLE
Duport Steels Ltd v Sirs [1980] 1 All ER 529	The House of Lords had to decide whether it was appropriate to grant an injunction to restrain secondary picketing on the ground that it was not covered by statutory immunities concerning trade union action as part of a trade dispute.	The British Constitution is firmly based on the separation of powers in that Parliament makes the laws and the judiciary interpret them.
Matthews v Ministry of Defence [2003] 1 AC 1163	This was a negligence claim involving considerations of **Art 6 European Convention on Human Rights and Fundamental Freedoms.**	The executive must never be put in a position where it effectively decides a case in the sense that it could order a court to dismiss a case. What matters is whether the effect of a legal provision is to give the executive a right to make decisions about people's rights which should be made by the judicial branch of government.
R (on the application of Al Rawi and others) v Secretary of State for Foreign and Commonwealth Affairs and another [2007] 2 WLR 1219	The Court of Appeal had to decide whether the courts must review the substance of an executive decision in human rights cases.	The role of the executive is to make decisions where it has access to special information or expertise or where the nature and consequences of the decision require accountability to the legislature and to the electorate. The role of the judiciary is to make sure that the executive complies with all formal requirements, considers matters rationally, and makes decisions, especially where human rights issues are involved, in accordance with the principle of proportionality.
R v Secretary of State for the Home Department, ex p Fire Brigades Union [1995] 2 All ER 244	See Chapter 3 on the rule of law.	Parliament, the executive, and the courts each have their distinct and largely exclusive domain. Parliament has a largely unchallengeable right to make whatever laws it thinks right. The executive carries on the administration of the country. The courts interpret the laws and see that they are obeyed.

Topic	'Constitutional Practice and Principle in the Article 50 Litigation'
Author/Academic	Richard Ekins
Viewpoint	This article considers, with reference to the ruling in *R (on the application of Miller) v Secretary of State for Exiting the European Union* (2017), the constitutional issues involved in the UK's service of notice of its withdrawal from the EU under **Art 50 TEU**. It goes on to reflect on the arguments raised in the case, the significance of the dissenting judgments, and how the decision intervenes in the relationship between the government and Parliament.
Source	(2017) 133 Law Quarterly Review 347–353

Topic	'Unpacking Separation of Powers: Judicial Independence, Sovereignty and Conceptual Flexibility in the UK Constitution'
Author/Academic	Roger Masterman and Se-shauna Wheatle
Viewpoint	This article considers the extent to which the UK doctrine of separation of powers exerts a normative influence on judicial decision-making. It goes on to examines the evolving constitutional significance of the doctrine, and how it manifests itself in judicial discourse through variants that are hierarchical, weakly normative, strongly normative, and constitutionally fundamental. It also outlines the context-specific nature of the variants.
Source	[2017] Public Law 469–487

Topic	'Legalism in Constitutional Law: Judging in a Democracy'
Author/Academic	Philip Sales
Viewpoint	This article discusses the author's experience as one of the judges subjected to media criticism for his role in *R (on the application of Miller) v Secretary of State for Exiting the European Union*. It also reviews key aspects of judging in a democracy, including legalism's role in constitutional law, the courts' responsibilities in the system of government, their interpretive duties, and their responsibility in safeguarding democratic politics.
Source	[2017] Public Law 687–707

Topic	'Constitutional Practice and Principle in the Article 50 Litigation'
Author/academic	Richard Ekins
Viewpoint	Considers, with reference to the ruling in *R (on the application of Miller) v Secretary of State for Exiting the European Union*, the constitutional issues involved in the UK's service of notice of its withdrawal from the EU under **Art 50 TEU**. Reflects on the arguments raised in the case, the significance of the dissenting judgments, and how the decision intervenes in the relationship between the government and Parliament.
Source	(2017) 133 Law Quarterly Review 347–353

Topic	'Political Constitutionalism and the Judicial Role: A Response'
Author/Academic	Paul Craig
Viewpoint	Discusses the challenges faced by political constitutionalists seeking to delineate the proper scope of judicial review in the UK.
Source	(2011) 9(1) International Journal of Constitutional Law 112–131

Topic	'Political Constitutionalism and the Human Rights Act'
Author/Academic	Richard Bellamy
Viewpoint	Evaluates the view that the **HRA 1998** gives excessive powers to the courts.
Source	(2011) 9(1) International Journal of Constitutional Law 86–111

 EXAM QUESTIONS

Essay question 1

Explain the functions and organs of government within the UK. What is meant by the separation of powers and what evidence is there that it is accepted as a legal principle?

Essay question 2

To what extent is the British system of government based on a fusion or separation of powers?

Online Resource

For outline answers to these essay questions, as well as interactive key cases and multiple-choice questions, please visit the online resources.
www.oup.com/he/faragher-concentrate7e

Concentrate Q&As

For more questions and answers on public law, see the *Concentrate Q&A: Public Law* by Richard Clements.

Go to the end of this book to view **sample pages**.

5 Parliamentary government and the legislative process

- The UK legislature is the monarch in Parliament.

- The UK Parliament is bicameral, with two chambers namely the House of Commons and the House of Lords.

- The House of Lords, which is composed of life peers, senior bishops, and some hereditary peers, protects the constitution and initiates and revises legislation.

- The House of Commons, which is composed of constituency representatives organized on party lines under the whip system, is the principal legislative chamber and plays a significant role in scrutinizing the executive.

- Both the House of Commons and the House of Lords are representative chambers but only the House of Commons is composed of elected representatives.

- Members of the House of Commons are elected according to the 'first past the post' electoral system.

- An Act of Parliament is a bill which has, at common law, received the separate and simultaneous assents of the House of Commons and the House of Lords as well as the Royal Assent.

- Under the **Parliament Acts 1911** and **1949** a bill may become an Act of Parliament by receiving the assent of the House of Commons and the Royal Assent.

- Public bills, which originate largely within government departments, pass between the House of Commons and the House of Lords and undergo scrutiny in committees set up by each House.

- There are alternative electoral systems, based on proportional representation, some of which are used within the UK.

- Part of the legislative function within the UK has been devolved to the Scottish Parliament, the National Assembly for Wales, and the Northern Ireland Assembly.

 REVISION TIP

You should begin your process of revision by understanding the structure, functions, and membership of the UK Parliament. This is important background information which will help you understand the material presented later in this chapter and in Chapter 6.

What is Parliament?

The UK has a parliamentary system of government. The UK Parliament is formally known as the Parliament of Great Britain and Northern Ireland. It was created, following the **Government of Ireland Act 1920**, by **s 2(1) Royal and Parliamentary Titles Act 1927**. The UK Parliament is bicameral. This means that, apart from the Queen, there are two legislative chambers: one is called the House of Lords; the other is called the House of Commons. They work separately and simultaneously.

The monarch's duties in Parliament

The monarch summons, opens, prorogues, and dissolves Parliament. The monarch also authorizes parliamentary general and by-elections and grants the Royal Assent to bills which have passed their necessary parliamentary stages. The monarch also appoints parliamentary officers like the Clerk of the Parliaments and the Clerk and Chief Executive of the House of Commons. Although the monarch may delegate their powers to commissioners, they are the only person who has the legal power to exercise these legal and formal powers.

Parliament comes to an end at the conclusion of the five-year period stipulated by the **Parliament Act 1911** and the **Fixed Term Parliaments Act 2011**. The **Fixed Term Parliaments Act 2011** fixes the date of the next general election at 5 May 2022, and provides for five-year fixed terms. It includes provisions to allow the Prime Minister to alter the date by up to two months by Order. There are also two ways in which an election could be triggered before the end of the five-year term:

1. if a motion of no confidence is passed and no alternative government is found;

2. if a motion for an early general election is agreed either by at least two-thirds of the House or without division.

Subject to these statutory provisions, before a general election can be held, the Prime Minister is legally obliged to go to the monarch and ask them to prorogue and dissolve Parliament and authorize a general election. Acting on the Prime Minister's advice, the monarch will then by royal proclamations via the Privy Council, authorize the prorogation and dissolution of Parliament and authorize the general election by writ.

Party leadership contests and hung parliaments may raise questions concerning how the monarch might exercise their powers. By convention, there is no need for Parliament to be dissolved if the Prime Minister loses their position as leader of the party in power. They merely offer their resignation to the monarch who accepts it and offers the post of Prime Minister to the new leader. There are important constitutional conventions which come into play both defining and informing what the monarch can and cannot do. If there is a hung parliament Rodney Brazier in *Constitutional Practice*, 3rd edn (1999), ch 3 says that the monarch's legal power to appoint a Prime Minister must be used to enhance the democratic process rather than to pre-empt it. So far as possible, the monarch must keep out of the process of government formation. Where there is a hung parliament, the monarch should stand back and let elected politicians decide the shape of the government. If the politicians fail to produce a way forward in a hung parliament, the monarch might receive each of the party leaders in turn. Brazier concludes that if a majority coalition government is proposed, rather than the more usual outcome in a hung parliament of a minority government taking office, then such a coalition should be appointed only if the party leaders can work out the details and present a copper-bottomed agreement to the monarch.

An example of the more usual outcome in a hung parliament followed the result of the 2017 general election after which the Conservative Party was the largest party in the House of Commons but lacked an overall majority. The outcome was a minority Conservative government supported by a Confidence and Supply Agreement with the Ulster Democratic Unionist Party (DUP). Under it the DUP agreed to support the government in votes in the UK Parliament on all motions of confidence, the Queen's Speech, the budget, finance bills, supply and appropriation legislation, and estimates. The DUP also agreed to support the government on legislation pertaining to the UK's exit from the EU and legislation pertaining to national security. Support on other matters was agreed on a case-by-case basis.

The monarch grants the Royal Assent to bills which have passed their parliamentary stages and a bill cannot become a valid Act of Parliament without the Royal Assent. There is a binding constitutional convention which requires the monarch to grant the Royal Assent as a matter of course if it has passed its required parliamentary stages. Another question, commonly raised, concerns whether the monarch might legitimately refuse the Royal Assent. After the **Human Rights Act 1998** came into force the question was raised as to whether the monarch might refuse the Royal Assent on the ground that they cannot be compelled to do anything as head of state which violates their right to freedom of speech, conscience, or religion. Robert Blackburn in 'The Royal Assent to Legislation and a Monarch's Fundamental Human Rights' [2003] Public Law 205 suggests two possible answers. The first, according to Blackburn, is opened up by the **Human Rights Act 1998** itself and relies on the **Regency Acts 1937–1953**. The second focuses on the meaning of 'Royal Assent'. The monarch could either (1) declare that they are not available for the performance of their duties as head of state due to fundamental human rights grounds of conscience, so that a regent could be temporarily appointed for the purpose of granting the Royal Assent; or (2) define 'Royal Assent' as a narrow duty to certify that a bill has passed through all its necessary parliamentary stages. Both here and in a later article entitled 'Monarchy and the Personal Prerogatives' [2004] Public Law 546, Blackburn favours the second answer and concludes that the Royal Assent is like a certificate that the bill has passed through all its necessary parliamentary stages; and the monarch cannot refuse the Royal Assent on the grounds of personal views or beliefs.

Rodney Brazier in *Constitutional Practice* offers the following guiding principles. The monarch's legal right to refuse the Royal Assent still exists but must be exercised in a way which is compatible with the political principle of democracy. The modern constitution ought to require political decisions, and responsibility for them, to be taken by politicians and (where appropriate) the electorate, not by the head of state. If a bill seeks to subvert the democratic basis of the constitution the monarch should either grant the Royal Assent under vigorous private protest or insist on a dissolution of Parliament and a general election.

The House of Lords

Under the **House of Lords Act 1999** the House of Lords consists of life peers, senior bishops of the Church of England, and hereditary peers.

Disclaimer and disqualification

Under the **Peerage Act 1963** hereditary peers may disclaim their titles for life and thus become eligible for membership of the House of Commons. Aliens, bankrupts, persons under the age of 21, and persons sentenced to imprisonment for treason may not sit in the House of Lords.

The functions and business of the House of Lords

There are four significant constitutional functions of the House of Lords:

- The House of Lords is the 'Protector of the Constitution'.
- The House of Lords is the place where many private and public bills are introduced into Parliament.
- The House of Lords may scrutinize and amend public bills.
- The House of Lords scrutinizes the executive through critical debates and examination on the floor of the House and in select committees.

The Protector of the Constitution: the role of the Constitution Committee of the House of Lords

The Constitution Committee of the House of Lords examines public bills to identify, investigate, and assess the implications of constitutional issues. The Committee also takes annual evidence from the Minister for the Constitution, the Lord Chancellor, the Lord Chief Justice of England and Wales, and the President of the Supreme Court. It played a significant role in scrutinizing the European (Withdrawal) Bill. The committee found that the bill raised 'a series of profound, wide-ranging and interlocking constitutional concerns' relating to:

- undermining legal certainty;
- challenging the relationship between the legislature and the executive; and
- the consequences for the devolved administrations and their relationship with the UK Government.

The Salisbury Doctrine

The House of Lords shall not, at its second or third reading, reject a government bill which has come from the House of Commons based on an electoral mandate from the nation. An electoral mandate from the nation means something contained in a general election manifesto. This is the Salisbury Doctrine or Salisbury Convention.

The House of Commons

Minors, aliens, peers, clerics, psychiatric patients, bankrupts, persons convicted of corrupt or illegal practices, prisoners, excess ministers, members of other legislatures, holders of public office, and holders of offices for profit under the Crown may not sit in the House of Commons.

Expulsion

The House may declare a disqualified member's seat vacant or may expel a member for whatever reason it pleases.

The principal functions of the House of Commons

The House of Commons exclusively initiates financial legislation. It sustains, checks, and balances the power of the government. It also represents the interests and grievances of constituents and promotes the interests of the nation in times of emergency. The House of Commons makes a leading contribution to the overall effectiveness of Parliament.

The House of Commons uses Question Time, debates, and Select Committees to carry out its functions.

Question Time

This occupies between 50 and 60 minutes and includes Prime Minister's Question Time. There are questions requiring oral answers, those requiring written answers, and private notice questions.

Debates

The House of Commons scrutinizes government policy in the second reading stage of a bill, substantive motions for debate moved by the government, substantive motions for debate moved by the opposition, the address in reply to the Queen's Speech, and the debate following budget proposals.

Select committees

These are smaller than **standing committees**. The select committee usually comprises up to 15 MPs with the various parties being represented according to their proportion of seats in the House. The types of select committee include the following:

Ad hoc committees

These committees are set up to look into and report on specific matters. Today much of the work which used to be done by such committees is now done by **Royal Commissions**, Tribunals of Inquiry, departmental committees, and committees of inquiry chaired by senior members of the judiciary.

Permanent select committees

The permanent, or regular, select committees of the House of Commons include the **Public Accounts Committee**, the Select Committee on European Legislation, the Select Committee on the Parliamentary Commissioner, the Select Committee of Privileges (now Standards and Privileges), and the Select Committees on services, selection, and procedure.

Departmental select committees

Government departments are scrutinized by select committees. The number of such committees depends on the number of government departments in existence at any given time.

The Parliamentary Commissioner for Administration

The Parliamentary Commissioner for Administration (the Ombudsman) was set up by the **Parliamentary Commissioner Act 1967**. This Act was subsequently amended by the **Parliamentary and Health Service Commissioners Act 1987** and the **Parliamentary Commissioner Act 1994**.

Purpose and jurisdiction

The purpose of the Ombudsman is to receive and deal with complaints from individuals who have suffered injustice because of maladministration. There is no statutory definition of maladministration. In 1966, Richard Crossman said that it includes bias, neglect, inattention, delay, incompetence, ineptitude, perversity, turpitude, and arbitrariness. Subsequently, this has been expanded to take into account categories of discrimination. The Ombudsman's jurisdiction is limited by **ss 5** and **6** and **Schs 2** and **3 Parliamentary Commissioner Act 1967**. There are detailed lists of excluded matters and bodies.

Procedure

According to **s 5 Parliamentary Commissioner Act 1967**, anyone who wishes to make a complaint has to go through an MP. In practice, if a complaint is made directly to the Ombudsman by a member of the public it is referred to an MP who, at their discretion, refers it back to the Ombudsman. If the complaint is accepted, the Ombudsman conducts a private inquiry according to the terms of **s 7 Parliamentary Commissioner Act 1967**. The end result of the investigation is a report which is considered by the Select Committee on Public Administration.

Where the Ombudsman finds maladministration remedial action can be recommended. Remedial action consists of payment of compensation, alterations of decisions or procedures, and giving an apology.

The Ombudsman has no power to require compliance with any recommendations.

LOOKING FOR EXTRA MARKS?

There have been a number of proposals for reform in this area and there are several useful publications available online at www.gov.uk/government/organisations/cabinet-office. You should look up these publications and think about how the Ombudsman service could be improved.

The electoral process

REVISION TIP

This topic is closely linked with the principle of democracy. This is a political principle and not easy to define. To avoid confusion, when you revise this part of the topic, stick to the key rules which apply to British constitutional law. Focus now on the legal right to vote in an election and what is meant by 'free elections'.

The right to vote in an election

At common law anyone qualified to vote in an election has the right to do so and may bring a claim for damages in tort against any person who illegally excludes them.

Ashby v White (1703) 92 ER 126, (1703) 92 ER 710, 1 ER 417

This was determined by the House of Lords, which overruled the decision of the Court of Queen's Bench and followed the dissenting judgment of Holt CJ from which the following key principles emerge. If a statute gives a right the common law will provide a remedy to maintain it where there is injury or damage. The court's jurisdiction to provide remedies for breaches of legal rights is not limited by parliamentary privilege.

Free elections

The principle of free elections was enacted by **Art 8 Bill of Rights 1689**, which provides that the parliamentary elections ought to be free. Moreover, **Protocol 1, Art 3 European Convention on**

Human Rights and Fundamental Freedoms (1953) provides that the High Contracting Parties undertake to hold free elections at reasonable intervals by secret ballot, under conditions which will ensure the free expression of the opinion of the people in the choice of the legislature. This was incorporated into UK law by the **Human Rights Act 1998**.

REVISION TIP

One of the important things to be clear about at this stage is that although democracy implies government by the people, in British constitutional law, the word 'people' does not mean the general population. You need to understand the nature and extent of the franchise, the electorate, and the organization of constituencies.

The franchise and the electorate

The franchise is the legal right to vote. The electorate is all those who have this right. The rules are found in the **Representation of the People Act 1983** as amended by the **Representation of the People Act 2000**. To qualify, an elector must be 18 years of age or over at the time of the election, be a British subject, or citizen of the Republic of Ireland (any EU national resident in the UK may vote in elections for the European Parliament), and not be subject to any legal disqualification.

The **Representation of the People Act 1989** allows UK citizens who live abroad to vote if they have been resident in the UK and registered as voters within the previous 20 years. Service personnel are entitled to be considered 'resident' providing that their absence results from service for the armed forces or the Crown overseas. Similar provisions apply to merchant seamen.

The **Representation of the People Act 2000** creates the concept of 'rolling' electoral registration. Thus an electoral register for any given constituency will be produced for a specific election based on an annual return as amended by any subsequent changes.

Section 3 Representation of the People Act 2000 deals with the residence requirements considered by registration officers when deciding whether or not to register a person as a voter. Regard will be had to the purpose of the residence and other circumstances. **Section 7** enables service voters to register on this basis provided the criteria under **s 3** are met. A person whose name is not on the register may not vote. It is a criminal offence to vote in more than one constituency (other than as a proxy for another elector). Even if a person's name is on the register, it is a criminal offence to vote if ineligible to do so. Those disqualified from voting include aliens, minors, mental defectives, and drunkards. Under the 2000 Act a person who is detained in a mental hospital as a voluntary patient may be registered as a voter provided their stay is sufficient in length for them to be regarded as resident in the mental hospital. Most convicted criminals serving sentences of imprisonment as well as persons convicted of corrupt or illegal practices at elections are disqualified from voting.

Constituencies

The delimitation of constituencies is a matter for Parliament. Prior to the enactment of the **Political Parties, Elections and Referendums Act 2000**, the determination of constituency boundaries was undertaken by four Boundary Commissions for England, Wales, Scotland, and Northern Ireland. Under the **Political Parties, Elections and Referendums Act 2000**, that task is transferred to the Electoral Commission.

The redistribution of seats is a controversial matter as political parties can lose 'safe' seats because of it. Although there have been a number of challenges in the courts to decisions of the Boundary Commissioners, none have succeeded.

R v Boundary Commission for England, ex p Foot [1983] QB 600

The Court of Appeal had to decide whether it had jurisdiction to decide if a decision of the Boundary Commission could be challenged on the ground that it had acted unreasonably. The Court of Appeal held that although there was no statutory right of appeal against a decision of the Boundary Commission, the High Court had jurisdiction to determine whether the Boundary Commission had properly carried out its statutory instructions. The rules followed by the Boundary Commission were guidelines only. The substantial obstacle to judicial review of the Boundary Commission was that it did not make decisions but recommendations for which it did not have to give reasons. The claimant would have to prove that the Boundary Commission's recommendations and conclusions were such that no reasonable commission could have made them. The claimants had failed to discharge their burden of proof in this case. Their claim for judicial review failed.

The Parliamentary Voting System and Constituencies Act 2011

Sections 10–14 update and set out the current powers of the Boundary Commission. **Section 11** of the Act provides that there shall be 600 constituencies within the UK of not more than 13,000 square kilometres unless it is at least 12,000 square kilometres and the Boundary Commission concerned is satisfied that it is not reasonably possible for the constituency to comply with that rule. The Act goes on to make further provisions for determining constituency boundaries.

Conduct of electoral campaigns: voting systems

The responsibility for the conduct of elections lies with the returning officer who is the sheriff of the county or mayor of the borough, depending on the constituency. Their authority is delegated to the registration officer for each constituency. Voting is by way of secret ballot. The candidate who receives the highest number of votes in each constituency is 'returned' as the Member of Parliament for that constituency. There is no requirement that a candidate must obtain a minimum percentage of the total vote to be elected. This system of voting is known as the 'first past the post' system.

Alternative voting systems (AV)

Single-member systems

The supplementary vote

With the supplementary vote, there are two columns on the ballot paper—one for the first choice and one for the second choice. Voters are not required to make a second choice if they do not wish to. Voters mark an 'X' in the first column for their first choice and a second 'X' in the second column for their other choice. Voters' first preferences are counted and if one candidate gets 50 per cent of the vote, then they are elected. If no candidate reaches 50 per cent of the vote, the two highest scoring candidates are retained and the rest of the candidates are eliminated. The second preferences on the ballot papers of the eliminated candidates are examined and any that have been cast for the two remaining candidates are given to them. Whoever has the most votes at the end of the process wins.

This system is used to elect the Mayor of London.

Multi-member systems

Single transferable vote (STV)

Each constituency would elect between three and five MPs depending on its size. Voters rank the candidates, putting a '1' for their favourite, a '2' for the next, and so on. If the voter's first-choice candidate does not need their vote, either because they are elected without it, or because they have too few votes to be elected, then the vote is transferred to the voter's second-choice candidate, and so on.

In this way, most of the votes help to elect a candidate and far fewer votes are wasted. An important feature of STV is that voters can choose between candidates both of their own and of other parties, and can even select candidates for reasons other than party affiliation. Thus, a voter wishing for more women MPs could vote for a woman from their own party and then all other women candidates, whatever party they stand for.

The system is used in the Australian Senate, the Republic of Ireland, Tasmania, Malta, and Northern Ireland for local elections and elections to the European Parliament.

Arguments used in favour

STV does more than other systems to guarantee that everyone gets their views represented in Parliament and that they have a say in what is done by their elected representatives. STV is the best option for putting the power in the hands of the voters and keeping MPs linked to the people who voted for them. Most voters can identify a representative that they personally helped to elect and can feel affinity with. Such a personal link also increases accountability.

Making Parliament reflect the views of the voters

Only a party or coalition of parties, who could attract more than 50 per cent of the electorate, could form a government. Any changes would have to be backed by a majority since public opinion is reflected fairly in elections under STV. This is far more important than that a government should be formed by only one political party.

It enables the voters to express opinions effectively. Voters can choose between candidates within parties, demonstrating support for different wings of the party. Voters can also express preferences between the abilities, or other attributes, of individual candidates.

It is simple for voters to use

There is no need for tactical voting. Voters can cast a positive vote and know that their vote will not be wasted whatever their choice is. It produces governments that are strong and stable because they are founded on the majority support of the electorate.

Weaknesses

The system does not produce such accuracy in proportional representation of parties as the party list or additional member systems. It breaks the link between *an individual* MP and their constituency. Constituencies would be three to five times larger than they are now but with three to five MPs. MPs may have to spend an excessive amount of time dealing with constituency problems and neglect the broader issues. There are critics who say that this system could lead to permanent coalition governments, but this would only happen if the voters as a whole want it. It is disliked by politicians, since it would remove power from them and give it to the electors, and many MPs with safe seats would lose the security they feel now.

Mixed systems

Additional member system (AMS)

Several variants of AMSs have been proposed, but basically they are a combination of the 'first past the post' system and party list voting. The purpose is to retain the best features of 'first past the post' while introducing proportionality between parties through party list voting.

Each voter has two votes, one vote for a single MP via 'first past the post' and one for a regional or national party list. Half the seats or more are allocated to the single-member constituencies and the rest to the party list. The percentage of votes obtained by the parties in the party list vote determines their overall number of representatives; the party lists are used to top up the 'first past the post' seats gained by the party to the required number. So if a party has won two seats in the constituencies but in proportion to its votes should have five, the first three candidates on its list are elected in addition.

The system is used in Germany and it was also chosen by New Zealand in a referendum in 1993 (although in New Zealand it is called Mixed Member Proportional Representation or MMP). The new Scottish Parliament and the Welsh Assembly were both elected by AMS in May 1999 and 2003 as was the London Assembly in May 2000.

Arguments used in favour

It results in broadly proportional representation along party lines while ensuring that there is a directly accountable MP for each constituency. It retains a number of single-member constituencies. It has produced strong and stable governments in Germany (but not single party governments). Each elector has at least one effective vote. Even if they see no chance of winning in the single-member constituency, people can use their second vote for a party they support and still have a limited say through an additional member. The separation of the vote allows the voter to make an expression of popular approval or disapproval which is not possible under 'first past the post'. Because the first vote does not affect a party's total representation, a voter can use it to express personal support for a candidate without necessarily helping that candidate's party. AMS would give people the government they wanted, keeping the link between MPs and voters as well as giving some value to all votes, via the additional members.

Weaknesses

It combines many of the faults of 'first past the post' with many of the defects of the list systems of proportional representation. Half of all MPs are not directly accountable to any voters, just to their party leadership, and have no constituency. It creates two types of MP, one with a constituency role and duties and one without such a base. To retain some constituency MPs, constituencies would have to increase in size. The parties would retain power over selecting candidates for constituency seats and would have complete control over choosing their Additional Members. Those who are under-represented today may not fare any better under AMS.

The Independent Commission on the Voting System (the Jenkins Report) made a number of significant recommendations, the most important of which was that the best alternative for Britain to the 'first past the post' system is a two-vote mixed system which can be described as either limited AMS or AV top-up.

The **Parliamentary Voting System and Constituencies Act 2011** provided for a referendum to determine whether the first past the post system ought to be replaced by AV. The referendum was held on 5 May 2011. The result favoured the retention of the first past the post system for general elections.

 REVISION TIP

Important legislative functions have been delegated under the principle of devolution. You should study this closely.

The legislative process

REVISION TIP

Your performance in essay and problem questions will be greatly improved if you learn and understand the meaning of relevant terminology. In particular, it will help you to recognize what an essay question is about and to select relevant material.

A bill is a draft statute, introduced into Parliament which, if passed, becomes an Act of Parliament. There are public, private, and hybrid bills.

A public bill seeks to make or change the law affecting people's rights and obligations generally in all or part of the UK. A private bill aims to confer upon or regulate the rights and obligations of individuals and corporate bodies. A hybrid bill concerns the general law and the rights and obligations of individuals and corporations.

At common law an Act of Parliament is a bill which has received the separate and simultaneous assents of the House of Lords and the House of Commons and the Royal Assent.

Stockdale v Hansard **(1839) 112 ER 1112**

This was determined by Lord Denman CJ. The question was whether the House of Commons could extend its own privileges by resolution.

It was held that the House of Commons cannot make or amend laws by resolution. For this purpose legislation is required which has received the simultaneous and separate assents of the House of Commons and the House of Lords plus the Royal Assent.

Bowles v Bank of England **[1913] 1 CH 57**

The principle in the case above was accepted and applied in this case by Parker J. The issue here was whether a resolution of the Committee of the House of Commons for Ways and Means could, once adopted by the House of Commons, authorize the Crown to levy and collect taxes before the annual Finance Bill had become an Act of Parliament.

The judge held that legislation was required before the Crown could levy and collect taxes and that a resolution was not equivalent to an Act of Parliament because it had not received the necessary assents.

The Parliament Acts 1911 and 1949 and the meaning of Act of Parliament

Under the **Parliament Acts 1911** and **1949**, bills may become Acts of Parliament without the assent of the House of Lords if the Lords fail within one month to pass a bill certified as a Money Bill by the Speaker of the House of Commons or refuse in two successive sessions, whether of the same Parliament or not, to pass a public bill which has been passed by the Commons in those two sessions, provided that one year has elapsed between the date of the bill's second reading in the Commons in the first of those sessions and the date of the third reading in that House in the second of those sessions.

The only exception is a bill which seeks to extend the life of a Parliament for more than five years. Examples include the **Welsh Church Act 1914**, the **Government of Ireland Act 1914**, the **Parliament Act 1949**, the **War Crimes Act 1991**, the **European Parliamentary Election Act 1999**, the **Sexual Offences (Amendment) Act 1999**, and the **Hunting Act 2004**.

Jackson v Attorney General [2006] 1 AC 262

The House of Lords, among other things, held that the purpose of the **Parliament Act 1911** was to restrict the power of the House of Lords to defeat bills which had been passed by the House of Commons. **Section 2(1) Parliament Act 1911** creates a parallel way in which any public bill introduced into the House of Commons can become an Act of Parliament. The 1911 Act applies to any public bill and for this reason there is no basis for implying any exceptions beyond those expressly mentioned in the 1911 Act. Accordingly, the **Parliament Act 1949** and the **Hunting Act 2004** are valid Acts of Parliament.

 REVISION TIP

Especially when answering essay questions, students think that they can impress their examiners by writing all they know about parliamentary procedure, whether or not it is required to answer the question. Remember, all you really have to do in an examination is answer the questions. Do not give examiners more than they want. You will not get extra marks for doing so.

Most bills originate from within the government. The scope for legislative initiatives by individual MPs is very limited. The legislative process is in three stages. The first stage concerns the period before publication of the bill. The second stage is the passage of the bill through Parliament. The third stage concerns the coming into force of the Act after the bill has received the Royal Assent.

The allocation of time in the House of Commons

The allocation of time to parliamentary business in the House of Commons is achieved by Programme Motions, Programme Orders, and Closure Motions.

Programme Motions in the House of Commons

A timetable for the passage of a government bill through the House of Commons is agreed by MPs when it receives its second House of Commons reading. This is done by tabling a Programme Motion.

Programme Orders in the House of Commons

A Programme Order gives effect to the agreed timetable proposed by the Programme Motion.

Closure Motions in the House of Commons

The Speaker of the House of Commons may close a debate and ask the House to vote on an issue. This is called a division. An MP may ask the Speaker to do this by tabling a Closure Motion which may require the support of at least 100 MPs. The discretion of the Speaker in this matter is absolute.

The role of backbenchers: private members' bills

Public bills may be sponsored by individual members of the House of Commons or House of Lords. These are called **private members' bills** because they do not form part of the government's legislative programme. They are allocated a very limited amount of parliamentary time which seriously reduces their chances of becoming law. All that a member or Lord needs to provide is the short title by which the bill will be known and a long title which briefly describes what the bill does.

Private members' bills can by introduced by the ballot, the ten-minute rule, and presentation.

The ballot

At the beginning of the parliamentary year a ballot is held to decide which of all the members who wish to introduce a bill will be allocated debating time. One day is usually allocated to the first seven bills drawn from the ballot. These are called ballot bills.

Ten-minute rule

The sponsor of a bill introduced under this rule is given ten minutes to speak in favour of the issue addressed by the bill. Another member may speak against it for ten minutes. This procedure is commonly used to raise awareness of an issue.

Presentation

Any member may introduce a bill in this way as long as they have previously given notice of their intention to do so. Members formally introduce the title of the bill but do not speak in support of it. These bills rarely become law.

Private members' bills introduced into the House of Lords

A similar procedure applies where a private members' bill is introduced into the House of Lords. If it passes its House of Lords stages it proceeds to the House of Commons if an MP is prepared to support it.

Raising objections to a private members' bill

Anyone who objects to a private members' bill can write to their MP or to a Member of the House of Lords or to a minister, if the bill has government support. Members of the public may lobby Parliament directly. See Fig 5.1.

Private bills

Private bills are subject to the same procedural requirements as public bills. One important difference, however, is that the House of Lords may veto a private bill. There is also no Report Stage in the House of Lords for private bills. In addition, a private bill will not be debated at the second reading stage unless objections to its provisions have been raised. If there are objections a private bill is sent to the Opposed Bill Committee. If there are no objections it goes to the Unopposed Bill Committee.

After the committee stage the bill is reported to the House and its subsequent stages.

Figure 5.1 Public bill procedure diagram

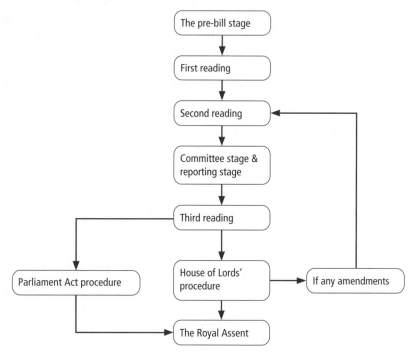

Delegated legislation

What is delegated legislation?

Parliament may give legislative powers to the executive by statute. Statutes which do this are called enabling Acts. Delegated legislation is law made by the executive when exercising these powers. The enabling Act contains general provisions and then empowers the executive to make more detailed law covering the subject matter of the relevant legislation. These take effect as if they are part of the enabling Act. An example of this is the **Criminal Justice Act 2003**. This empowers the Secretary of State to make codes of practice which the police use when issuing cautions.

Types of delegated legislation

Delegated legislation can take the form of Statutory Instruments, Orders in Council, Regulations, Rules, Orders, Schemes, Warrants, Bylaws, and Directions.

Parliamentary scrutiny of Statutory Instruments

Statutory Instruments form the largest group of delegated legislation. Many Statutory Instruments take effect on a stipulated date without parliamentary scrutiny. One of three parliamentary procedures may apply where an enabling Act requires a Statutory Instrument to be laid before Parliament. Some Statutory Instruments are laid before Parliament for information only. No further action is taken. Others take effect unless there is a motion or prayer of annulment passed by either House. This is called a *negative resolution procedure*. Statutory Instruments which must be approved by Parliament before they take effect follow the *affirmative resolution procedure*. The Joint Committee on Statutory Instruments looks at General Statutory Instruments to make sure that they comply with the provisions of the enabling Act.

The advantages of delegated legislation

Parliamentary time may be allocated more effectively if the enabling statute concentrates on the general principles and provisions. The executive takes responsibility for carrying these principles into effect by making detailed regulations as and when required. This is especially useful in emergencies or rapidly changing circumstances. Statutory Instruments often contain detailed provisions affecting local or technical issues requiring the kind of specialist expertise which can be found within departments of state. Because the process of making delegated legislation is quicker and less complex than passing or amending Acts of Parliament it promotes flexible government.

The disadvantages of delegated legislation

It undermines the separation of powers by giving too much legislative power to the executive especially where the rights and obligations of the general public are concerned. It makes the process of law-making less democratic by giving Parliament less time to scrutinize measures before they become law. It can lead to undesirable levels of sub-delegation especially where local authorities are empowered to make bylaws. Not enough parliamentary time is given to scrutinizing delegated legislation and there is simply too much delegated legislation for the general public to keep up with the law.

Covid-19 legislation and regulations

The executive has made extensive use of delegated legislation in its attempts to deal with the coronavirus pandemic, exercising its powers under the **Public Health (Control of Diseases) Act 1984**, Social Security and Welfare Reform Acts, and the **Coronavirus Act 2020** which became law on 25 March 2020.

The emergency procedure contained in **s 45R Public Health (Control of Diseases) Act 1984** was used to pass the following regulations:

- **Health Protection (Coronavirus) Regulations 2020**, which were made and laid before Parliament on 10 February 2020;
- **Health Protection (Notification) (Amendment) Regulations 2020**; and
- **Health Protection (Coronavirus, Business Closure) (England) Regulations 2020**.

The Social Security and Welfare Reform Acts were used to pass:

- **Employment and Support Allowance and Universal Credit (Coronavirus Disease) Regulations 2020**; and
- **Charges to Overseas Visitors (Amendment) Regulations 2020**.

These regulations gave the executive extensive powers, including giving police constables the power to detain individuals and impose restrictions on travel and other activities where they had reasonable grounds to believe an individual had coronavirus and posed a risk to others. They also resulted in extensive business closures.

The Coronavirus Act 2020

The **Coronavirus Act 2020** has 102 sections and 29 Schedules. The provisions of the Act, which are time-limited for two years, enable the government to restrict or prohibit public gatherings, control or suspend public transport, order businesses such as shops and restaurants to close, temporarily detain people suspected of Covid-19 infection, suspend the operation of ports and airports, temporarily close educational institutions and childcare premises, enrol medical students and retired healthcare workers in the health services, relax regulations to ease the burden on healthcare services, and assume control of death management in particular local areas. The government has stated that these powers may be 'switched on and off' according to the medical advice it receives. The Act formally postpones the local elections originally scheduled for May 2020 and grants the UK and relevant devolved governments the power to postpone any other election, local referendum, or recall petition until 6 May 2021. Local councillors, elected mayors, and Police and Crime Commissioners originally due for election in 2020 will serve three-year terms after their election in 2021, rather than the normal four years, in order to maintain the normal election cycle.

The constitutional sources which determine how Parliament works

Apart from statutes like the **Parliament Acts 1911** and **1949**, the **Royal Assent Act 1967**, and the **Fixed Term Parliaments Act 2011** the sources governing parliamentary procedure are:

- ancient usage;
- Standing Orders of the House of Commons and the Standing Orders of the House of Lords; and
- Speakers' Rulings in the House of Commons.

Ancient usage is a set of rules contained in the orders and resolutions of the House of Commons. They are recorded in the journals of the House of Commons dating back to the seventeenth century. Examples of ancient usage include:

- the requirement that a bill be read three times in each House;
- the practice of the House of Commons sitting as a Committee of the Whole House when considering certain types of bills; and
- the procedure governing the work of select committees.

Ancient usage is akin to the common law of Parliament.

The Standing Orders of the House of Commons and the House of Lords set out how the business of each House can be best carried out and determine the current rules of debate. The rules governing the election of the Speaker of the House of Commons are contained in the Standing Orders of the House of Commons. The Standing Orders of each House are like a set of internal statutes.

As far as the House of Commons is concerned, the rulings of the Speaker on points of order which are recorded in Hansard form a third source of parliamentary procedure. There is no equivalent in the House of Lords. The Lord Speaker may not give rulings. Speakers' rulings are the parliamentary equivalent of case law. In the House of Lords, rulings are given by the Leader of the House.

The Speaker's statement on 19 March 2019

Following repeated government defeats on motions concerning the EU Withdrawal Agreement, MPs expressed concern that the House of Commons was being repeatedly asked to pronounce on the same fundamental proposition and asked for a ruling from the Speaker. In response, the Speaker made a statement in which he referred to a rule dating from 1604 stated in the 24th edition of 'Erskine May', p 397, which said that 'A motion or an amendment which is the same, in substance, as a question which has been decided during a session may not be brought forward again during that same session ... Attempts have been made to evade this rule by raising again, with verbal alterations, the essential portions of motions which have been negatived. Whether the second motion is substantially the same as the first is finally a matter for the judgment of the Chair.' Applying this rule, the Speaker held that the government could not schedule a third vote on the EU Withdrawal Agreement unless it was substantially different from the previous motions voted on by the House. In coming to his decision, the Speaker took into account precedents in which former Speakers between 1870 and 1921 had recognized the rule and considered themselves bound by it. He also stated that there was a good reason for the rule. It is a necessary rule to ensure the sensible use of the House's time and proper respect for the decisions that it takes.

Constitutional conventions underpinning parliamentary government in the UK

The most significant constitutional conventions which underpin Parliament are:

- the monarch must act on the advice of the Prime Minister;
- the monarch must appoint a member of the House of Commons as Prime Minister who has the confidence of the House, which means that under normal circumstances they will be the leader of the political party with a majority of seats in the House of Commons;
- all Cabinet ministers, as well as other members of the government appointed by the monarch, must be members of the House of Commons or the House of Lords;
- the monarch must assent to any bill that has received the assent of either House of Parliament (or the House of Commons alone under the **Parliament Acts 1911** and **1949**);
- ministers are individually and collectively responsible to Parliament.

The political and legal theories underpinning parliamentary government

There are four principles which underpin parliamentary government.

- The UK parliamentary system of government allowing political parties based on divergent political theories to participate and contribute to the process of debates and making laws.
- The executive is accountable to both Parliament and the courts for the way it exercises its powers.
- Pluralistic liberal political ideas, prohibiting discrimination and promoting fair and impartial judicial procedures, underpin the rules governing the relationship between the citizen and the state especially concerning civil and political rights.
- Legislation should benefit society as a whole and not protect and promote the personal interests of those in power or the interests of limited sections of society.

LOOKING FOR EXTRA MARKS?

The issues discussed in this chapter can give rise to some very elaborate arguments. John Alder and Keith Syrett in *Constitutional & Administrative Law*, 11th edn (2017), discuss a wide variety of political ideas, including liberal pluralism, which underpin constitutional law in the UK. You should read their discussion of these theories and follow up the issues raised here in your recommended standard textbook. You should also read the articles recommended in the Key debates.

The devolution of the legislative function

Scotland

The Scottish Parliament is set up by **s 1 Scotland Act 1998**.

The Scottish Parliament can legislate generally, subject to the restrictions in **ss 28** and **29** and **Sch 4 Scotland Act 1998**. Acts of the Scottish Parliament are subordinate legislation because they owe their validity to the **Scotland Act 1998**. They can be set aside by the courts and over-ridden by Acts of the UK Parliament. According to **s 28** the validity of the procedure leading to an enactment does not affect the Act's validity. But Acts of the Scottish Parliament that are outside its competence are not law. Where a measure is ambiguous it must be interpreted narrowly in favour of its validity according to **s 101 Scotland Act 1998**.

Restrictions

The Scottish Parliament cannot, except in minor respects, amend the **Scotland Act 1998**. It cannot alter law outside Scotland. It cannot override EU law or rights binding under the **Human Rights Act 1998**. UK ministers have the exclusive powers to bring EU law into effect. It has taxation powers limited to altering the basic rate of income tax by three pence in the pound.

Reserved matters

Many important matters are reserved matters on which only the UK Parliament can legislate. They include important constitutional provisions such as matters affecting the Crown (but not the exercise of the Royal Prerogative), the civil service, the registration and funding of political parties, the Union with England, the UK Parliament, the higher Scottish courts, international relations, defence, national security, treason, fiscal, economic, and monetary policy, currency, financial services and markets, money laundering, border controls, transport safety and regulation, media policy, employment regulation, certain health matters, and the regulation of key professions and social security.

The devolution of legislative competence to the Scottish Parliament does not affect the ability of Westminster to legislate for Scotland even in relation to devolved matters. But, under the so-called Sewel Convention, the Westminster Parliament will not normally legislate with regard to devolved matters in Scotland without the consent of the Scottish Parliament.

The Scotland Act 2012

The **Scotland Act 2012** makes changes to the devolution settlement for Scotland and gives effect to many of the recommendations as set out in the Commission on Scottish Devolution's (Calman Commission) final report, *Serving Scotland Better: Scotland and the United Kingdom in the 21st Century*, published in June 2009. The Act follows the Coalition Government's commitment to 'implement the proposals of the Calman Commission' in *The Coalition: Our Programme for Government*, published in May 2010. The Act also makes a number of technical amendments to the **Scotland Act 1998** not related to the Calman Commission's report, but which will update the operation of the devolution settlement. The Act achieves many of its aims by way of amendment to the **Scotland Act 1998**. As well as bringing in a new Scottish rate of income tax and borrowing powers worth £5 billion, the **Scotland Act 2012** hands powers over air guns, drink-driving, and speeding limits to the Scottish Parliament. It also devolves stamp duty, land tax, and landfill tax, and gives the Scottish Parliament a role in appointments in broadcasting and the Crown Estate. In addition, there are new procedures for Scottish criminal cases that go to the UK Supreme Court.

The Scotland Act 2016

The **Scotland Act 2016** recognizes the permanence of the Scottish Parliament and the Scottish Government, requiring a referendum before either of them can be abolished, and grants further powers to the Scottish Parliament and the Scottish Government.

Wales

The **Government of Wales Act 1998** establishes a National Assembly for Wales (the Welsh Assembly) consisting of 60 Assembly Members (AMs). Forty AMs were elected on a 'first past the post' basis from constituencies identical with parliamentary constituencies and a further 20 AMs were elected from five electoral regions, four from each region. The Welsh Assembly's powers, whether transferred by Orders in Council or conferred directly by Act of Parliament, include a large number of subordinate order-making powers (including some powers enabling the Assembly to amend primary legislation), but the Assembly was not empowered by the 1998 Act to make primary legislation for Wales.

The **Government of Wales Act 2006** provides that the Welsh Assembly is no longer a corporate body, makes amendments to the electoral law, creates the Welsh Assembly Government, and deals with some issues concerning the powers of the Secretary of State for Wales.

The legislative competence of the Welsh Assembly

The Welsh Assembly was reconstituted as a separate legislature following elections in May 2007. **Section 94** and **Sch 5 Government of Wales Act 2006** give the Welsh Assembly the power to make laws called Measures of the National Assembly for Wales (Assembly Measures). The legislative competence of the Welsh Assembly is set out in Sch 5. An Assembly Measure is within the legislative competence of the Welsh Assembly if it relates to agriculture, fisheries, forestry, rural development, ancient monuments, historic buildings, culture, economic development, education, and training. In March 2011 a referendum was held in Wales to determine whether the Welsh Assembly should be given further legislative powers in accordance with the provisions of **Pt 4** of the 2006 Act. The result of the referendum was that 63.5 per cent of people voted yes and 36.5 per cent voted no. The Welsh Assembly will, in the future, be able to make laws for Wales on subjects for which the Assembly and the Welsh Assembly Government are already responsible, without needing permission from the UK Parliament first.

The Wales Act 2014

The purpose of the **Wales Act 2014** is to implement some of the recommendations of the Silk Commission. The Act's provisions include the following:

- Devolving stamp duty, business rates, and landfill tax to Wales and enabling the Welsh Assembly to replace them with new taxes specific to Wales. Further taxes can also be devolved, with the agreement of the UK Parliament and the Welsh Assembly.
- Providing for a referendum in Wales on whether an element of income tax should be devolved. If there is a vote in favour then the Welsh Assembly will be able to set a Welsh income tax rate. Fluctuations in revenues will be managed by new borrowing powers for Welsh ministers.
- Extending Welsh Assembly terms permanently from four to five years.
- Removing the prohibition on candidates in Welsh Assembly elections from standing in a constituency and also being on the regional list.
- Prohibiting Welsh Assembly members from also being MPs.
- Formally changing the Welsh Assembly Government's name to the Welsh Government.
- Clarifying the position of the First Ministers between dissolution of the Assembly and an Assembly election.
- Allowing Welsh ministers to set a limit for the amount of housing debt that individual local housing authorities in Wales may hold. The UK Treasury will limit the total Welsh housing debt.
- Requiring the Law Commission to provide advice and information to Welsh ministers on the law reform matters that they referred to the Commission.

The Wales Act 2017

The **Wales Act 2017** recognizes the National Assembly for Wales and the Welsh Government as permanent among the UK's constitutional arrangements, with a referendum required before either can be abolished. The Act also recognizes that there is a body of Welsh law made by the National Assembly for Wales. This does not change the single England and Wales jurisdiction. The **Wales Act 2017** also moves Wales from a conferred matters model to a reserved matters model which is used in Scotland under the **Scotland Act 1998**. This Act also repeals the provision of the **Wales Act 2014** for a referendum in Wales on the devolution of income tax. The **Wales Act 2017** also gives extra powers to the National Assembly for Wales and the Welsh Government. In particular the Act gives the National Assembly for Wales the power to amend sections of the **Government of Wales Act 2006** relating to the operation of the National Assembly for Wales and the Welsh Government within the UK, including control of its electoral system (subject to a two-thirds majority within the parliament for any proposed change). The Act also extends the legislative powers of the National Assembly for Wales and the executive powers of the Welsh ministers relating to control of road signs, speed limits, onshore oil and gas extraction, harbours, rail franchising, and consumer advocacy and advice. The Act also de-volves power concerning the management of Ofcom in Wales.

REVISION TIP

The process of legislative devolution has been particularly problematic in Northern Ireland. You should consider the issues carefully.

Northern Ireland

The **Northern Ireland Act 1998** set up the Northern Ireland Assembly. This was suspended by the **Northern Ireland Act 2000**. The Northern Ireland Assembly ceased to function from October 2002. The **Northern Ireland Assembly (Elections and Periods of Suspension) Act 2003** postponed the date of the poll for the election of the next Northern Ireland Assembly from 29 May 2003, set by the **Northern Ireland Assembly Elections Act 2003**, and provided a mecha-nism for setting the date of the next poll. The **Northern Ireland Act 2006** recalled the members of the Northern Ireland Assembly to sit in a '2006 Assembly' whose focus was to provide a forum for the parties to begin preparations for devolved government. It set a deadline of 24 November 2006 for the parties to have made sufficient progress to allow for devolution to be fully restored. The next legislative step was the **Northern Ireland (Miscellaneous Provisions) Act 2006**. This Act made provision concerning:

- registration of electors;
- the Chief Electoral Officer for Northern Ireland (CEO);
- donations for political purposes;
- devolution of policing and justice;
- extension of the amnesty period for arms decommissioning;
- loans to the Northern Ireland Consolidated Fund;
- a single wholesale electricity market;
- financial assistance for energy purposes;
- sustainable development;
- extending certain provisions of the **Serious Organised Crime and Police Act 2005 (SOCAP)** to Northern Ireland;

- the health and safety of police officers; and
- the duty to fill judicial vacancies.

The **Northern Ireland (St Andrews Agreement) Act 2006** set up a transitional Assembly. A poll was held on 7 March 2007. Following this, a permanent Assembly was set up. The Assembly was in a period of suspension until January 2020, after it collapsed in January 2017 due to policy disagreements between its power-sharing leadership, particularly following the Renewable Heat Incentive scandal. In January 2020, the British and Irish governments agreed on a deal to restore devolved government in Northern Ireland.

LOOKING FOR EXTRA MARKS?

You should follow up this subject by reading the articles recommended under Key debates as well as by reading your recommended standard textbook.

KEY CASES

CASE	FACTS	PRINCIPLE
Ashby v White (1703) 92 ER 126, 710	The Court of Queen's Bench and the House of Lords had to decide whether a person deprived of an opportunity to vote when they had a legal right to do so had a cause of action in tort.	If a statute gives a right the common law will provide a remedy to maintain it where there is injury or damage in spite of parliamentary privilege.
R v Boundary Commission for England, ex p Foot [1983] QB 600	The Court of Appeal had to decide whether it had jurisdiction to decide if a decision of the Boundary Commission could be challenged.	The Court of Appeal held that the court would not intervene unless the claimant could prove that the Boundary Commission's recommendations and conclusions were such that no reasonable commission could have made them.

KEY DEBATES

Topic	'Brexit as Constitutional "Shock" and Its Threat to the Devolution Settlement: Reform or Bust'
Author/Academic	Noreen Burrows and Maria Fletcher
Viewpoint	The authors of this article argue that the devolution settlement between Scotland and the UK Parliament cannot withstand the 'constitutional shock' of Brexit and that the Joint Ministerial Committee (EU Negotiations) has not proved a successful forum for the exchange of views between the UK and the devolved administrations.
Source	[2017] 1 Judicial Review 49–57

Topic	'Miller: Legal and Political Fault Lines'
Author/Academic	Paul Daly
Viewpoint	This article reflects on the ruling in *R (on the application of Miller) v Secretary of State for Exiting the European Union* (2017), and suggests that it can be understood with reference to the fault lines between: (1) form and substance regarding devolution and the relationship between UK and EU law; (2) the old and new constitutions; and (3) legal and political accountability. Examines the legislative response to the judgment.
Source	[2017] (Nov) Public Law Supp, Brexit Special Extra Issue 73–93

Topic	'The Strange Reconstitution of Wales'
Author/Academic	Richard Rawlings
Viewpoint	This article reflects on the complex constitutional arrangements applicable to a devolved Wales under the **Wales Act 2017**. It goes on to discuss the successive phases of Welsh devolution legislation, the dynamics of the draft Wales Bill 2015, the approach of the shadow draft Bill, and the revised position under the Wales Bill 2016. It also examines the move to a reserved powers model of devolution in the 2017 Act, the influence of Scottish devolution law, and the impact of Brexit.
Source	[2018] Public Law 62–83

Topic	'"Brexit" in the Supreme Court'
Author/Academic	Scott Blair
Viewpoint	This is the first in a series of articles. It considers, with reference to the role of the Scottish Parliament, elements of the Supreme Court decision in *R (on the application of Miller) v Secretary of State for Exiting the European Union* concerning the UK's process of withdrawal from the EU and the associated scope of prerogative powers.

Topic	'"Brexit" in the Supreme Court'
Source	(2017) 76 Scottish Human Rights Journal 3–8

Topic	'The Supreme Court's Judgment in *Miller*: In Search of Constitutional Principle'
Author/Academic	Mark Elliott
Viewpoint	This article criticizes, due to its treatment of arguments of constitutional principle, the majority judgment in *R (on the application of Miller) v Secretary of State for Exiting the European Union* on whether the UK Government could exercise its prerogative power to initiate the UK's withdrawal from the EU, and whether the devolved legislature's consent had to be obtained prior to commencing the withdrawal process.
Source	(2017) 72 Cambridge Law Journal 257–288

EXAM QUESTIONS

Essay question 1

Critically assess whether proportional representation or 'first past the post' ought to be adopted in general elections to the House of Commons.

Essay question 2

Explain the extent to which the legislative powers of the UK Parliament have been permanently delegated to the Scottish Parliament and the Welsh and Northern Ireland Assemblies.

Online Resources

For outline answers to these essay questions, as well as interactive key cases and multiple-choice questions, please visit the online resources.
www.oup.com/he/faragher-concentrate7e

Concentrate Q&As

For more questions and answers on public law, see the *Concentrate Q&A: Public Law* by Richard Clements.

Go to the end of this book to view **sample pages**.

Parliamentary sovereignty

6

KEY FACTS

- The legislative supremacy of Parliament is a jurisdictional question: Parliament has unlimited power to make and unmake laws and, once the courts have determined that a bill has become an Act of Parliament, they have no jurisdiction to override it or set it aside.

- Cases following the House of Lords' decision in *Pepper v Hart* (1992) suggest that the courts may be willing to exercise their jurisdiction to interpret statutes more generously.

- Although any legislative provision may be expressly repealed by Parliament, the courts have jurisdiction to determine whether an Act of Parliament is a constitutional statute and immune from the common law doctrine of implied repeal.

- The **Human Rights Act 1998** requires the courts to interpret statutes in a way which is consistent with Convention rights and enables the High Court in England and Wales to make declarations of incompatibility.

- The effect of **s 2(1)** and **(4) European Communities Act 1972** is that the provisions of subsequent statutes are enacted without prejudice to the directly enforceable EU rights of nationals of any member state of the EEC.

- Substantive EU rights prevail over the express terms of any domestic law, including primary legislation, made or passed after the coming into force of the 1972 Act, even in the face of plain inconsistency between the two.

The jurisdictional question

REVISION TIP

Problem questions commonly focus on this issue. Remember that, in problem questions, you are not concerned with the political consequences of legislation or contextual issues. You are concerned with the legal principles governing the courts' powers to apply and interpret legislation.

Essay questions might ask you to consider contextual issues concerning the relationship between the courts and Parliament. This links up with the separation of powers (see Chapter 4).

Parliamentary sovereignty is a fundamental principle of UK constitutional law. In England, it originates from the **Bill of Rights 1688/9**, the **Act of Settlement 1701**, and the **Acts of Union with Scotland in 1706** and **1707**. AV Dicey in *Introduction to the Study of the Law of the Constitution* (1885) said that parliamentary sovereignty means that Parliament has 'the right to make or unmake any law whatsoever; and further, no person or body is recognised by the law as having a right to override or set aside the legislation of Parliament'. This was affirmed by the UK Supreme Court in *R (on the application of Miller) v Secretary of State for Exiting the European Union* (2017).

This is a jurisdictional principle: it tells the courts what they can and cannot do with an Act of Parliament. It focuses on the relationship between Parliament and the courts. When we looked at the separation of powers we considered cases in which the judges explored and determined the boundaries of this relationship. Parliament has the ultimate power to make and unmake laws. Any limitation coming from the **Human Rights Act 1998**, EU law, or devolution is self-imposed and can be undone by future legislation. The Supreme Court in *R (on the application of Miller) v Secretary of State for Exiting the European Union* also observed that the development of parliamentary sovereignty went hand in hand with the development of an independent judiciary, the role of which is to uphold and further the rule of law. Judges impartially identify and apply the law in every case brought before the courts. It is not open to judges to apply or develop the common law in a way which is inconsistent with the law as laid down by Acts of Parliament. Furthermore, the Supreme Court also recognized a close relationship between the development of parliamentary sovereignty and the separation of powers. The Supreme Court observed that by the end of the twentieth century, the great majority of what had previously been prerogative powers, at least in relation to domestic matters, had become vested in the three principal organs of the state, the legislature (the two Houses of Parliament), the executive (ministers and the government more generally), and the judiciary (the judges).

LOOKING FOR EXTRA MARKS?

There is considerable debate about whether, in the light of developments in EU law, devolution, and the passing of the **Human Rights Act 1998**, Dicey's idea of parliamentary sovereignty is becoming increasingly outdated and irrelevant. See the Key debates section for further reading.

Can Parliament alter its own constitution?

If Parliament can make or unmake any law it likes, can Parliament alter its own constitution? It appears that Parliament does have this power. Current case law determines that Parliament has the power to alter its own constitution for certain purposes. This is illustrated by the following decision of the House of Lords.

Jackson v Attorney General [2006] 1 AC 262

The House of Lords had to decide whether the **Parliament Act 1949**, which amended the **Parliament Act 1911**, was invalid because it was passed without the consent of the House of Lords in accordance with the procedure contained in **s 2 Parliament Act 1911**. If the 1949 Act were invalid the **Hunting Act 2004** would also be invalid. The House of Lords held that there is no constitutional principle, or principle of statutory interpretation, which prevents a legislature from altering its constitution in accordance with the provisions of a statute which empowers it to do so, for the purpose of altering the empowering statute.

The development of the rule that no person or body has the right to override or set aside legislation

In the constitutional turmoil of the seventeenth century there were suggestions that the courts might have the power to question the validity of an Act of Parliament if it was:

- against common right or reason, repugnant, or impossible to perform (*Dr Bonham's Case* (1610));
- against natural equity (*Day v Savage* (1615));
- contrary to the law of God in scripture (*R v Love* (1651)); and
- contrary to the rules of natural justice (*City of London v Wood* (1702)).

Challenges based on substance

In the UK there is no equivalent to the principle stated by Chief Justice Marshall in the United States Supreme Court decision in *Marbury v Madison* (1803) that a statute which is repugnant to the constitution is void. In the Privy Council decision in *Madzimbamuto v Lardner Burke* (1969), Lord Reid said that while many might think that it would be morally or politically unconstitutional for Parliament to do certain things, this does not diminish or undermine the legal power of Parliament to legislate. If Parliament chooses to do them, the courts cannot hold the resulting Act of Parliament invalid.

Cheney v Conn [1968] 1 All ER 779

Ungoed-Thomas J said that anything enacted in a statute cannot be unlawful. Statute is the highest form of law within the UK and it is not for a court to say that an Act of Parliament is illegal.

See also *Mortensen v Peters* (1906) and *R v Jordan* (1967).

Procedural challenges: the enrolled bill rule

The enrolled bill rule is that the courts have no jurisdiction, once a bill has become an Act, to consider:

1. the way in which a bill is introduced into Parliament and what happened either before or during its progress through Parliament; and

2. whether Parliament or its officers were misled by fraud.

These principles were laid down in:

- *Edinburgh & Dalkeith Railway v Wauchope* (1842);
- *Lee v Bude and Torrington Junction Railway* (1871); and
- *Pickin v British Rail Board* (1974).

Express and implied repeal

REVISION TIP

In problem questions you may be asked to consider whether the provisions of an Act of Parliament can be protected from subsequent changes. The first thing you must do is make sure that you understand the distinction between implied and express repeal.

Acts of Parliament may amend, abolish, or replace common law rules: this means that if something entirely governed by common law rules is subsequently entirely covered by the provisions of an Act of Parliament, it is the Act of Parliament which applies in place of the common law. Although an Act of Parliament which is in force can amend, abolish, and re-place common law rules as far as the Act of Parliament applies, it is possible for the courts to refer to pre-existent common law rules when interpreting the provisions of new Acts of Parliament.

Parliament changes statute law by the process of repeal. There are two types of repeal, namely, express repeal and implied repeal. Express repeal is a statement in an Act declaring that the provisions of an earlier statute are no longer in force or are replaced with the provisions of the new Act. Implied repeal is a common law rule. Laws LJ in *Thoburn v Sunderland City Council* (2003) said that implied repeal may occur where Parliament enacts successive statutes which on the true construction of each of them make irreducibly inconsistent provisions. In such a case the outcome is that the earlier statute is impliedly repealed by the later.

The way in which the courts perceive their jurisdiction changes with time. According to Avory J in *Vauxhall Estates Ltd v Liverpool Corporation* (1932) no Act of Parliament can ef-fectively provide that no future Act shall interfere with its provisions. In *Ellen Street Estates, Ltd v Minister of Health* (1934) Maugham LJ said that the legislature cannot bind itself as to the form of subsequent legislation. By this he meant that it is impossible for Parliament to enact that, in a subsequent statute dealing with the same subject matter, there can be no implied repeal. If, in a subsequent Act, Parliament plainly says that an earlier statute is being to some extent repealed, effect must be given to that intention just because it is the will of the legislature.

There now seems to be an exception to the rule. In *Thoburn v Sunderland City Council* (2003) Laws LJ draws a distinction between ordinary and constitutional statutes. He went on to make the following points:

- A constitutional statute concerns the relationship between the citizen and the state and/ or fundamental human rights.
- Ordinary statutes may be impliedly repealed. Constitutional statutes may not.
- For the repeal of a constitutional statute, the court must find express words in the later statute which irresistibly show that Parliament intended to repeal the former constitutional statute.

Can the jurisdiction of the court over an Act of Parliament be enlarged?

There are some instances where courts seem willing to expand their jurisdiction over Acts of Parliament. These include:

- reference to parliamentary material in statutory interpretation;
- the use of entrenchment clauses and prospective formulae; and
- the **Human Rights Act 1998**.

Reference to parliamentary material in statutory interpretation

The courts do not normally permit parliamentary material to be used as evidence when interpreting statutes. This is partly based on **Art 9 Bill of Rights 1689** which provides that the freedom of speech and debates or proceedings in Parliament ought not to be impeached or questioned in any court or place outside Parliament. There are now exceptions to this rule based on the following principles:

- subject to parliamentary privilege, parliamentary material may be allowed where:
  - legislation is ambiguous or obscure or leads to absurdity;
  - the material is a statement by a minister or sponsor of a bill and any additional parliamentary material necessary to understand such statements and their effect; and
  - the statements are clear;

- if Parliament enacts legislation after making clear statements in both Houses, it is appropriate to refer to parliamentary material if there is any ambiguity concerning the Act's nature and scope; and
- there is nothing to prevent material in parliamentary speeches being admitted as evidence where the court is considering not only the meaning of the provisions of the statute but also the intention behind it.

Pepper v Hart [1992] 3 WLR 1032

The first principle was determined by the House of Lords in this case.

The claimants challenged a decision of the Inland Revenue concerning assessment of tax. The assessment was based on **ss 61** and **63 Finance Act 1976**. The claimants alleged that these provisions were ambiguous. An enlarged Appellate Committee of the House of Lords chaired by the Lord Chancellor, Lord Mackay, had to decide whether parliamentary material could be used in aiding the interpretation of legislation.

It was held that parliamentary material may be used to assist in the interpretation of legislation in cases where such legislation is ambiguous or obscure.

R v Secretary of State for Foreign and Commonwealth Affairs, ex p Rees-Mogg [1994] QB 552

The second principle was determined by Lloyd LJ in this case.

The claimant sought judicial review of the Foreign Secretary's decision to ratify the **Treaty on European Union** (1992). The claimant's evidence included large extracts from parliamentary statements made by ministers which were reported in Hansard. The claimant relied on *Pepper v Hart*. The Secretary of State argued that *Pepper v Hart* did not apply. Judicial review was refused and *Pepper v Hart* was not applied because there were no ambiguities in the relevant statutes. But had there been any ambiguities it would have been appropriate to apply *Pepper v Hart*.

Marshall, in [1993] Public Law 402, said that *Ex p Rees-Mogg* (1994) means that **Art 9 Bill of Rights 1689** protects Members of Parliament from civil liability for what they say in debates and parliamentary proceedings. It does not prevent judicial scrutiny of parliamentary material where the courts have to decide on the legal effect of resolutions of either House. He concluded that the courts have jurisdiction to consider parliamentary material where:

- this was necessary to uphold the will of the Queen in Parliament; or
- a statute refers to parliamentary proceedings or resolutions and it is necessary to refer to them to determine what the statutory provisions mean.

Lord Browne-Wilkinson, in the Privy Council decision in *Prebble v Television New Zealand Ltd* (1995), said that the courts and Parliament recognize their respective constitutional roles. The courts will not allow any challenge to what is said or done within Parliament in performance of its legislative functions and protection of its privileges.

Entrenchment clauses and prospective formulae

 REVISION TIP

Make sure that you understand the difference between these formulae. This will help you spot them in an examination problem question and apply the correct law.

Entrenchment clauses and prospective formulae are statutory provisions which aim to protect an Act of Parliament from amendment or repeal. Entrenchment clauses in a statute require a special procedure to be followed before an Act of Parliament can be amended or repealed. This can be in the form of a referendum or poll or two-thirds majority. An example of such a clause appears in **s 1 Northern Ireland Act 1998**. This provides that Northern Ireland will remain part of the UK until a majority of the electorate gives its consent to a change in a poll.

 LOOKING FOR EXTRA MARKS?

RFV Heuston, in *Essays in Constitutional Law* (1964), considers the legal effect of entrenchment clauses in many jurisdictions and suggests that, in some contexts, they may bind a legislature as to the manner and form of legislation. You should read about this and think about whether it is possible to bind the Westminster Parliament in the same way.

The speeches of Lord Steyn and Baroness Hale in *R (Jackson) v Attorney General* (2006) suggest that there may be some judicial support in this country for entrenchment clauses. The main issue in this case was whether there is any constitutional principle or principle of statutory interpretation which prevents a legislature from altering its constitution in accordance with the provisions of a statute which empowers it to do so, for the purpose of altering the empowering statute. The **Hunting Act 2004**, which made the hunting of wild animals with dogs unlawful, received the Royal Assent in November 2004. It was enacted under **s 2 Parliament Act 1911**, which laid down the circumstances in which, save for stated exceptions, 'any public Bill' could be enacted without the consent of the House of Lords, as amended by **s 1 Parliament Act 1949**. That provision reduced by a year the period which had to elapse before the Lords' consent could be dispensed with. The claimants, who opposed the banning of fox hunting, contended that the 1949 Act was invalid because the provisions of the 1911 Act had been relied on to enact it, whereas the 1911 Act could only be amended with the consent of the House of Lords. They sought declarations that the 1949 Act was not an Act of Parliament and was consequently of no legal effect and that, accordingly, the **Hunting Act 2004** was not an Act of Parliament and was not of legal effect.

The House of Lords decided that there was no constitutional principle or principle of statutory construction which prohibited a legislature from altering its own constitution by enacting alterations to the instrument from which its powers derived by virtue of powers in the same instrument, if the powers extended so far. Baroness Hale said quite plainly that: 'If Parliament can do anything, there is no reason why Parliament should not decide to redesign itself, either in general or for a particular purpose.'

Lord Steyn elaborates on this. He begins by drawing a distinction between the 'static' and 'dynamic' concepts within the legal definition of Parliament. The static element within the definition is that Parliament consists of the House of Commons, the House of Lords, and the monarch. The dynamic element, according to Lord Steyn, is that the constituent parts of Parliament work together separately and simultaneously to make law. Under normal circumstances, they must each give their assent to a bill. He went on to say that an ordinarily constituted Parliament could 'redistribute legislative power in different ways'. Such a redefinition cannot be disregarded.

A prospective formula seeks to protect a statute from amendment or repeal by saying that its provisions prevail over those of subsequent statutes or that future statutes shall be construed and have effect subject to its provisions.

The Human Rights Act 1998 and parliamentary sovereignty

Section 3 Human Rights Act 1998 obliges the courts to interpret statutes in accordance with Convention rights as far as it is possible to do so. **Section 4** gives the High Court in England and Wales the jurisdiction to issue a declaration of incompatibility. Moreover, **s 2** obliges the courts to take into account the decisions of the European Court of Human Rights when making decisions involving rights contained in the **European Convention on Human Rights and Fundamental Freedoms (ECHR)**. None of this affects the validity of an Act of Parliament and the government is not bound by a declaration of incompatibility to amend incompatible legislation.

The judicial use of **ss 3** and **4** is illustrated by the House of Lords' decision in *Ghaidan v Godin-Mendoza* (2004). In this case the House of Lords determined that, subject to the limitation of doing what is possible, **s 3** gives the courts jurisdiction to modify the meaning of words used in statutes. If the court finds that **s 3** requires this, it is bound only to interpret the statute in accordance with the underlying thrust of the legislation. The court is not bound to follow the exact form of words used in the Act. In this way a court can interpret any statute in a way which is compatible with Convention rights, as far as it is possible to do so, without crossing the constitutional boundaries preserved by **s 3**.

The courts have no jurisdiction to declare a statute invalid. But in *International Transport Roth GmbH v Secretary of State for the Home Department* (2003) Laws LJ said:

- the British system is moving away from parliamentary supremacy towards constitutional supremacy;
- although Parliament, subject to the EU, has unlimited legislative powers, the common law now recognizes and endorses the notion of constitutional or fundamental rights;

- these rights are contained in the **ECHR** incorporated as Convention rights under the **Human Rights Act 1998**;

- this creates tension between legislative sovereignty and the vindication of fundamental rights;

- in reconciling the competing claims of parliamentary sovereignty and fundamental constitutional rights, the courts must, first, acknowledge the legislative supremacy of Parliament subject to a rule of construction that fundamental rights will not be over-ridden by a statute unless the words used expressly and specifically show that it was the intention of Parliament to do so; and

- the courts, second, have to strike a balance between the claims of the democratic legisla-ture and the claims of the constitutional right by determining and measuring the degree or margin of deference it pays to the democratic decision-maker.

Laws LJ went on to say:

- greater deference is to be paid to an Act of Parliament than to a decision of the executive or to a subordinate measure;

- there is more scope for deference where the **ECHR** requires a balance to be struck, and less where the right is unqualified;

- greater deference will be due to the democratic powers where the subject matter lies within their constitutional responsibility, and less when it lies within the constitutional responsibility of the courts; and

- greater or lesser deference will be due according to whether the subject matter lies within the expertise of the courts.

Issues concerning the sovereignty of parliament and the judicial policy of the UK domes-tic courts in relation to following and applying the jurisprudence of the European Court of Human Rights arose following the decision of the European Court of Human Rights in *Hirst v United Kingdom (No 2)* (2005) that although all prisoners may not be entitled to vote in UK elections, a blanket ban on all British prisoners exercising the right to vote was contrary to the **ECHR**. Another case raising sovereignty issues and the question of whether the UK Supreme Court was obliged to follow Strasburg jurisprudence rather than simply take it into account, was the European Court of Human Rights decision in *Vinter v United Kingdom* (2013) in which the Court decided that life sentences without any prospect of release or review amounted to inhuman or degrading treatment or punishment, and thus are a violation of the **ECHR**.

These cases subsequently resulted in negative legal and political comment. Two views emerged. Both centred around how **Art 46 ECHR**, which obliged member states to 'abide by the final judgment of the Court in any case to which they are parties', should be interpreted. The first was stated by the Joint Committee on the Draft Voting Eligibility (Prisoners) Bill (2013). It concluded that:

> Parliament remains sovereign, but that sovereignty resides in Parliament's power to withdraw from the Convention system; while we are part of that system we incur obligations that cannot be the subject of

cherry picking. A refusal to implement the Court's judgment would not only undermine the international standing of the UK; it would also give succour to those states in the Council of Europe who have a poor record of protecting human rights and who may draw on such an action as setting a precedent that they may wish to follow.

The second view was stated by Lord Sumption, in *R (on the application of Chester) v Secretary of State for Justice* and *McGeogh v Lord Advocate* (2013), who asserted that under the UK's constitutional arrangements Parliament is sovereign. It can overrule, through the legislative process, any decision of the UK Supreme Court. He went on to say that should Parliament disagree with a decision of the Strasbourg Court, Parliament was under no legal obligation, under **Art 46 ECHR**, to take general measures to get rid of the violations found by the Court.

The Independent Human Rights Act Review 2021

The Independent Human Rights Act Review was set up in December 2020 to consider how the **Human Rights Act 1998** is working in practice and whether any change is needed. It will focus on the relationship between the domestic courts and the European Court of Human Rights.

The relationship between domestic courts and the European Court of Human Rights

The Review will examine how **s 2 Human Rights Act 1998**, and the relevant jurisprudence of the European Court of Human Rights, have been interpreted and applied by the UK courts when determining a question that has arisen in connection with a Convention right.

The Review will address the following questions:

- How has the duty to 'take into account' the jurisprudence of the European Court of Human Rights been applied in practice?

- Is there a need for any amendment of **s 2**?

- When taking into account the jurisprudence of the European Court of Human Rights, how have domestic courts and tribunals approached issues falling within the margin of appreciation permitted to states under that jurisprudence?

- Is any change required?

- Does the current approach to 'judicial dialogue' between domestic courts and the European Court of Human Rights satisfactorily permit domestic courts to raise concerns as to the application of European Court of Human Rights jurisprudence having regard to UK circumstances?

- How can such dialogue be strengthened and preserved?

LOOKING FOR EXTRA MARKS?

There has been a substantial amount of case law on s 3 **Human Rights Act 1998**. It is a hot topic. You should, therefore, supplement your revision by referring to Chapter 14 and your recommended standard textbook.

KEY CASES

CASE	FACTS	PRINCIPLE
Ellen Street Estates, Ltd v Minister of Health [1934] 1 KB 590	The Court of Appeal had to decide whether the provisions of a statute could be impliedly repealed because of the provisions of an earlier statute.	The legislature cannot bind itself as to the form of subsequent legislation.
International Transport Roth GmbH v Secretary of State for the Home Department [2003] QB 728	Laws LJ discussed the effect of the **Human Rights Act** on statutory interpretation and the legal doctrine of legislative supremacy.	Since the coming into force of the **Human Rights Act**, the common law now recognizes a distinction between constitutional or fundamental rights on the one hand and other kinds of rights on the other.
R (on the application of Jackson) v Attorney General [2006] 1 AC 262	The House of Lords had to decide whether the **Parliament Act 1949** and the **Hunting Act 2004** were valid Acts of Parliament.	The purpose of the **Parliament Act 1911** was to limit the power of the House of Lords to block the bill which had been approved by the House of Commons. The 1911 Act applies to any public bill subject only to the exceptions contained in the 1911 Act. There is no constitutional principle, or principle of statutory interpretation which prevents a legislature from altering its constitution, in accordance with the provisions of a statute which empowers it to do so, for the purpose of altering the provisions of the empowering statute.
Stockdale v Hansard (1839) 112 ER 1112	The court had to decide whether the House of Commons, by its own resolution, could extend its privileges and immunities.	The Lord Chief Justice held that the privileges and immunities of Parliament could be extended only by legislation which required the separate and simultaneous estates of the House of Commons and the House of Lords as well as the Royal Assent.
Thoburn v Sunderland City Council [2003] QB 151	The question was whether the **European Communities Act 1972** was capable of being impliedly repealed.	Ordinary statutes may be impliedly repealed. Constitutional statutes may not.

KEY DEBATES

Topic	'Legislative Freedom in the United Kingdom'
Author/Academic	Richard Ekins
Viewpoint	Evaluates the claims that the legislative freedom of the UK Parliament is limited by: Scottish devolution; the duties with respect to EU law laid down in the **s 2 European Communities Act 1972**; the provisions of the **Human Rights Act 1998**; and judicial assessments of whether the process of producing particular legislation adhered to the rule of law.
Source	(2017) 133 Law Quarterly Review 582–605

Topic	'Revisiting the "Manner and Form" Theory of Parliamentary Sovereignty'
Author/Academic	Han-Rhou Zhou
Viewpoint	Assesses whether the theory that UK statutes are only valid if they have been subjected to formal or procedural 'manner and form' conditions is compatible with parliamentary sovereignty by examining: (1) the lessons that can be learned from cases in Commonwealth jurisdictions on the binding effect of manner and form conditions; (2) the treatment of manner and form theory by the House of Lords' judgment in *R (on the application of Jackson) v Attorney General*; and (3) the views of Parliament and senior officials of the legislative branch.
Source	(2013) 129 Law Quarterly Review 610–638

Topic	'Parliamentary Sovereignty under the New Constitutional Hypotheses'
Author/Academic	Jeffrey Jowell
Viewpoint	Reviews the jurisdiction of the courts over Acts of Parliament in the light of the **Human Rights Act 1998** and other developments.
Source	[2006] Public Law 562

Topic	'*R (Miller) v Secretary of State for Exiting the European Union*: Three Competing Syllogisms'
Author/Academic	Nicholas Aroney
Viewpoint	This article sets out the two competing syllogisms put forward by the parties in *R (on the application of Miller) v Secretary of State for Exiting the European Union* (2017) on whether the UK's power to withdraw from the EU could be exercised by Crown prerogative or required authorization by Act of Parliament. The author argues that the Supreme Court formulated a third syllogism, and explains how this avoided the dualist approach to domestic and international law.
Source	(2017) 80 Modern Law Review 726–745

EXAM QUESTIONS

Problem question

Assume that, in order to reduce the cost of the National Health Service to the taxpayer, the Health Services Act 2019 is passed which provides that all those receiving medical treatment must pay a fee according to a fixed scale contained in the Act. Section 2 provides that 'provisions of this Act are to take precedence over Acts passed or to be passed'. Section 3 provides that 'this Act is not to be amended or repealed unless the consent of the British Medical Council and the Royal College of Surgeons is obtained'.

The scheme proves very unpopular and the Health Services (Amendment) Act 2021 is passed. This statute abolishes all fees. Neither the British Medical Council nor the Royal College of Surgeons is consulted.

Elizabeth has received a bill from her doctor following a blood transfusion. She refuses to pay, relying on the Health Services (Amendment) Act 2021. Her doctor relies on the Health Services Act 2019.

Advise Elizabeth as to whether she has to pay her doctor's bill.

See the Outline Answers section in the end matter for help with this question.

Essay question

Critically assess Dicey's assertions that Parliament can make or unmake any law it wishes and that an Act of Parliament cannot be overridden or set aside by the courts.

 Online Resources

For an outline answer to this essay question, as well as interactive key cases and multiple-choice questions, please visit the online resources.
www.oup.com/he/faragher-concentrate7e

 Concentrate Q&As

For more questions and answers on public law, see the *Concentrate Q&A: Public Law* by Richard Clements.

Go to the end of this book to view **sample pages**.

7 The monarchy and the Royal Prerogative

KEY FACTS

- In terms of legal formality, the British Constitution is monarchical.

- The reigning monarch (king or queen) is the head of state of the United Kingdom of Great Britain and Northern Ireland.

- As such, the reigning monarch is the titular head of the executive, legislature, and the judiciary, commander in chief of the armed forces, and Supreme Governor of the Church of England.

- The primary legal source of the monarch's personal powers and privileges is an ancient branch of the Common Law called the Royal Prerogative supplemented by statutes like the **Bill of Rights 1689**.

- Constitutional conventions have fundamentally shaped the exercise of the personal powers of the monarch when acting as head of state.

- The attributes and privileges given to the monarch as head of state are that the monarch can do no wrong, the monarch is never an infant, the monarch never dies, and the monarch is inviolable.

The head of state

Every country with an organized government has a head of state. There are different types of heads of state. Some are executive heads of state who actively exercise legal and political power and others are non-executive heads of state whose powers are purely legal and formal. They do not participate in the political process. Most heads of state are elected. Others, like the British monarch, take office under the hereditary principle.

The UK monarch as head of state

REVISION TIP

Having a clear idea of the constitutional role and powers of the monarch will help you to understand the context in which the Royal Prerogative has been delegated to members of the executive. This topic also links up with what you have studied in Chapters 5 and 6 and what you will study in Chapter 8. You should also bear in mind the separation of powers.

In its legal form the UK Constitution is monarchical. The UK is a constitutional monarchy: the monarch exercises their legal powers as part of a parliamentary system of government. The reigning monarch is the head of state of the United Kingdom of Great Britain and Northern Ireland, Supreme Governor of the Church of England, Commander in Chief of the Army, Navy, and Air Force, nominal head of the judiciary, and head of the legislature.

The monarch is also head of state of their other Realms and Territories and Defender of the Faith. When exercising their personal legal powers as head of state, the reigning monarch is sometimes referred to as the Crown or the sovereign. The country in which a monarch performs their legal role as head of state is on some occasions called a kingdom or realm.

The constitutional role and duties of the British monarch

The constitutional role and duties of the British monarch are set out in the current version of **s 3 Coronation Oath Act 1688**. The monarch governs the people of the UK. This implies that the monarch is the legal and formal head of the executive and the legislature. The monarch must also 'cause law and justice in mercy to be executed in all judgments'. This implies that the monarch's role includes being the constitutional head of the judicial system. All this may create the somewhat mis-leading impression that the British monarch is an all-powerful head of state with unlimited power. This is not the case in practice. The British monarch does not participate in the political process of government. Many of the duties which were anciently carried out personally by the monarch are today carried out by members of the executive who as members of the legislature are accountable to Parliament. There is also an independent judiciary. When the monarch exercises their personal powers they always act on the advice of ministers and in particular the Prime Minister.

The monarch and the Privy Council

The Privy Council is one of the oldest parts of government. It supports the legal proposition that the UK is a constitutional monarchy because all the government ministers who are appointed to participate in its policy work must be MPs or Lords who are accountable to Parliament. The ministerial head of the Privy Council is the President of the Privy Council. The Privy Council Office provides secretariat services for the Privy Council (that part of Her Majesty's Government which advises on the exercise of prerogative powers and certain functions assigned to the reigning monarch and the Privy Council by Act of Parliament).

The monarch's duties and the executive

The monarch is the legal and formal head of the executive. Ministers are commonly referred to collectively as 'Her Majesty's Government'. The executive or the government is sometimes referred to collectively as the Crown. Originally the monarch exercised the supreme executive, legislative, and judicial power of the state in person, and the Crown and the person of the monarch were synonymous legal entities. Over the course of modern history, particularly following the enforced abdication of James II and enactment of the **Bill of Rights (1688** or **1689)**, legal and constitutional distinctions have emerged between the personal and political capacities of the monarch and the king or queen as an individual person and the monarchy as a public institution. The expression 'the Crown' now describes the collective structure of central government in the UK.

The Queen appoints the Prime Minister as well as all the other Secretaries of State and ministers who form Her Majesty's Government. She appoints diplomats and signs state papers. She is also legally empowered to grant honours, declare war, make peace, conduct foreign affairs, and attend to the execution and administration of the law. The monarch cannot reject the final advice of her ministers without the likely consequences of their resignation, which would bring the monarchy into controversy. Walter Bagehot in his book entitled *The English Constitution* (1865–1867) described the sovereign's rights as:

- the right to be consulted;
- the right to encourage; and
- the right to warn.

Sir William Heseltine (the Queen's Private Secretary) wrote to *The Times* in 1986 following reports of disagreements between the Prime Minister (Mrs Thatcher) and the Queen on policy. Sir William made three points. First, the sovereign has the right to counsel, encourage, and warn the government. She is entitled to have opinions on government policy and express them to her chief minister. Second, whatever personal opinions the sovereign may hold or may have expressed to her government, she is bound to act on the advice of her ministers. Third, the sovereign is obliged to treat her communications with the Prime Ministers as entirely confidential between the two of them.

The monarch's duties and the judiciary

The constitutional status of the judiciary is underpinned by its origins in the Royal Prerogative and its legal relationship with the Crown, dating from the medieval period when the Royal Prerogative was exercised by the monarch personally. The monarch was and is the constitutional source and fountain of justice from whom the jurisdiction of the UK courts is formally derived. But the monarch cannot personally act in any office connected with the administration of justice or order an arrest. This was determined by the Court of King's Bench in **Prohibitions Del Roy** (1607). Signing official documents confirming the appointment or dismissal of judges and signing Orders in Council bringing into force the reports delivered by the Judicial Committee of the Privy Council on appeal are the only significant practical duties the monarch performs in the judicial branch of government.

The privileges and immunities of the British monarch

REVISION TIP

Again, essay questions can focus on this topic. You should also refer to the Key cases and Key debates sections at the end of this chapter for further material.

The common law gives the monarch privileges and immunities. Their practical purpose is to ensure that the monarch can properly carry out the constitutional duties which we have looked at earlier in this chapter in the public interest. They also make sure that the process of government runs smoothly. Today the following privileges and immunities apply:

1. The monarch never dies.

This means that the monarch's successor can normally act as head of state immediately following the death of a reigning monarch. They do not have to wait for the coronation. The death of a king or queen is legally known as the demise of the sovereign. The word demise in this context signifies the immediate transfer of the right to act as head of state. Receiving and accepting the right to act as head of state is called accession to the throne. The act of accession is done by proclamation issued jointly by the House of Lords, the Privy Council, and the Lord Mayor of the City of London.

2. The monarch is never an infant.

This is the key principle in **The Duchy of Lancaster Case** (1561). The law does not take into account the age of the monarch when they act as head of state. Anything done by the monarch acting in their constitutional role as head of state cannot be legally challenged on the ground that they were under the age of 18 when it was done.

3. The monarch's person is inviolable.

This means that a reigning monarch cannot be arrested, detained, or imprisoned.

4. The monarch can do no wrong.

A monarch cannot be held legally accountable for their conduct as head of state or the consequences of decisions taken collectively by the government or individually by ministers. At common law the courts have no jurisdiction over the monarch in person. This applies to civil and criminal proceedings. The monarch cannot be sued in their own courts. Two possible exceptions are a petition of right granted with the permission of the Attorney General and an action brought against the Attorney General for a declaration affecting the monarch's rights. This immunity does not extend to the other members of the royal family. One of the consequences of this privilege is that the monarch cannot be forced to appear as a witness in a criminal trial.

LOOKING FOR EXTRA MARKS?

There is a lot of debate as to whether the monarch has 'personal powers' or 'reserve powers' under the Royal Prerogative to be used in exceptional cases only. There is even disagreement over the precise words to be used to describe them. Compare the views of R Blackburn in 'Monarchy and the Personal Prerogatives' [2004] Public Law 546 with those of Rodney Brazier in 'Monarchy and the Personal Prerogatives: A Personal Response to Professor Blackburn' [2005] Public Law 45.

The constitutional sources of the monarch's powers, privileges, and immunities

In the context of the unwritten British constitution, the legal basis of the monarchy and the powers and duties of the monarch is the Royal Prerogative. This has been defined in various ways. Blackstone, in his *Commentaries on the Laws of England* (1765–1769) defined the Royal Prerogative as the special pre-eminence which the king has over and above all other persons, and out of the ordinary course of common law, in right of his royal dignity.

This definition indicates that the original and oldest primary source of the monarch's personal powers is the common law. The key words in this definition are 'pre-eminence' and 'dignity'. Blackstone's definition focuses on the status of the monarch given to them by law. The law gives the king or queen a pre-eminent legal status. They become the Chief Executive Officer of the state. The law gives the reigning monarch the power to carry out the unique duties associated with their legal status as head of state through the executive, legislative, and judicial organs and function of government, which we have already discussed (see Table 7.1). They are not based on agreement or the consent of the governed. They are incidental to the legal status of being a king or queen and acting as head of state. Blackstone's definition was accepted by Hale LJ in *R v Secretary of State for Health, ex p C* (2000) at 405 who emphasized the unique status of the monarch and the organs of central

Table 7.1 The monarch and the organs and functions of government

THE EXECUTIVE	THE LEGISLATURE	THE JUDICIARY
• The head of state • Commander in Chief • Appoints Prime Minister	• Summons and opens Parliament • Dissolves Parliament • Grants the Royal Assent	• Head of the judiciary • Appoints judges

government on the basis that some of their powers come from the common law under the Royal Prerogative.

AV Dicey in the *Law of the Constitution*, 8th edn (1915), p 421 defines the Royal Prerogative as the residue of discretionary power left in the hands of the Crown, whether exercised by the monarch or their ministers. This view of the Royal Prerogative was judicially accepted by Lord Dunedin in the House of Lords' decision in ***Attorney General v De Keyser's Royal Hotel*** (1920).

REVISION TIP

You will note that Dicey said that the Royal Prerogative is a 'residue'. One of the implications of this is that the Royal Prerogative cannot be enlarged as a source of executive power. Consideration of the following cases will help you understand this.

Two major developments have strongly influenced the Royal Prerogative. The first development is parliamentary sovereignty. The key constitutional principles applied by the Supreme Court in ***R (on the application of Miller) v Secretary of State for Exiting the European Union*** (2017) include the following assertions which limit the exercise of the Royal Prerogative:

- although ministers generally enjoy a power freely to enter and to terminate treaties without recourse to Parliament, they are not normally entitled to exercise any power they might otherwise have if it results in a change in UK domestic law unless an Act of Parliament, so provides;

- the government cannot make or withdraw from a treaty that amounts to a 'major change to UK constitutional arrangements' without an Act of Parliament; and

- because the EU Treaties are a source of domestic law and domestic rights, ministers cannot alter them using the Royal Prerogative alone.

Furthermore, in ***R (on the application of Miller) v The Prime Minister*** (2019) the Supreme Court developed the law further by stating and applying the following key principles:

- The powers exercised by the executive under the Royal Prerogative are limited by the principle of parliamentary sovereignty.

- The protection of parliamentary sovereignty from threats posed to it by the use of prerogative powers by the executive is a legitimate role of the court.

- The sovereignty of Parliament is capable of being undermined if the prerogative is used by the executive for the purpose of preventing Parliament from exercising its legislative authority for as long as the executive pleases.

- As a result, the power to prorogue cannot be unlimited and must therefore be subject to judicial review.

- Upon finding that the prerogative power to advise the monarch to prorogue Parliament has been exercised unlawfully by the Prime Minister, the court is entitled to declare that the resulting prorogation is null and void.

The second development is the influence of binding constitutional conventions which control the exercise of the monarch's formal legal powers.

The relationship between the Royal Prerogative and statute

The key principle, accepted and applied by the Supreme Court in *R (on the application of Miller) v Secretary of State for Exiting the European Union* (2017) is that, prerogative powers, however well established, may be curtailed or abrogated by statute. The statutory curtailment or abrogation may be by express words or by necessary implication. It is inherent in its residual nature that a prerogative power will be displaced in a field which becomes occupied by a corresponding power conferred or regulated by statute. Two further principles were recognized by the Supreme Court:

- it is a fundamental principle of the UK constitution that, because the Royal Prerogative does not enable ministers to change statute law or common law, ministers must exercise prerogative powers in a way which is consistent both with the common law as laid down by the courts and with statutes as enacted by Parliament; and

- ministers cannot frustrate the purpose of a statute or a statutory provision, for example by emptying it of content or preventing its effectual operation.

Can the Royal Prerogative powers exercised by the monarch be subject to legal scrutiny?

In *Council of Civil Service Unions v Minister for the Civil Service (GCHQ)* (1984) the House of Lords said that executive action is not immune from judicial review merely because it is carried out in pursuance of a power derived from the Royal Prerogative. A minister exercising power under the Prerogative might, depending on the justiciability of its subject matter, be under the same duty to act fairly as in the case of action taken under a statutory power.

Concerning justiciability, Lord Roskill thought that, as well as others, the grant of honours, the dissolution of Parliament, the making of treaties, and the appointment of ministers were not open to legal scrutiny by the courts.

The key principles in the above case were applied by the House of Lords in the following case.

> **R (on the application of Bancoult) v Secretary of State for Foreign and Commonwealth Affairs (No 2) [2009] 1 AC 453**
>
> The House of Lords had to decide whether the Crown's Prerogative power to legislate by Order in Council on the advice of its ministers in relation to an overseas territory is susceptible to judicial review.

The key principle is that Prerogative legislation, made on the advice of ministers, is reviewable by the courts in the same way as Prerogative acts. The basis of review is illegality, irrationality, and procedural impropriety.

The Supreme Court, in *R (on the application of Miller) v Secretary of State for Exiting the European Union* (2017), stated that there are two categories of case where exercise of the Prerogative can have important legal consequences.

- Where it is inherent in the Prerogative power that its exercise will affect the legal rights or duties of others. Thus, the Crown has a Prerogative power to decide on the terms of service of its servants, and it is inherent in that power that the Crown can alter those terms so as to remove rights, albeit that such a power is susceptible to judicial review.

- Cases where the effect of an exercise of Prerogative powers is to change the facts to which the law applies. Thus, the exercise of the Prerogative to declare war will have significant legal consequences: actions which were previously lawful may become treasonable, and some people will become enemy aliens, whose property is liable to confiscation.

The most significant area in which ministers exercise the Royal Prerogative is the conduct of the UK's foreign affairs. This includes diplomatic relations, the deployment of armed forces abroad, and, particularly in point for present purposes, the making of treaties. Subject to any restrictions imposed by primary legislation, the general rule is that the power to make or un-make treaties is exercisable without legislative authority and that the exercise of that power is not reviewable by the courts.

The Royal Prerogative and constitutional conventions

 REVISION TIP

It is important to remember that the way in which the monarch exercises their legal constitutional powers under the Royal Prerogative is governed by significant conventions. This links up with Chapter 2, which you may wish to review at this point in your revision to make sure you understand the distinction between law and convention.

The way the monarch exercises their powers is greatly determined by **constitutional conventions**. A monarch must act on the advice of ministers, appoint a member of the House of Commons, who has the confidence of the House, as Prime Minister, appoint government ministers, upon the Prime Minister's recommendation, who are members of either the House of Commons or the House of Lords, normally accept any recommendation made by the Prime Minister to dissolve Parliament, and grant the Royal Assent to every bill passed by Parliament.

How the British monarchy is financed

The Queen's work as head of state is financed on a yearly basis by the government out of funds approved by Parliament. This is called the Sovereign Grant and is provided under **s 1 Sovereign Grant Act 2011**. The Queen also receives a private income from the Duchy of Lancaster. The Prince of Wales receives separate provision out of the Duchy of Cornwall. The Keeper of Her Majesty's Privy Purse must keep proper accounting records relating to the royal household and prepare a statement of such accounts for each financial year, in accordance with any Treasury directions, and give a copy of the statement to the Comptroller and Auditor General for audit and a copy of the statement and the Comptroller's report on it must be laid before Parliament.

Succession to the throne

At common law the hereditary principle determines who can be the monarch and act as head of state. The **Act of Settlement (1700 or 1701)** lays down the legal conditions governing succession to the throne. A Roman Catholic cannot be a British monarch. The **Succession to the Crown Act 2013** makes important changes to the law. **Section 1** provides that, 'in determining the succession to the Crown, the gender of a person born after 28 October 2011 does not give that person, or that person's descendants, precedence over any other person (whenever born)'. **Section 2** provides that, 'a person is not disqualified from succeeding to the Crown or from possessing it as a result of marrying a person of the Roman Catholic faith'. This section applies retrospectively where the person concerned is alive at the time the Act comes into force. Provisions concerning the monarch's consent to certain royal marriages are contained in **s 3**. **Section 3(1)** provides that a person who (when the person marries) is one of the six persons next in the line of succession to the Crown must obtain the consent of Her Majesty before marrying. **Section 3(3)** stipulates that 'the effect of a person's failure to comply with **subsection (1)** is that the person and the person's descendants from the marriage are disqualified from succeeding to the Crown'. **Section 3(4)** expressly repeals the **Royal Marriages Act 1772** which provided that, subject to certain exceptions, a descendant of King George II may marry only with the consent of the sovereign.

Abdication and retirement

A British monarch acts as head of state for life. There is no law or constitutional convention providing for a monarch's retirement. The only abdication to occur in modern times was that of Edward VIII in 1936, who executed an Instrument of Abdication which declared his vacation of the throne. An Act of Parliament was also passed which gave legal effect to the Instrument of Abdication and provided for the alteration in the line of succession.

The death of the monarch

In ancient times the death of a monarch effectively dissolved all the organs and functions of government. This is no longer the case. To ensure continuity of government the monarch never dies. The death of a reigning king or queen is legally called the demise of the sovereign. The word 'demise' in this context means the immediate transfer of the legal right to act as head of state to the heir to the throne. The word 'sovereign' in this context means that sovereignty is being transferred. Sovereignty is the legal right to act as head of state. The acquisition of the right to act as head of state is legally known as accession to the throne.

KEY CASES

CASE	FACTS	PRINCIPLE
Council of Civil Service Unions v Minister for the Civil Service [1985] AC 374	The Civil Service Union challenged a decision to ban trade union membership at GCHQ on national security grounds.	Although this case was mainly concerned with the justiciability of Royal Prerogative powers delegated to the executive, Lord Roskill (*obiter*) said that powers to dissolve Parliament, appoint ministers, and grant honours 'as well as others' were not justiciable.
M v Home Office [1993] 3 WLR 433	Among other things, the House of Lords had to decide whether the High Court had the power to issue an injunction against the Crown and, if so, was the Home Secretary, in either their personal or ministerial capacity, in contempt of court for ignoring it.	This case draws attention to the fact that the term 'the Crown' is capable of having two meanings, namely, the monarch and the executive, to which the monarch's powers have been delegated.
Prohibitions del Roy (1607) 77 ER 1342	The Court of King's Bench had to decide whether the monarch had any right to take part in the judicial process.	The monarch cannot take part in any criminal or civil action or influence the decision of any court of justice. The monarch cannot issue a warrant of arrest.

KEY DEBATES

Topic	*'Miller*: The Prerogative and Constitutional Change'
Author/Academic	Cormac Mac Amhlaigh
Viewpoint	This article reflects on the scope of prerogative powers under the UK Constitution, and their relationship to statute, in light of *R (on the application of Miller) v Secretary of State for Exiting the European Union* (2017) on whether the UK Government could rely on prerogative power to give notice under **Art 50 Treaty on European Union (TEU)** of the intention to withdraw from the EU, or whether statutory approval was required.
Source	(2017) 21(3) Edinburgh Law Review 448–454

Topic	'A Simple Application of the Frustration Principle: Prerogative, Statute and *Miller*'
Author/Academic	Robert Craig
Viewpoint	Robert Craig argues that the judgment in *R (on the application of Miller) v Secretary of State for Exiting the European Union*, on whether notification of an intention to withdraw from the EU under **Art 50 TEU** was within prerogative powers, was correctly decided. It reviews the constitutional issues underpinning the case, and suggests why *Miller* does not fall within the abeyance principle but rather exemplifies the application of the frustration principle.
Source	[2017] (Nov) Public Law Supp, Brexit Special Extra Issue, 25–47

Topic	'*Miller*, Structural Constitutional Review and the Limits of Prerogative Power'
Author/Academic	Paul Craig
Viewpoint	This article discusses constitutional law issues raised by the ruling in *R (on the application of Miller) v Secretary of State for Exiting the European Union* (2017). Reviews the facts of the case, the stages of analysis when considering prerogative powers, case law on the limits of such powers, and how these were interpreted in *Miller*. It also examines the distinctions between the majority and dissenting views in the case, and suggests why the majority was correct.
Source	[2017] (Nov) Public Law Supp, Brexit Special Extra Issue, 48–72

Topic	'Legislating about the Monarchy'
Author/Academic	Rodney Brazier
Viewpoint	Considers the reasons why very little legislation about the monarchy has been enacted in recent times, including the reluctance of politicians to engage with the political consequences of changes to the status quo and the parliamentary barriers to such constitutional reform. It discusses the issues of legislative methodology that would be raised by legislation about the monarchy. It assesses the likelihood that such legislation will be enacted in the future, particularly with the accession of HRH Prince of Wales.
Source	(2007) 66 Cambridge Law Journal 86–105

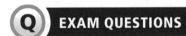 **EXAM QUESTIONS**

Problem question

Assume that there is a general election which results in a hung parliament. The Prime Minister refuses to resign because the party formerly in opposition does not have an overall majority. There are discussions about the form the next government should take. The Liberal Democrats say that they will join a coalition only if an electoral system based on proportional representation forms part of the new government's legislative programme. The Scottish and Welsh Nationalist Parties inform the Prime Minister that they will agree to a coalition government provided Scotland and Wales are given independence. All this is strongly opposed by the MPs belonging to the Prime Minister's own party who want him to lead a minority government.

Advise the Queen's Private Secretary as to the legal and political rules governing the Queen's role, if any, in the appointment of the Prime Minister and the formation of the next government under these circumstances.

See the Outline Answers section in the end matter for help with this question.

Essay question

Explain what is meant by Royal Prerogative and the extent to which it is susceptible to legal scrutiny.

Online Resources

For an outline answer to this essay question, as well as interactive key cases and multiple-choice questions, please visit the online resources.
www.oup.com/he/faragher-concentrate7e

Concentrate Q&As

For more questions and answers on public law, see the *Concentrate Q&A: Public Law* by Richard Clements.

Go to the end of this book to view **sample pages**.

8 The executive

Central, devolved, and local government

KEY FACTS

- The monarch is the formal head of the executive and the Prime Minister, who is also First Lord of the Treasury and Minister for the Civil Service, advises the monarch on the exercise of all executive powers.

- The Cabinet deals with all matters concerning the collective responsibility of the government as well as the formulation of government policy and putting it into effect via the parliamentary legislative process.

- Central government in the UK is organized into departments of state led by Secretaries of State and other ministers whose work is coordinated by the Cabinet.

- Every Secretary of State and minister, including the Prime Minister, is responsible to Parliament and subject to the jurisdiction of the courts.

- The Welsh Assembly Government, the Scottish Government, and the Northern Ireland Executive exercise devolved executive powers within the UK.

- The executive includes the police and armed forces, and Parliament, through legislation, grants executive powers to local authorities.

REVISION TIP

Make sure you are aware of the meaning of basic legal terms before you revise this topic in detail.

The executive

The executive consists of the reigning monarch who is legally the head of state, the Prime Minister, Cabinet, Secretaries of State, Ministers of the Crown, departments of state, non-departmental public bodies, devolved administrative organizations, local authorities, the police, and the armed forces. See Fig 8.1.

REVISION TIP

This topic links up with the separation of powers covered in Chapter 4. It is also provides a foundation for your understanding of judicial review covered in Chapters 11 to 13.

The Prime Minister

REVISION TIP

When you revise this topic you must remember the significant relationship between law and convention within the British Constitution. This topic links with Chapters 2 and 4.

Appointment

The Prime Minister is appointed by the reigning monarch. The monarch's powers are governed by binding constitutional conventions. The outgoing Prime Minister offers their resignation to the monarch who accepts it. Their successor is summoned to the monarch's presence and asked to form a new government.

Figure 8.1 The UK executive

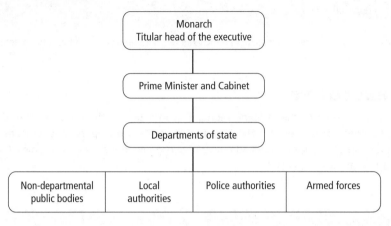

Following a general election, this takes place as soon as possible after the result is known, or if there is a hung parliament within a reasonable time if a coalition agreement has to be negotiated. Parliament may object to unreasonable delay.

Powers and duties

The Prime Minister's powers come from the Royal Prerogative and statute. The Prime Minister may advise the monarch on:

- the exercise of all prerogative powers concerning the government;
- the appointment of senior members of the judiciary;
- heads of the intelligence and security services; and
- senior officers of the Church of England.

In conjunction with the Secretary of State for Defence, the Prime Minister is responsible for senior appointments in the armed forces. The Prime Minister makes recommendations for honours and life peerages. The Prime Minister may also:

- determine the size and membership of the Cabinet;
- control the agenda of the Cabinet;
- create and disband Cabinet Committees; and
- exercise general control over the Cabinet Office by receiving reports from the Secretary of the Cabinet, the Deputy Prime Minister, and the First Secretary of State or other bodies.

As we saw in Chapter 5, the **Fixed Term Parliaments Act 2011** modifies the power of the Prime Minister to advise the monarch on the exercise of powers formerly under the Royal Prerogative to dissolve Parliament and permit a general election.

The Prime Minister and the civil service

The Prime Minister is Minister for the Civil Service. **Section 3 Constitutional Reform and Governance Act 2010** provides that the Minister for the Civil Service has the power to manage the civil service. This includes, among other things, the power to make appointments. The agreement of the Minister for the Civil Service is required in matters concerning the remuneration of civil servants (including compensation payable upon leaving the civil service) or the conditions on which civil servants may retire. In exercising their power to manage the civil service, the Minister for the Civil Service shall have regard to the need to ensure that civil servants who advise ministers are aware of the constitutional significance of Parliament and of the conventions governing the relationship between Parliament and Her Majesty's Government.

The Prime Minister's Office

The Prime Minister has an office with a principal private secretary and private secretaries, a diary secretary, a secretary for appointments, a political secretary, parliamentary private secretaries, press secretaries, and a parliamentary clerk. They also have a Policy Unit, and an Adviser on Efficiency and Effectiveness.

Death or resignation

The death, resignation, or dismissal of the Prime Minister does not automatically lead to a general election or a change of government or the resignation of the other members of the Cabinet. Any changes in Cabinet membership may be made by the Prime Minister's successor.

REVISION TIP

Again, remember the constitutional conventions discussed in Chapter 2. They have an important role to play in the way the Cabinet works.

The Cabinet

Membership

Members of the Cabinet are chosen by the Prime Minister and appointed by the monarch. The Cabinet may vary in size. In January 2021 the Cabinet consisted of 22 members.

Functions

The Cabinet deals with questions which concern the **collective responsibility** of the government because they raise major issues of policy or because they are of critical importance to the public, and deal with unresolved arguments between departments. In addition, the Cabinet determines the policy to be submitted to Parliament, including decisions as to the contents of the Queen's Speech and the legislative timetable, and the broad economic policy within which the Chancellor of the Exchequer formulates the budget.

Committees

There are standing and ad hoc Cabinet Committees. Standing Committees are permanent. **Ad hoc committees** are set up and empowered by the Cabinet as and when required to deal with current matters of importance. Cabinet Committees may include members who are not part of the Cabinet itself. Particulars of Cabinet committees have been published periodically since 1992.

The Cabinet in relation to the monarch

The monarch does not attend Cabinet meetings. The Prime Minister does so on the monarch's behalf. Ministerial discussions are communicated to the monarch, who is entitled to be fully informed before being asked to approve and sign any documents which are sent via the Prime Minister.

Unanimity of advice

The advice given to the monarch by the Cabinet ought to be unanimous. The monarch may not inquire into any differences of opinion within the Cabinet, or express any political views except to ministers, or seek advice elsewhere. The monarch may listen to the views of others without commenting on them.

Collective Cabinet responsibility

Collective Cabinet responsibility is a constitutional convention. Lord Widgery CJ in **Attorney General v Jonathan Cape Ltd** (1976) said that collective Cabinet responsibility means that any policy decision reached by the Cabinet has to be supported thereafter by all members of the Cabinet whether they approve of it or not, unless they feel compelled to resign. Geoffrey Marshall in *Ministerial Responsibility* (1989) identified three elements in this convention:

- The confidence principle: this means that a government must have the confidence of the House of Commons to remain in power.
- The unanimity principle: this means that, with the exception of free votes authorized by the Prime Minister in Cabinet or an agreement to differ, all the members of the government must speak and vote together in Parliament.
- The confidentiality principle: this principle allows frank ministerial discussion within Cabinet and government.

In practice this means that:

- a minister must not vote against government policy;
- a minister must not speak against government policy;
- all decisions are decisions of the whole government; and
- a former minister must not reveal Cabinet secrets.

The breakdown of collective Cabinet responsibility during meaningful vote procedure under s 13 of the European Union (Withdrawal) Act 2018

On 13 March 2019, during the vote under **s 13 European Union (Withdrawal) Act 2018** on whether Parliament would not approve withdrawal from the EU without a deal under any circumstances, 13 Conservative front benchers, including four Cabinet ministers, defied the Prime Minister by abstaining. Under normal circumstances, under the Constitutional convention of collective Cabinet responsibility, they would have been obliged to resign. None of the Cabinet ministers resigned. Although subsequently denied, it was alleged that they had been advised by a senior official that they were not obliged to resign because they did not actually vote against the motion. The only front bencher, who was not a Cabinet minister, to vote against the motion did resign.

REVISION TIP

This area illustrates how the Royal Prerogative, explained in Chapter 7, is delegated to the members of the executive. You should review the relevant parts of Chapter 2.

Secretaries of State

A Secretary of State has delegated authority from the monarch to act in the name of the Crown. They are normally Cabinet ministers and Members of Parliament, to which they are accountable.

Under the **European Communities Act 1972** the First Secretary of State is designated minister for transport, consumer protection, the collection of information, employment, medicinal products, and the European agricultural policy.

Departments of state

These implement policies and advise ministers. They are staffed by politically impartial civil servants funded by Parliament. They often work alongside local authorities, non-departmental public bodies, and other government-sponsored organizations. Some departments are responsible for the whole of the UK; others are responsible for England and Wales, Scotland, or Northern Ireland. Many departments are headed by ministers. Others are headed by non-ministerial office holders for whose conduct ministers are accountable to Parliament.

Non-departmental public bodies

These are regional or national public bodies which work independently of ministers. There are executive non-departmental public bodies and advisory non-departmental public bodies.

The effect of the Public Bodies Act 2011

The **Public Bodies Act 2011** empowers ministers to abolish or reform those public bodies listed in its schedules, in order to increase accountability and control costs. **Section 1** enables a minister, by order, to abolish any public body or office specified in **Sch 1** and to transfer any or all of its functions to an 'eligible person', defined as a minister, the Scottish ministers, a Northern Ireland department, or the Welsh ministers, any other person exercising public functions, a company limited by guarantee, a community interest company, a cooperative society, a community benefit society, a charitable incorporated organization, or a body of trustees, or other unincorporated body.

The civil service

Part 1 Constitutional Reform and Governance Act 2010 removes the Royal Prerogative from the management of the civil service and gives the Minister for the Civil Service (the Prime Minister) statutory authority to manage the civil service. The only exceptions are security vetting and the management of the parts of the Civil Service of the State (listed in **s 1**) which are not covered by the provisions in **Pt 1**. The Secretary of State for Foreign and Commonwealth Affairs is given a parallel power to manage the diplomatic service. The Act requires that a code of practice should ensure that civil servants carry out their duty with integrity, honesty, objectivity, and impartiality. The responsibility for appointments to the civil service and hearing complaints is given to the Civil Service Commission. All appointments are to be made on merit on the basis of fair and open competition. The fair and open competition requirement does not apply to special advisers. There is also a requirement for a separate code of conduct for special advisers which provides that special advisers may not authorize the expenditure of public funds, exercise any power in relation to the management of any part of the civil service (except in relation to other special advisers), or otherwise exercise any statutory or prerogative power.

The Civil Service Commission

The Civil Service Commission performs the functions of the former Civil Service Commissioners. The First Civil Service Commissioner and the other Civil Service Commissioners are members of the new Civil Service Commission. Transitional arrangements will enable those serving as Civil Service Commissioners automatically to move across to the new commission.

Parliamentary accountability

REVISION TIP

This topic provides a foundation for judicial review. See Chapters 11 to 13.

Apart from collective responsibility each minister is responsible and must answer to Parliament for their own acts and policies and for all that is done by civil servants in their department. This is called the *Crichel Down Principle* which was formulated by the House of Commons after the Crichel Down Affair (1954). In giving an account to Parliament a minister must not knowingly mislead Parliament. They must protect a civil servant who has carried out their explicit order, and must defend a civil servant who acts properly in accordance with the policy laid down by the minister. Except on an important issue of policy or where a claim to individual rights is seriously involved, where an official makes a mistake or causes some delay the minister should acknowledge the mistake and accept the responsibility although they are not personally involved. They should then state that they will take corrective action in the department. Where action has been taken by a civil servant of which the minister disapproves and has no previous knowledge, and the conduct of the official is reprehensible, there is no obligation on a minister to endorse what they believe to be wrong or to defend what are clearly shown to be errors of their officers. They remain, however, constitutionally responsible to Parliament for the fact that something has gone wrong, although this does not affect their power to control and discipline their staff.

Although in principle ministers are expected to give an account of their departments and answer questions in Parliament, they may refuse to answer questions on a number of grounds, for example that they concern confidential commercial information, or advice received by a minister from a civil servant, or that the information asked for cannot be obtained without undue expense. As far as making amends is concerned there is no legally coercive mechanism to enforce this where no unlawful conduct is involved if the minister does not wish to make amends. A person complaining of injustice in consequence of maladministration may ask a Member of Parliament to refer the matter to the Parliamentary Commissioner for Administration. A minister may be called upon in Parliament to make amends or resign if found to be personally at fault, for example if they are found to have committed an error of judgement or to have been negligent in office. If the fault is not that of the minister but of a civil servant it seems there is no duty to resign, though there is still a notional duty to make amends for the fault. In practice ministers do not resign even in the face of parliamentary criticism unless, for instance, they do so voluntarily on the basis that they accept personal responsibility for what has gone wrong or they lose the support of the Prime Minister or the Cabinet, or their own backbenchers, or they consider that they are too much of an embarrassment to the government to carry on in office.

REVISION TIP

Looking at the principles of individual ministerial responsibility and collective Cabinet responsibility now will help you to understand the role of Select Committees and the Parliamentary Commissioner for Administration (the Ombudsman) discussed in the next chapter. You should also review what you learned about the distinction between law and convention. See Chapter 2.

The Ministerial Code

The Ministerial Code is a document which sets out rules and standards for government ministers in the UK. Separate codes exist for ministers of the Scottish Government, the Northern Ireland Executive (based on the St Andrews Agreement), and the Welsh Government. Codes of conduct for ministers were amongst a range of initiatives designed to respond to perceptions of the erosion of ministerial accountability, and to preserve public trust in the institutions of Cabinet government. Written guidance for British Cabinet ministers began as 'Questions of Procedure for Ministers' (QPM), which was a confidential document, prepared by the Cabinet Office to assist ministers, and which dates from the 1980s. The earliest published form of the Code was when the QPM was released by the Major Government in 1992 and further editions have been adapted based on suggestions and recommendations from the Committee on Standards in Public Life. The first edition to be entitled 'Ministerial Code' was Tony Blair's 1997 set of rules. The most recent version was released in May 2010 (it being a convention for each new Prime Minister to issue their own). When Gordon Brown came into office in June 2007 he appointed Sir Philip Mawer, who was Parliamentary Commissioner for Standards, as the Independent Adviser on Ministers' Interests—a form of enforcer to conduct investigations and give confidential advice. The Adviser under Tony Blair was Sir John Bourn who was Comptroller and Auditor General. The Cabinet Secretary is responsible for clearing ministers' financial matters. The Code is currently administered by the propriety and ethics group within the Cabinet Office.

The Code has ten sections, and one annex.

Section 1—Ministers of the Crown: this section is an introduction, setting out the role of ministers to the government, to Parliament, and to the people. It directs ministers to 'behave in a way that upholds the highest standards of propriety', to uphold the principle of collective responsibility, and to avoid conflicts of interest.

Section 2—Ministers and the government: this sets out the precise rules of collective responsibility. It also states that ministers should relinquish all government material when ceasing to hold a role, and provides rules on access to government papers by former ministers (eg those writing memoirs may wish to check the documents from their time in office). This set of rules are known as the 'Radcliffe rules'.

Section 3—Ministers and appointments: this sets out the rules regarding special advisers (temporary civil servants who are political agents of the minister), how many each minister may appoint, and their powers and duties. Also covered is the appointment of parliamentary private secretaries (PPS) (backbenchers who act as an unpaid secretary to the minister, to gain experience and credit with the party), whose appointment would require written authority from the Prime Minister. PPSs are not members of the government, but are expected to form part of the payroll vote, and support all government initiatives in the House of Commons.

Section 4—Ministers and their departments: this looks at the machinery of government (the structure of government departments and how responsibilities can be transferred), and how ministers should ensure that their work is covered during any absence from London, even for constituency business.

Section 5—Ministers and civil servants: this section has regard to ministerial relationships with the civil service. It states that ministers 'must uphold the political impartiality of the Civil Service, and not ask civil servants to act in any way which would conflict with the *Civil Service Code*'.

Section 6—Ministers' constituency and party interests: this directs ministers to refrain from using government property and resources in their role as an MP. For example, political leaflets must not be distributed at the expense of public funds. Ministers with a conflict of interest between their government role and their constituency (eg a transport minister may have to balance the desire of their constituents not to have a new airport built near their town, with their government duties) are simply advised to act cautiously; 'ministers are advised to take particular care'.

Section 7—Ministers' private interests: this section requires ministers to provide their permanent secretary with a complete list of any financial interests they have. In March 2009, this list was released to the public for the first time. It is collated and made available by the Cabinet Office. Officials sometimes need to restrict 'interested' ministers' access to certain papers, in order to ensure impartiality. Guidelines are set out as to maintaining neutrality for ministers who are members of a trade union. No minister should accept gifts or hospitality from any person or organization when a conflict of interest could arise. A list of gifts, and how they were dealt with on an individual basis, is published annually.

Section 8—Ministers and the presentation of policy: this section stipulates that speeches, interviews, and news releases should all be cleared with the Number 10 Press Office, to ensure synchronicity of timing and clarity of content. Ministers should not practise 'regular journalism' without the permission of the Office. No minister may publish a book about their ministerial experiences while in office. Former ministers require manuscripts to be cleared by the Cabinet Secretary, under the 'Radcliffe rules'.

Section 9—Ministers and Parliament: under this section ministers should not make oral statements to Parliament without prior approval from the Prime Minister. Any other minister or MP to be mentioned in such a statement should be notified beforehand.

Section 10—Travel by ministers: official government transport, paid for by public funds, should normally only be used on government business, except where security requires that it be used even for personal transport. All travel should be cost-effective, and any trips abroad should be kept to a minimum. All overseas delegations costing more than £500 have their details published annually. Members of the Cabinet have the authority to order special (non-scheduled) flights, but this power should only be used when necessary. In the event of a minister being summoned home on urgent government business, the cost of the round trip will be paid for from public funds. There are also rules relating to the use of official cars and air miles gained by official travel.

The seven principles of public life

These principles were first published by the Committee on Standards in Public Life in 1995. They are as follows:

- *Selflessness*: ministers should act entirely in the public interest.

- *Integrity*: no financial obligations should be accepted if they could undermine the minister's position.

- *Objectivity*: when making appointments, decisions should be based on merit.
- *Accountability*: all public office holders are accountable, and should cooperate with all scrutiny procedures.
- *Openness*: all decisions should be justified, and information should be restricted only when necessary for the public interest.
- *Honesty*: public office holders are required, by duty, to be honest in all their dealings and business.
- *Leadership*: the principles should be supported and upheld by leadership and example.

Legal accountability

In *R v Secretary of State for the Home Department, ex p Oladehinde* (1991) the House of Lords (per Lord Griffiths) said that when a statute places a duty on a minister it may be exercised by a member of their department for whom they accept responsibility and for whose conduct they are legally accountable. Moreover Lord Woolf said, in *M v Home Office* (1993), that there appears to be no reason in principle why, if a statute places a duty on a specified minister or other official which creates a cause of action, an action cannot be brought for breach of statutory duty claiming damages or for an injunction against the specified minister personally by any person entitled to benefit from the cause of action.

REVISION TIP

The accountability of the executive to the judiciary links up with the rule of law discussed in Chapter 3 as well as the separation of powers discussed in Chapter 4. It provides a foundation for what you will study in Chapter 12 on judicial review. It is very important not to restrict your revision to the minimum number of topics required by the assessment.

Devolution

Through the process of devolution, executive powers within the UK have been given to executive organizations in Scotland, Wales, and Northern Ireland.

Scotland

Under the current system of devolution executive functions are carried out by the Scottish Government. This is set up by **Pt II Scotland Act 1998** as amended by **Pt 2 Scotland Act 2012**. The Scottish Government consists of the First Minister, the Scottish ministers, and the Scottish Law Officers. The First Minister is a member of the Scottish Parliament and appointed by the Queen. The Scottish ministers are also members of the Scottish Parliament. They are appointed by the First Minister and approved by the Scottish Parliament. The Scottish Law Officers are the Lord

Advocate and the Solicitor General for Scotland. These are appointed, upon the recommendation of the First Minister and with the agreement of the Scottish Parliament, by the Queen. There are also junior Scottish ministers who are appointed to assist the Scottish Executive. These are members of the Scottish Parliament and are appointed by the First Minister with the approval of the Scottish Parliament. Executive powers were and continue to be transferred to the Scottish Government within the legislative competence of the Scottish Parliament. There are general provisions for this in the **Scotland Act 1998**. The **Scotland Act 2016** declares that the Scottish Parliament and the Scottish Government are considered permanent parts of the UK's constitutional arrangements and will not be abolished without a decision of the people of Scotland. It also recognizes that the UK Parliament will not normally legislate in relation to devolved matters without the consent of the Scottish Parliament, whilst retaining the sovereignty to do so. Generally, this Act transfers powers to the Scottish Parliament and the Scottish Government to rebalance reserved responsibilities.

Wales

Public authorities serving Wales are the Secretary of State for Wales, the Welsh Office, the Welsh Language Board, and the Auditor General for Wales. The current law is contained in the **Government of Wales Acts 1998–2006** as amended by the **Wales Act 2014**.

The Government of Wales Act 1998

Sections 52–55 Government of Wales Act 1998 set up the Welsh Assembly. The Assembly is empowered to elect the Assembly First Secretary. The Assembly First Secretary is empowered to appoint Assembly Secretaries. The Assembly must establish certain committees. Where additional committees are established, they must (unless they exist solely to provide advice) be elected to reflect the party balance in the Assembly. Sub-committees may also be formed. The Assembly must establish certain committees including the Welsh Administration Ombudsman, the Welsh Development Agency, the Development Board for Rural Wales, the Land Authority for Wales, and Housing for Wales.

The Government of Wales Act 2006

The **Government of Wales Act 2006** as amended by the **Wales Act 2014** establishes the Welsh Government as an entity separate from, but accountable to, the Assembly. It deals with the appointment and remuneration of the First Minister and other ministers and deputy ministers; creates the office of Counsel-General to the Welsh Assembly Government and makes provision for appointment to it; and authorizes the appointment of staff (who are civil servants) in support of the Assembly Government. It provides for the exercise of statutory functions by ministers in their own right (rather than as delegates of the Assembly), and places duties on them in respect of carrying out regulatory impact assessments in connection with Welsh subordinate legislation, and duties in respect of equality of opportunity, sustainable development, and the Welsh language. Ministers will also be required to engage with stakeholders through consultation mechanisms with business, local government, and the voluntary sector.

Northern Ireland

The head of the executive in Northern Ireland is the Secretary of State for Northern Ireland acting on behalf of the reigning monarch. Executive powers within Northern Ireland are exercised by the Northern Ireland Executive, the members of which are appointed by the Secretary of State. The **Northern Ireland Act 1998** contained provisions concerning the Government of Northern Ireland including the creation of the Northern Ireland Assembly. This was suspended by the **Northern Ireland Act 2000**.

The Northern Ireland institutions, including the Northern Ireland Assembly, were suspended in October 2002. Plans to restore a devolved executive in Northern Ireland were contained in the **Northern Ireland Act 2006**. Government proposals, incorporated in this Act, involved bringing together Assembly members to participate in a process to select a Northern Ireland Executive, comprising a First Minister, a deputy First Minister, and Northern Ireland ministers. The Northern Ireland Executive was suspended, along with the Northern Ireland Assembly, in January 2017. Since then the Westminster Parliament has passed a series of budgetary statutes and the **Northern Ireland (Executive Formation and Exercise of Functions) Act 2018** which made provisions which allowed Northern Ireland's public bodies and services to continue to function. Since January 2020, when the Northern Ireland Assembly resumed, the First Minister and deputy First Minister are nominated respectively by the largest parties of the largest and second largest political designations in the Assembly. Ministers of the executive, with the exception of the Minister of Justice, are nominated by the political parties in the Northern Ireland Assembly. The number of ministers which a party can nominate is determined by its share of seats in the Assembly. The Minister of Justice is appointed through a nomination made by the First Minister and deputy First Minister acting jointly and approved by a cross-community resolution of the Assembly. The First Minister and deputy First Minister act jointly and each minister has responsibility for a specific Northern Ireland government department.

The European Union (Withdrawal) Act 2018

Section 11, together with **Sch 2**, and **s 12 European Union (Withdrawal) Act 2018** confer important powers on devolved institutions and make important amendments to the **Scotland Act 1998**, the **Northern Ireland Act 1998**, and the **Government of Wales Act 2006**. **Schedule 2**, which is brought into force by **s 11**, confers powers on the devolved administrations which correspond to the powers conferred on the UK Government under **ss 8** and **9**. **Section 12 European Union (Withdrawal) Act 2018** removes the requirements that the devolved legislatures and the devolved administrations can only legislate or act in ways that are compatible with EU law. It then inserts powers into each of those Acts to apply, by regulations, a temporary 'freeze' on devolved legislative or executive competence in specified areas, so that in those areas the current parameters of devolved competence are maintained.

London: the Mayor and the Greater London Authority

Section 1 Greater London Authority Act 1999 creates the Greater London Authority. **Section 2** says that the Greater London Authority shall consist of the Mayor of London and an Assembly for London called the London Assembly.

 LOOKING FOR EXTRA MARKS?

You should now go to the Key debates section and read the recommended articles. There is a lot of material on devolution issues in Scotland, Wales, and Northern Ireland to be found online. You should follow this up.

Cities and Local Government Devolution Act 2016

The aim of this Act is to devolve powers and budgets to boost local growth in England, by devolving far-reaching powers over economic development, transport, and social care to large cities which choose to have elected mayors. The Act also:

- streamlines the process for making changes to existing combined authorities and establishing and changing the area of a combined authority or an economic prosperity board, and removes geographical limitations as to the establishment of combined authorities and economic prosperity boards;
- makes certain other changes to arrangements for local governance;
- amends the **National Health Service Act 2006** to provide for joint and devolved exercise of functions (including provisions about sharing and control of patient data);
- provides National Park Authorities with a functional power of competence;
- inserts provision into the **Local Transport Act 2008** to enable the establishment of Sub-national Transport Bodies, enabling decision-making over strategic transport schemes to be devolved below national level.

Local government

England

England consists of the combined areas of the counties, districts, and unitary authorities created by the **Local Government Acts 1972, 1985**, and **1992**. It also consists of Greater London and the Metropolitan Police District, formed by the **London Government Act 1963, the Local Government Act 1985**, the **Police Act 1996**, and the **Greater London Authority Act 1999**. Under s 2(1) London Government Act 1963 the administrative area of Greater London means the combined areas of the London boroughs, the City of London, the Inner Temple, and the Middle Temple. Under the **Greater London Authority Act 1999** and the **Police and Social Responsibility Act 2011**, the Metropolitan Police District means Greater London, excluding the City of London and the Inner Temple and the Middle Temple.

LOOKING FOR EXTRA MARKS?

Attempts to extend devolution to the English regions have been less successful than in Scotland, Wales, and Northern Ireland. There has also been some opposition to proposed local government reforms in England. You should follow this up in your recommended standard textbook and look up the journal articles available online and think about the future of England within a devolved UK.

Wales

Following the **Local Government (Wales) Act 1994**, Wales consists of 22 unitary authorities.

Scotland

Following the **Local Government (Scotland) Act 1994**, Scotland is the combined areas of 29 unitary authorities and three island authorities. Under the **Island of Rockall Act 1972**, as amended by **s 214(2)** and **Sch 27, Pt II, para 202 Local Government (Scotland) Act 1973**, the Island of Rockall is part of Scotland.

Northern Ireland

Section 43(2) Northern Ireland Constitution Act 1973 provides that Northern Ireland consists of the parliamentary counties of Antrim, Armagh, Down, Fermanagh, Londonderry, and Tyrone and the parliamentary boroughs of Belfast and Londonderry.

The effect of the Localism Act 2011 on local government powers and functions

Part I Localism Act 2011 extends the power of local authorities, from county councils to parish councils, to 'do anything that individuals generally may do' as long as that is not limited by some other Act. It deals with the standards expected of council members, with the keeping of registers of interests and, in an important change, it allows members to have expressed prior views about a topic and also contribute towards a decision on that topic, without the risk of making the decision invalid.

KEY CASES

CASE	FACTS	PRINCIPLE
M v Home Office [1991] 3 All ER 537	The House of Lords had to decide whether the Home Secretary was subject to the compulsory jurisdiction of the court.	There appears to be no reason in principle why, if a statute places a duty on a specified minister or other official which creates a cause of action, an action cannot be brought for breach of statutory duty claiming damages or for an injunction, against the specified minister personally by any person entitled to benefit from the cause of action.
R v Secretary of State for the Home Department, ex p Oladehinde [1991] 1 AC 254	The House of Lords had to decide whether the Home Secretary was legally responsible for the conduct of immigration officers.	When a statute places a duty on a minister it may generally be exercised by a member of their department for whom they accept responsibility and for whose conduct they are accountable.
R v Skinner [1968] 2 QB 700	The question to be considered by the court was whether the minister could delegate a decision to use breathalysing equipment.	Ministers are not expected to take every decision entrusted to them by Parliament. If a decision is made on their behalf by one of their officials, then that is the minister's constitutional decision.

KEY DEBATES

Topic	'The Multifaceted Constitutional Dynamics of UK Devolution'
Author/Academic	P Leyland
Viewpoint	Assesses the unanticipated constitutional impact of devolution in Scotland, Wales, and Northern Ireland, including some of the controversies it has raised in each of the four UK jurisdictions. It compares devolution to federalism.
Source	(2011) 9(1) International Journal of Constitutional Law 251–273

Topic	'Pulling a Trigger or Starting a Journey? Brexit in the Supreme Court'
Author/Academic	David Feldman

Topic	'Pulling a Trigger or Starting a Journey? Brexit in the Supreme Court'
Viewpoint	This article comments on *R (on the application of Miller) v Secretary of State for Exiting the European Union* (2017) on whether: the government could rely on its prerogative power to notify the EU of the UK's decision to trigger **Art 50 Treaty on European Union**; and consent to give notice was required from the devolved Governments of Northern Ireland, Scotland, and Wales.
Source	(2017) 76 Cambridge Law Journal 217–223

Topic	'Taking Local Government Seriously: Democracy, Autonomy and the Constitution'
Author/Academic	S Bailey and M Elliott
Viewpoint	Assesses the effectiveness of attempts by central government to strengthen local democracy. It discusses the role and degree of autonomy of local government, including its relationship with central government, and key conditions influencing the quality of local democracy, in particular the organization and internal structure of local government and the related electoral process. Outlines reasons for the lack of success of central government attempts to strengthen local government and local democracy. It also considers relevant legislative changes and proposals for reform.
Source	(2006) 59(3) Parliamentary Affairs 420–436

Topic	'*Miller*: Legal and Political Fault Lines'
Author/Academic	Paul Daly
Viewpoint	Reflects on the ruling in *R (on the application of Miller) v Secretary of State for Exiting the European Union*, and suggests that it can be understood with reference to the fault lines between: (1) form and substance regarding devolution and the relationship between UK and EU law; (2) the old and new constitutions; and (3) legal and political accountability. Examines the legislative response to the judgment.
Source	[2017] (Nov) Public Law Supp, Brexit Special Extra Issue 73–93

Topic	'The Reconstruction of Constitutional Accountability'
Author/Academic	Diana Woodhouse
Viewpoint	Considers the definition of constitutional accountability which requires ministers to be accountable for the actions of themselves and their departments and suggested reformulation of theory which concentrates on role rather than causal responsibility.
Source	[2002] Public Law 73–90

EXAM QUESTIONS

Problem question

Assume that the government introduces a bill into Parliament to make all universities private companies. All the members of the Cabinet support the bill except the Home Secretary. He has spoken out against the bill on television and in Parliament. The Prime Minister also discovers that, owing to a mistake made by civil servants at the Home Office, the cost of introducing identity cards is 500 per cent more than reported to the House of Commons. There are calls for the Home Secretary's resignation.

Advise the Home Secretary as to:

* whether he is obliged to resign; and
* his parliamentary and legal responsibility, if any, for the errors made by the team of civil servants at the Home Office.

See the Outline Answers section in the end matter for help with this question.

Essay question

Explain the principle of devolution and the extent to which executive powers have been devolved equally throughout the UK.

Online Resources

For an outline answer to this essay question, as well as interactive key cases and multiple-choice questions, please visit the online resources.
www.oup.com/he/faragher-concentrate7e

Concentrate Q&As

For more questions and answers on public law, see the *Concentrate Q&A: Public Law* by Richard Clements.

Go to the end of this book to view **sample pages**.

9 European Union law and institutions

- The European Union is a supranational legal order based on treaties and general legal principles.

- The institutions of the European Union exercise legislative, executive, and judicial powers.

- The sources of EU law are Treaties, Regulations, Directives, Decisions, and judgments of the Court of Justice of the European Union (CJEU), formerly the European Court of Justice (ECJ).

- Decisions of the ECJ (now the CJEU) assert that human rights form part of the general principles of EU law and **Art 6 Treaty on European Union (TEU)** has the effect of giving formal recognition that human rights, especially those protected by the **European Convention on Human Rights (ECHR)**, are part of EU law and are protected by the ECJ.

- **Article 50 TEU** prescribes the procedure by which a member state can withdrawal from the EU.

- The key statutes governing the process by which the UK left the EU are the **European Union (Notification of Withdrawal) Act 2017**, the **European Union (Withdrawal) Act 2018**, and the **European Union (Withdrawal Agreement) Act 2020**.

- The present relationship between the EU and the UK is governed by the **EU–UK Trade and Cooperation Agreement** (2020) as implemented by the **European Union (Future Relationship) Act 2020**.

REVISION TIP

Before reading this chapter, please refer to your study guides and other materials provided as part of your course to check coverage and emphasis. This chapter primarily focuses on the impact of EU law on UK constitutional law issues.

EU Treaty framework since 1957

The **Treaty of Rome** (1957) established the European Economic Community. Other treaties of constitutional significance are the **Merger Treaty** (1967), **the Single European Act 1987**, the **Treaty on European Union** (1992), the **Treaty of Amsterdam** (1999), the **Treaty of Nice** (2001), and the **Treaty of Lisbon** (2007).

EU institutions

The main institutions are the Council of Ministers, European Commission, European Parliament, and the CJEU. Other bodies like the Economic and Social Committee and the Committee of the Regions play important decision-making roles.

Sources of EU law

REVISION TIP

In your plan you should revise this topic in conjunction with human rights, dealt with in Chapter 14, and parliamentary sovereignty dealt with in Chapter 6. Substantive EU law, the institutional structure of the EU, and EU history is covered more fully in the *EU Law Concentrate*.

Apart from the Treaties mentioned earlier, other sources of EU law are Regulations, Directives, Decisions, and Decisions of the CJEU, the jurisdiction of which concerns the interpretation of the Treaties, Regulations, and Decisions, the recognition and development of general principles of law, and the development of doctrines such as direct effect.

General principles in EU law

General principles form a body of 'unwritten' law, stated and applied by the ECJ and the General Court designed to assist it in its duties and to fill the gaps in the law. These general principles are not to be confused with the fundamental principles of EU law as expressed in the **EC Treaty**. The general principles include proportionality, equality, legitimate expectation, legal certainty, the right to a hearing, duty to give reasons, right to due process, and legal professional privilege.

Human rights in EU law

REVISION TIP

Here it is important to focus on how the ECJ, as well as the European Court of Human Rights, have come to play a leading role in the protection of human rights in the EU. The influence of the EU on human rights and the relationship between civil and political rights on the one hand, and economic and social rights on the other is a hot topic. There is considerable debate and this might be the subject of an essay question. Supplement your reading, first, be consulting your recommended public law textbook and, second, by looking up the articles and other materials mentioned later in this chapter.

The original **Treaty of Rome** lacked a catalogue of fundamental human rights. In some of its early case law, the ECJ denied that human rights were part of EC law. A turning point in its case law was *Stauder v City of Ulm* (1969) in which the ECJ decided that human rights would be protected as part of the 'general principles of law'. **Article 6 TEU** has the effect of giving formal recognition that human rights, especially those protected by the **ECHR**, are part of EU law and are protected by the ECJ. Some of the earlier cases mentioned in this chapter can now be considered under the various articles of the **ECHR**.

The EU Charter of Fundamental Rights

The **EU Charter of Fundamental Rights (the EU Charter)** sets out in a single text, for the first time in the EU's history, the whole range of civil, political, economic, and social rights of European citizens and all persons resident in the EU. These rights are divided into six sections. These are Dignity, Freedoms, Equality, Solidarity, Citizens' Rights, and Justice.

They are based, in particular, on the fundamental rights and freedoms recognized by the **ECHR**, the constitutional traditions of the EU member states, the Council of Europe's **Social Charter**, the **Community Charter of Fundamental Social Rights of Workers**, and other international conventions to which the EU or its member states are parties.

The **Treaty of Lisbon Protocol (No 30)** contains the following provisions concerning the **EU Charter**.

1. The jurisdiction of the UK courts to declare national law inconsistent with the fundamental rights guaranteed by the **EU Charter** is not extended.

2. In particular, and for the avoidance of doubt, nothing in **Title IV EU Charter** creates justiciable rights applicable to Poland or the UK except insofar as Poland or the UK has provided for such rights in its national law.

3. **Article 2** provides that to the extent that a provision of the Charter refers to national laws and practices, it shall only apply to Poland or the UK to the extent that the rights or principles that it contains are recognized in the law or practices of Poland or the UK.

Direct effect under EU law

REVISION TIP

This is a topic of fundamental importance and comes up in examinations on a regular basis. You should, therefore, revise this thoroughly. Your understanding of the subject will improve greatly if you acquire a comprehensive knowledge of the case law.

The Treaty Articles referred to here are those contained in the **Treaty of Rome** (1957) as amended by the **TEU** which came into effect on 1 November 1993. The 1957 Treaty Articles appear in brackets.

Regulations

As defined in **Art 288(2) [249] (ex 189(2)) EC**: a Regulation shall have general application. It shall be binding in its entirety and directly applicable in all member states.

Decisions

Article 288(4) [249] (ex 189) EC provides that: a Decision shall be binding in its entirety upon those to whom it is addressed.

Directives

Article 288(3) [249] (ex 189) EC provides that: a Directive shall be binding as to the result to be achieved upon each member state to which it is addressed, but shall leave to the national authorities the choice of form and method.

Member states must implement the provisions within the time limit laid down in the Directive. **Directives** have a different character from **Regulations**—they are important in the harmonization programme of the Community.

The authors of the Treaty did not intend that Directives should have direct effect; however failure by member states to fulfil their obligation under **Art 288(3) [249] (ex 189) EC** led the ECJ to apply the principle of direct effect (albeit to a limited extent). This was decided in the following case.

Van Duyn v Home Office [1974] ECR 1337

Miss Van Duyn, a Dutch woman, was refused leave to enter the UK where she wished to take up a job with the Church of Scientology. Her action against the Home Office was based on Community law guaranteeing the free movement of workers (**Art 48** and **Directive 64/221/EEC**). The High Court made a reference to the ECJ.

The ECJ held that **Art 3** of the Directive relied upon was capable of conferring rights on individuals which the courts of member states were under an obligation to protect.

Two further principles are important.

The first of these is that the binding nature of a Directive, which constitutes the basis for the possibility of relying on the Directive before a national court, exists only in relation to 'each Member State to which it is addressed'. It follows that a Directive may not of itself impose obligations on an individual and that a provision of a Directive may not be relied upon as such against such a person. This principle was determined by the ECJ in **Marshall v Southampton AHA** (1986) in which the Court determined that the claimant could rely on an anti-discrimination Directive against the state regardless of the capacity in which the latter was acting.

The second is that the provisions of a Directive can be relied on against organizations or bodies which are subject to the authority or control of the state or have special powers beyond those which result from the normal rules applicable between individuals. This was formulated by the ECJ in **Foster v British Gas** (1991). The key issue here was whether the defendant was part of the state. The Court held that the Directive could be relied upon.

Failure to transpose a Directive into national law

Article 10 (ex 5) provides that member states shall take all appropriate measures, whether general or particular, to ensure fulfilment of the obligations arising out of the Treaty or resulting from action taken by the institutions of the Community. They shall facilitate the achievement of the Community's tasks. They shall abstain from any measure which could jeopardize the attainment of the objectives of the Treaty.

Francovich v Italian State [1991] ECR I-5357

Directive 80/987/EEC required member states to set up guarantee funds in the event of an employer becoming insolvent. Italy failed to implement the Directive. F found himself denied the protection envisaged by the Directive.

It was held that it is a principle of Community law that the member states are obliged to make good any loss and damage caused to individuals by breaches of Community law for which they can be held responsible.

This principle is subject to three conditions: (1) the result prescribed by the Directive should entail the grant of rights to individuals; (2) it should be possible to identify the content of those rights on the basis of the provisions of the Directive; and (3) there must be a causal link between the breach of the state's obligation and the loss and damage suffered by the injured parties.

The ECJ decided that F could claim no effective rights as the provisions of the Directive lacked sufficient unconditionality.

These principles were applied by the ECJ in **Dillenkofer v Federal Republic of Germany** (1997).

The legal background to the UK's withdrawal from the EU

 REVISION TIP

You should now reconsider the doctrine of parliamentary sovereignty and assess its compatibility with the principle of the supremacy of EU law presented here.

The UK joined the European Community on 1 January 1973 under the terms of the **Treaty of Accession 1972**. This Treaty was incorporated into UK law by the **European Communities Act 1972**. If there is conflict between EU law and national law, which prevails? According to the ECJ, the European Community is a new legal order of international law for the benefit of which the states have limited their sovereign rights and a legal system which forms an integral and binding part of the legal systems of member states involving a permanent transfer of rights and obligations.

Any subsequent unilateral act which is incompatible with the concept of the Community cannot prevail. This was determined by the ECJ in *NV Algemene Transport-Expedite Onderneming van Gend en Loos v Nederlandse Administratie der Belastigen* (1963) and *Costa v ENEL* (1964). The English courts first considered the effect of this doctrine on the sovereignty of Parliament in the following case.

Blackburn v Attorney General [1971] 1 WLR 1037

The claimant brought two actions against the Attorney General claiming declarations to the effect that, by signing the **Treaty of Rome**, Her Majesty's Government would irreversibly surrender in part the sovereignty of the Queen in Parliament and in so doing would be acting in breach of the law. Eveleigh J upheld the order of the master striking out the statements of claim as disclosing no reasonable causes of action. The claimant appealed to the Court of Appeal. Lord Denning said that although, in theory, Parliament cannot bind its successors and declare an Act of Parliament to be irreversible, legal theory must, at times, give way to practical politics and that sovereignty is a political fact for which no purely legal authority can be constituted.

The declarations were refused.

Sections 2 and **3 European Communities Act 1972** give legal effect in England and Wales to any rights and obligations created by the EC Treaties. They also make available, without question, any remedies or procedures provided by the EC Treaties. This was determined by Lord Denning MR in *HP Bulmer Ltd and Another v J Bollinger SA and Others* (1974). The Court of Appeal had to decide whether a matter concerning EC rights should be referred to the ECJ. Both the trial judge and the Court of Appeal refused to refer the matter on the ground that it was not necessary to do so. While the **European Communities Act 1972** remained in force,

EU law was supreme. But ultimate sovereignty was, at least in legal theory, retained by the Queen in Parliament because the **European Communities Act 1972** could always be expressly repealed by any future Parliament. Lord Denning MR in *Macarthies v Smith* (1979) said that if Parliament deliberately passed an Act intending to repudiate the **EC Treaty** expressly, the courts would have no choice but to follow the provisions of the Act.

One consequence of membership of the EU was the development of a purposive approach to the interpretation of statutes. One example of this was *Pickstone v Freemans* (1989). Here, the Court of Appeal took a purposive approach to **s 1(2)(c) Equal Pay Act 1970** to allow reliance on the section in harmony with **Art 119 EEC Treaty**. Similarly, in *Lister v Forth Dry Dock & Engineering Co Ltd* (1990) the House of Lords determined that regulations enacted in 1981 were expressly enacted for the purpose of complying with **Council Directive 77/187/EEC** which provides for the safeguarding of employees' rights on the transfer of a business. The courts of the UK are under a duty to give a purposive construction to the regulations in a manner which would accord with the decisions of the ECJ on the Directive.

In *R v Secretary of State for Transport, ex p Factortame Ltd* (1990) (*Factortame (No 1)*) the High Court requested a preliminary ruling from the ECJ to determine the compatibility of the **Merchant Shipping Act 1988** with the **EC Treaty**. As the ruling would take some two years to be given and in the meantime the applicants would suffer serious loss if they were unable to operate their vessels, interim temporary injunctions were sought. The High Court granted an interim order against the Crown that pending the final determination of the cases the relevant parts of the 1988 Act be disapplied in relation to the applicants and that the registration under the **Merchant Shipping Act 1894** continue.

The Secretary of State appealed and the Court of Appeal reversed the decision of the High Court. The Court of Appeal held as a matter of English law that the English courts had no jurisdiction to disapply an Act of Parliament. This conclusion was based on the presumption that an Act of Parliament was compatible with EC law until it is declared to be incompatible. The conclusion was also based on an old common law rule that an injunction cannot be granted against the Crown.

The House of Lords subsequently agreed with the Court of Appeal. The House of Lords referred to the ECJ the question of whether there was an overriding principle of EC law, that a national court was under an obligation to provide an effective interlocutory remedy to protect rights, having direct effect under EC law where a seriously arguable claim to such rights was advanced and the party claiming those rights would suffer irredeemable damage if they were not effectively protected in the meantime.

The ECJ replied first to the question referred to it by the House of Lords. The reply was that any rule of national law which acts as the sole obstacle to interim relief being granted in a case concerning EC law, must be set aside. In response, the House of Lords restored the interim order granted by the High Court which disapplied the relevant provisions of the **Merchant Shipping Act 1988**.

Later, the ECJ delivered a ruling to the earlier reference from the High Court. The ECJ said that the system governing the regulation of British fishing vessels in the 1988 Act was contrary to EC law.

> ### *Equal Opportunities Commission v Secretary of State for Employment* [1995] 1 AC 1
>
> The Equal Opportunities Commission claimed that the provisions of the **Employment Protection (Consolidation) Act 1978** resulted in indirect discrimination against women which was contrary to EC law, in particular **Art 119 EC** and the Directives on equal pay and equal treatment.
>
> The House of Lords made a declaration that the threshold provisions breached EC law.

Following *Factortame (No 1)* substantive Community rights prevailed over the express terms of any domestic law, including primary legislation, made or passed after the coming into force of the 1972 Act, even in the face of plain inconsistency between the two. This was determined by Laws LJ in the Administrative Court's decision in *Thoburn v Sunderland City Council* (2003) (see Key cases).

In May 2010, the Coalition Government took office. Many politicians were deeply concerned that the courts were getting ready to dispense with Dicey's assertion that Parliament could make or unmake any law. The UK Supreme Court seemed to be evolving into a constitutional court with the power to override Acts of Parliament which were repugnant to EU law. Parliament's reply was **s 18 European Union Act 2011** which provided that directly applicable or directly effective EU law referred to in **s 2(1) European Communities Act 1972** falls to be recognized and available in law in the UK only by virtue of that Act. **Section 18** was a declaratory provision which confirmed that directly applicable or directly effective EU law took effect in the UK only as a result of the existence of an Act of Parliament. This section was enacted to address concerns that the doctrine of parliamentary sovereignty may in the future be eroded by decisions of the courts by providing in statutory form that directly effective and directly applicable EU law only takes effect in the UK legal order through the will of Parliament and by virtue of an Act of Parliament. It was designed to provide clear authority which can be relied upon to counter arguments that EU law constitutes a new higher autonomous legal order derived from the EU Treaties or international law and principles which have become an integral part of the UK's legal system independent of statute. This section did not, however, alter the existing relationship between EU law and UK domestic law.

The legal process of leaving the EU

Article 50(1) TEU (the Lisbon Treaty) (2007) provides that any Member State may decide to withdraw from the Union in accordance with its own constitutional requirements. **Article 50(2)** provides that a member state which decides to withdraw shall notify the European Council of its intention. In the light of the guidelines provided by the European Council, the Union shall negotiate and conclude an agreement with that state, setting out the arrangements for its withdrawal, taking account of the framework for its future relationship with the Union. That agreement shall be negotiated in accordance with **Art 218(3) Treaty on the Functioning of the European Union**. It shall be concluded on behalf of the Union by the Council, acting by a qualified majority, after obtaining the consent of the European Parliament. Under **Art 50(3)**

the Treaties shall cease to apply to the state in question from the date of entry into force of the withdrawal agreement or, failing that, two years after the notification referred to in **para 2**, unless the European Council, in agreement with the member state concerned, unanimously decides to extend this period.

Can Art 50 be revoked unilaterally?

A member state that has notified its intention to withdraw from the EU may revoke that notification in accordance with its own constitutional requirements by means of submitting an unequivocal and unconditional statement in writing to the European Council at any point before a withdrawal agreement comes into force, or before the conclusion of the two-year time period subject to any possible unanimous extensions. The result will be that the withdrawing state will remain within the EU under terms that are unchanged as regards its status as a member state. This was determined by the CJEU in *Wightman v Secretary of State for Exiting the European Union* (2018).

The UK statutory framework

Following the **European Referendum Act 2015**, a referendum was held in the UK and Gibraltar on 23 June 2016 on whether the UK should remain a member of the EU. Nearly 33.5m people, some 72 per cent of registered voters, voted in the referendum and 52 per cent of those who voted, voted to leave the EU.

Following the decision of the Supreme Court in *R (on the application of Miller) v Secretary of State for Exiting the European Union* (2017), the **European Union (Notification of Withdrawal) Act 2017** received the Royal Assent on 16 March 2017. This gave the Prime Minister power to notify the European Council of the UK's intention to withdraw from the EU under **Art 50(2) TEU**. This notification was given on 29 March 2017. On 13 November 2017, the government announced its intention to bring forward a new Act to implement the Withdrawal Agreement in domestic law. This confirmed that the major policies set out in the Withdrawal Agreement would be given effect in domestic law through new primary legislation rather than by secondary legislation.

The **European Union (Withdrawal) Act 2018** received the Royal Assent on 26 June 2018. Its purpose was to give effect to withdrawal and to provide a functioning statute book when the UK left the EU. On 14 November 2018, the government published a draft of the Withdrawal Agreement (agreed at negotiator level). This Agreement was agreed by European leaders on 25 November 2018 and laid before Parliament on 26 November 2018.

The Agreement was subject to votes in the House of Commons, as prescribed by **s 13 European Union (Withdrawal) Act 2018**, on 15 January and 12 March 2019. The Withdrawal Agreement alone, without the Political Declaration, was voted on by the House of Commons on 29 March 2019. The Withdrawal Agreement was rejected in all these votes. The Withdrawal Agreement was also subject to the take note motions in the House of Lords. On 22 March 2019, the European Council and the UK agreed to an extension to the **Art 50** period until 22 May

2019, provided the Withdrawal Agreement was approved by the House of Commons before 29 March 2019, or otherwise until 12 April 2019 (**Council Decision (EU) 2019/476**). The definition of 'exit day' in the **European Union (Withdrawal) Act 2018** was amended by the **European Union (Withdrawal) Act 2018 (Exit Day) (Amendment) Regulations 2019** to reflect this, having been approved by the House of Commons and the House of Lords on 27 March 2019.

On 5 April 2019, the then Prime Minister wrote to the then President of the European Council seeking a second extension of the **Art 50** period. On 11 April 2019, the European Council and the UK agreed an extension to the **Art 50** period until 31 October 2019 (**Council Decision (EU) 2019/584**). The extension could be terminated early if the Withdrawal Agreement was ratified and came into force before that date. Following the conclusion of the European Council, a statutory instrument, the **European Union (Withdrawal) Act 2018 (Exit Day) (Amendment) (No 2) Regulations 2019**, was made under the negative procedure on 11 April amending the definition of 'exit day' in the **European Union (Withdrawal) Act 2018** to 31 October 2019 at 11.00 pm.

On 23 May 2019, Prime Minister Theresa May resigned. Following a change in government, Prime Minister Boris Johnson committed to negotiating a new Withdrawal Agreement. This Withdrawal Agreement was agreed by European leaders at the European Council on 17 October 2019. In addition, the government made a unilateral declaration concerning the operation of the 'Democratic consent in Northern Ireland' provision of the Protocol on Ireland/Northern Ireland, which was published on the same day. On 19 October 2019, the government laid before Parliament the new Withdrawal Agreement and new framework for the future relationship between the UK and the EU. On 21 October 2019, the European Union (Withdrawal Agreement) Bill was introduced to Parliament. The House of Commons voted for the Act at second reading, which passed by 329:299, but the House did not vote in favour of the timetable to debate the Act. On 30 October 2019, in accordance with the **European Union (Withdrawal) (No 2) Act 2019**, an amendment to the definition of 'exit day' was made to the **European Union (Withdrawal) Act 2018**, amending the day of exit to 31 January 2020. Parliament subsequently passed the **Early Parliamentary General Election Act 2019** to authorize a general election which was held in December 2019. On 19 December 2019, the European Union (Withdrawal Agreement) Bill was introduced to Parliament.

On 23 January 2020, the **European Union (Withdrawal Agreement) Act 2020** was passed into law. The principal purpose of the Act was to implement the Withdrawal Agreement, the separation agreement between the UK and the EEA EFTA (European Economic Area, European Free Trade Association) countries (EEA EFTA Separation Agreement) and the Swiss Citizens' Rights Agreement. On 31 January 2020, the UK left the EU and the Withdrawal Agreement concluded with the EU entered into force. The transition period provided for in the Agreement ended at 11pm on 31 December 2020. On 2 March 2020, the first round of negotiations began. The Agreements were agreed by the UK and EU on 24 December 2020. The UK and EU provisionally agreed to apply the Agreements from the end of the transition period ahead of ratification. On 30 December 2020, the European Union (Future Relationship) Bill was introduced to Parliament. The **European Union (Future Relationship) Act 2020** received the Royal Assent on 30 December 2020.

The legal basis of the present relationship between the UK and the EU

The legal basis of the relationship between the EU and the UK is the **EU–UK Trade and Cooperation Agreement (TCA)** (2020) as implemented by the **European Union (Future Relationship) Act 2020.**

The **TCA** covers:

- trade;
- governance;
- level playing field provisions;
- subsidies/state aid;
- fisheries;
- security;
- EU programmes;
- review and termination.

The key provisions of the **TCA** are:

- There will be no tariffs or quotas on trade in goods provided rules of origin are met. There are increased non-tariff barriers, but also measures on customs and trade facilitation to ease these.
- The Agreement is overseen by a UK–EU Partnership Council supported by other committees.
- There are binding enforcement and dispute settlement mechanisms covering most of the economic partnership, involving an independent arbitration tribunal.
- There is no role for the CJEU in the governance and dispute settlement provisions.
- Both parties can engage in cross-sector retaliation in case of non-compliance with arbitration rulings (through suspension of obligations, including imposition of tariffs). This cross-sector retaliation applies across the economic partnership.
- Both parties have the right to take countermeasures including imposition of tariffs, subject to arbitration, where they believe divergences are distorting trade. There is also a review mechanism where this occurs frequently.
- Both parties are required to have an effective system of subsidy control with independent oversight. Either party can impose remedial measures if a dispute is not resolved by consultation.
- Twenty-five per cent of the EU's fisheries quota in UK waters will be transferred to the UK over a period of five years. After this, there will be annual discussions on fisheries opportunities. Either party will be able to impose tariffs on fisheries where one side reduces or withdraws access to its waters without agreement. A party can suspend access to waters or other trade provisions where the other party is in breach of the fisheries provisions.

- A new security partnership provides for data sharing and policing and judicial cooperation, but with reduced access to EU databases. A new surrender agreement takes the place of the European Arrest Warrant. Cooperation can be suspended by either side swiftly in the case of the UK or a member state no longer adhering to the **European Convention on Human Rights**.

- Continued UK participation in some EU programmes: Horizon Europe (Research), Euratom Research and Training, ITER fusion, and Copernicus (satellite system).

- The **TCA** will be reviewed every five years. It can be terminated by either side with 12 months' notice, and more swiftly on human rights and rule of law grounds.

European Union (Future Relationship) Act 2020

The **European Union (Future Relationship) Act 2020** is divided into four parts.

- **Part 1** of the Act makes provision to implement the parts of the Agreements relating to security, including obligations about sharing and retaining criminal record data with EU member states.

- **Part 2** of the Act makes provision to implement certain parts of the Agreements relating to trade and other matters. This includes provision on sharing information on non-food product safety, sharing information about customs, powers to make regulations about the movement of goods, and amendments to certain laws relating to transport. Through **Part 2**, the UK has also decided to incorporate the social security provisions of the **TCA** directly into UK law, meaning individuals will be able to rely on these provisions before UK courts.

- **Part 3** of the Act makes provision about general implementation. It provides the UK Government and devolved administration with powers to make regulations to implement the **TCA**, the **Nuclear Cooperation Agreement**, and the **Security of Classified Information Agreement (SCIA)**, including regulations that can amend primary legislation ('Henry VIII powers'). **Schedule 5** includes provisions about the scrutiny of these regulations. There is also a general provision that, to the extent that the Agreements are not otherwise implemented, all 'existing domestic law' will be modified to ensure that the UK is compliant with its obligations under the **TCA** and **SCIA**.

- **Part 4** of the Act includes supplementary provisions.

The wider legal consequences of the UK leaving the EU
Retained and converted EU law

Section 2–4 European Union (Withdrawal) Act 2018 created two categories of retained EU law (see Table 9.1):

- preserved legislation;
- converted legislation.

Table 9.1 Retained EU law under the European Union (Withdrawal) Act 2018, ss 2–4

RETAINED EU LAW	CONVERTED LEGISLATION
Regulations made under **s 2(2)** or **Sch 2 para 1A European Communities Act 1972 (ECA)**	Direct EU legislation: EU Regulations EU Decisions
Other primary and secondary legislation with the same purpose as regulations under **s 2(2) ECA**	EU tertiary legislation Direct EU legislation as it applies with adaptations for the EEA
Other domestic legislation which relates to the above, or to converted legislation, or otherwise relates to the EU or EEA	Any other rights which are recognized and available in domestic law through **s 2(1) ECA** (eg directly effective rights contained in EU Treaties) The Act converts and incorporates this law as it existed immediately before exit day into domestic law.

The interpretation of EU law

Section 6(3) European Union (Withdrawal) Act 2018 provides that any question as to the meaning of unmodified retained EU law will be determined in UK courts in accordance with relevant pre-exit case law of the CJEU and general principles. This includes taking a purposive approach to interpretation where the meaning of the measure is unclear.

The supremacy of EU law

Section 5 European Union (Withdrawal) Act 2018 sets out two exceptions to the saving and incorporation of EU law provided for under **ss 2, 3, and 4**. The first exception is the principle of supremacy of EU law. As we have seen, the principle of supremacy means two things. First, it means that domestic law must give way if it is inconsistent with EU law. In the event of such inconsistency the court must disapply an Act of Parliament, or a rule of the common law, or strike down UK secondary legislation even if the domestic law was made after the relevant EU law. Second, it means that domestic law must be interpreted, as far as possible, in accordance with the wording and purpose of EU law. The effect of **s 5(1)** and **(2)** is that the principle of supremacy will not apply in respect of the disapplication of legislation which is passed or made on or after exit day. This means that if an Act of Parliament is passed on or after exit day which is inconsistent with EU law and which is preserved or converted by the Act, the new Act of Parliament will take precedence. Where, however, a conflict arises between pre-exit domestic legislation and retained EU law, **s 6(2)** provides that the principle of supremacy will, where relevant, continue to apply as it did before exit. The principle will not, however, be relevant to the provisions of the **European Union (Withdrawal) Act 2018** or to other legislation which was made in preparation for the UK's exit from the EU.

Concerning the obligation to interpret domestic law, as far as possible, in accordance with the wording and purpose of EU law, this obligation will not apply to domestic legislation passed or made on or after exit. **Section 6(2)**, however, preserves this duty in relation to domestic legislation passed or made before exit. **Section 6(3)** provides that the principle of supremacy can continue to apply to pre-exit law which is amended on or after exit day where that accords with the intention of the modifications.

The status of EU law after the UK left the EU is dealt with by **s 7 European Union (Withdrawal) Act 2018**. **Section 7(1)** stipulates that EU-derived domestic legislation which is saved by **s 2** will continue as legislation of the same type as it was before exit day. **Section 7(2)–(4)** restricts the way in which retained EU law brought in by **ss 3** and **4** can be amended by primary and subordinate legislation. Such law can be amended by:

- Acts or other primary legislation;
- powers to make subordinate legislation which explicitly or implicitly provide that they may amend such law (which includes the powers in **ss 8, 9**, and **23(1)** and **(6)** of the Act); and
- powers to make subordinate legislation which may amend such law by virtue of the glosses in **paras 3–8** (existing powers) or **10–12** (future powers) of **Sch 8**.

The *Francovich* principle

Sch 1 para 4 European Union (Withdrawal) Act 2018 provides that, subject to transitional arrangements, the right to claim damages against the state for breaches of EU law (*Francovich* damages) will not be available after exit. This provision does not affect any specific statutory rights to claim damages in respect of breaches of retained EU law or the case law which applies to the interpretation of any such provisions.

The present role of the CJEU

Section 6 European Union (Withdrawal) Act 2018 sets out how retained EU law is to be read and interpreted on and after exit day. **Section 6(1)** and **(2)** sets out the relationship between the CJEU and domestic courts and tribunals after exit. These subsections provide that:

- decisions of the CJEU made after exit day will not be binding on domestic UK courts and tribunals;
- domestic courts cannot refer cases to the CJEU on or after exit day; and
- domestic courts and tribunals are able to have regard to actions of the EU taken post-exit, including CJEU Decisions, where they are relevant to any matter the court or tribunal is considering.

The present legal status of the general principles

Schedule 1 European Union (Withdrawal) Act 2018 sets out detailed rules about how the general principles of EU law will apply after the UK leaves the EU. The main provisions of **Sch 1** are:

- Only the EU general principles which have been recognized in CJEU cases decided before exit will form part of domestic law after exit including some fundamental rights, non-retroactivity, and proportionality.

- There is no right of action in domestic law post-exit based on failure to comply with the EU general principles. Courts cannot disapply domestic laws post-exit on the basis that they are incompatible with the EU general principles.

- Subject to transitional arrangements, domestic courts will not be able to rule that a particular act was unlawful or quash any action taken on the basis that it was not compatible with the general principles. Courts will, however, be required under **s 6** to interpret retained EU law in accordance with the retained general principles.

The legal status of the EU Charter of Fundamental Freedoms under the European Union (Withdrawal) Act 2018

Section 5(5) European Union (Withdrawal) Act 2018 states that whilst the Charter will not form part of domestic law after exit, this does not remove any underlying fundamental rights or principles which exist, and EU law which is converted will continue to be interpreted in the light of those underlying rights and principles. **Section 5(6)** provides that further limited exceptions to the preservation and conversion of EU law have effect, as set out in **Sch 1**.

Human rights in the Trade and Cooperation Agreement

The **TCA** deals with the continued protection of civil and political rights and social rights.

The continued protection of civil and political rights is dealt with by **Art COMPROV.4 TCA** which covers democracy, the rule of law, and human rights. It provides that the parties shall continue to uphold the shared values and principles of democracy, the rule of law, and respect for human rights, which underpin their domestic and international policies. In that regard, the parties reaffirm their respect for the **Universal Declaration of Human Rights** and the international human rights treaties to which they are parties.

The protection of social rights is dealt with by **Art 6** and **Art 8** of the level playing field provisions. **Article 6(1)** applies to the following areas of current employment law including:

- fundamental rights at work;
- occupational health and safety standards;
- fair working conditions and employment standards;
- information and consultation rights at company level; and
- restructuring of undertakings.

Article 6(2) contains a non-regression rule in the following terms:

A Party shall not weaken or reduce, in a manner affecting trade or investment between the Parties, its labour and social levels of protection below the levels in place at the end of the transition period, including by failing to effectively enforce its law and standards.

To enforce this non-regression rule, there is a special rule on dispute settlement (**Art 6(4)**): in place of the general dispute settlement rules, **Art 9(1) to (3)** of the level playing field provisions apply.

The second set of relevant rules is found in **Art 8** of the level playing field provisions, on 'Other instruments for trade and sustainable development'. The key provision on labour standards in this chapter (**Art 8(3)**) refers expressly to social rights.

 KEY CASES

CASE	FACTS	PRINCIPLE
Francovich v Italy [1993] 2 CMLR 66	Italy had failed to implement **Council Directive 80/987/EEC** relating to the protection of employees in the event of the insolvency of their employer. F was an employee in a company which became insolvent and which owed him a substantial amount of unpaid salary which it was unable to pay. Under the Directive, Italy should have established a guarantee fund to ensure employees a certain minimum protection in cases such as this. F therefore sued in the Italian court for compensation from the Italian Government on the basis that it was at fault in not having implemented the Directive.	The ECJ decided that he could claim no effective rights as the provisions of the Directive lacked sufficient unconditionality.
NV Algemene Transport- Expeditie Onderneming van Gend en Loos v Nederlandse Administratie der Belastingen [1963] ECR 1	The Tariefcommissie, a Dutch administrative tribunal, made a reference to the European Court under **Art 177 Treaty of Rome** (1957).	The constitutional principle here is that the European Community is a new legal order with sovereign powers.
R v Secretary of State for Employment, ex p Equal Opportunities Commission [1995] 1 AC 1	The House of Lords had to consider, among other things, whether it had jurisdiction to declare a UK statute incompatible with EU law.	The Divisional Court had jurisdiction to declare that primary legislation was incompatible with Community law.
R v Secretary of State for Transport, ex p Factortame Ltd (No 1) [1990] 2 AC 85	The House of Lords had to consider its jurisdiction to disapply the provisions of a UK statute which was incompatible with EU law.	**Part II** of the 1988 Act was unambiguous. If the court were to order the Secretary of State to treat F as entitled to registration and F were unable to prove they were entitled to registration in the European Court, interim relief would have given F rights which contravened parliamentary intention and deprived British fishing vessels of a proportion of the quotas available.

CASE	FACTS	PRINCIPLE
Thoburn v Sunderland City Council [2003] QB 151	In four appeals the issue before the court concerned the introduction in accordance with the policy of the EU of compulsory systems of metric weights and measures.	The common law recognized a category of constitutional statutes, and the fundamental legal basis of the UK's relationship with the EU rested with domestic rather than European legal powers.

KEY DEBATES

Topic	'UK Referendum Practice and Regulation Needs Urgent Reform'
Author/Academic	Alan Renwick and Jess Sargeant
Viewpoint	This article highlights the 2018 publication of the 'Report of the Independent Commission of Referendums', and its recommendations for improving the use and conduct of referendums in UK politics. Discusses the growing popularity of political referendums, their role in a democratic system, and the report's main conclusions on their improved regulation, including greater transparency and legislative reforms.
Source	[2018] 5 European Human Rights Law Review 422–425

Topic	'Reversing a Withdrawal Notification Under Article 50 TEU: Can a Member State Change Its Mind?'
Author/Academic	Aurel Sari
Viewpoint	Considers whether member states can rescind their notice to withdraw from the EU under **Art 50 TEU** before it takes effect. Explains the applicable rules of interpretation under **Arts 31** and **32 Vienna Convention on the Law of Treaties (1969)**, the approach adopted in **R (on the application of Miller) v Secretary of State for Exiting the European Union** (2017), and the terms and context of **Art 50**. Suggests why the withdrawal of notice appears possible.
Source	(2017) 42(4) European Law Review 451–473

Topic	'Miller, Statutory Interpretation, and the True Place of EU Law in UK Law'
Author/Academic	Mikolaj Barczentewicz
Viewpoint	The author argues that the ruling in **R (on the application of Miller) v Secretary of State for Exiting the European Union** was incorrectly decided and the court should have found that notification of an intention to withdraw from the EU under **Art 50 TEU** was within prerogative powers. Reviews EU law's place within UK law and suggests how the court failed to give adequate answers to arguments involving interpretation of the **ECA 1972**.
Source	[2017] (Nov) Public Law Supp, Brexit Special Extra Issue 10–24

EXAM QUESTION

Essay question

With reference to relevant law, critically assess the nature and extent of the most significant legal consequences of the UK's departure from the EU.

Online Resources

For an outline answer to this essay question, as well as interactive key cases and multiple-choice questions, please visit the online resources.
www.oup.com/he/faragher-concentrate7e

Concentrate Q&As

For more questions and answers on public law, see the *Concentrate Q&A: Public Law* by Richard Clements.

Go to the end of this book to view **sample pages**.

10 Introduction to administrative law

The foundations and extent of judicial review

KEY FACTS

- Judicial review allows people with a sufficient interest to ask a judge to review the lawfulness of a decision of a public body carrying out its public functions and enactments where there is no right of appeal or where all avenues of appeal have been exhausted.

- Judicial review is based on the constitutional principles of the rule of law and the separation of powers.

- The defendant must be a public body, the subject matter of a claim must be a public law matter, and the claimant must have the right to claim.

- The court may refuse to exercise its jurisdiction on policy grounds.

- It may be necessary to consider whether judicial review has been limited or excluded by Parliament.

- Quashing orders, mandatory orders, and prohibiting orders must be claimed by judicial review procedure contained in the current **Civil Procedure Rules** and **s 31 Senior Courts Act 1981,** as amended by the **Civil Procedure Act 1997** and the **Civil Procedure (Modification of the Senior Courts Act) Order 2004**. Declarations, injunctions, and damages may be sought by judicial review procedure.

What is judicial review?

Judicial review allows a High Court judge to examine the lawfulness of decisions made by public bodies carrying out their public functions and 'enactments'.

'Public' means that the body making the decision is governmental and/or its decisions concern the general population as in a decision affecting the public. The term 'enactments' refers to the jurisdiction of the High Court in England and Wales to determine whether Acts of Parliament conflict with any directly effective provision of EU law as retained by the **European Union (Withdrawal) Act 2018** as amended by the **European Union (Withdrawal Agreement) Act 2020**, the jurisdiction of certain courts under **s 4 Human Rights Act 1998** to determine whether an Act of Parliament is compatible with Convention rights, and the High Court jurisdiction to review subordinate or delegated legislation.

Judicial review and appeals

Judicial review is available where no right of appeal exists or where such rights are exhausted.

REVISION TIP

In an examination question you may need to decide whether the decision in question is appropriately challenged by judicial review or by appealing against it. If so you must be prepared to explain fully the differences between judicial review and an appeal.

There are important differences between judicial review and an appeal. On appeal the claimant says that the decision of a lower court or tribunal is wrong mainly, but not exclusively, on points of law. The decision of the lower court or tribunal may be reversed. Other earlier decisions may be overruled. The appeal court or tribunal replaces the judgment of the lower court or tribunal with its own. Statutes providing an appeal process stipulate the court or tribunal which may hear the appeal as well as the procedure, time limits, and grounds of appeal.

In many cases judicial review focuses on the way public bodies make their decisions. The basis of such judicial review claims is not that a decision is wrong, unless the decision is so wrong that no reasonable public body could have reached it. In some cases, however, the court can review the substance of a public body's decision, for instance to determine whether its decision disproportionately interferes with a fundamental human right. In judicial review claims based on an alleged infringement of a Convention right under the **Human Rights Act 1998**, the court focuses on the practical outcome of the decision rather than the quality of the decision-making process.

The claimant must bring their claim within narrow technical grounds. These are considered in Chapters 11 to 13. Lord Diplock, in the House of Lords' decision in *Council of Civil Service Unions v Minister for the Civil Service* (1985) classified the grounds as illegality, irrationality, and procedural impropriety. Instead of substituting its own judgment, as it would in an appeal, the court may, in a judicial review, declare the decision void (empty of legal effect) by making a quashing order, or order the public body to do something by making a mandatory order, or order the public body not to do something by making a prohibiting order, or make a declaration that the defendant has acted unlawfully. Judicial review cannot be used to reverse or overrule or replace a decision.

The constitutional context of the supervisory jurisdiction

REVISION TIP

Review the chapters on the rule of law and the separation of powers (Chapters 3 and 4). Focus on the relationship between the judiciary and the executive and note the link between judicial review and the third part of Dicey's definition of the rule of law.

Judicial review forms the supervisory jurisdiction of the High Court in England and Wales. Claims are made to the Administrative Court. The constitutional basis for this is the rule of law and separation of powers. Judicial review gives effect to the principle that government must be conducted according to law. Judicial independence is vital. Although the basis of jurisdiction is statutory, the principles governing the role of the judiciary and the exact nature and scope of the supervisory jurisdiction have been developed by the judges in decided cases.

LOOKING FOR EXTRA MARKS?

You should look again at what senior members of the judiciary have said about the constitutional principle of the rule of law and the separation of powers as well as the opinions of leading academics. Many of these are well summarized in the leading textbooks. Be able to compare and contrast their opinions.

Is judicial review appropriate?

REVISION TIP

The first part of an answer to a problem question should focus on whether the defendant is a public body, whether its decisions are public law matters, and whether the claimant has the right to bring a claim for judicial review.

Judicial review must be appropriate. The important questions are: is the defendant a public body? And is the defendant's decision a public law matter? Both questions must be addressed.

Is the defendant a public body?

REVISION TIP

When answering a problem question look at the source of the defendant's powers. If the source of the defendant's powers is neither statute nor Royal Prerogative (see Chapter 7) apply *Datafin* (1987) and analyse the nature of the defendant's functions comprehensively.

The defendant must be a **public body**. In this context public means that a body is governmental. Executive organs of government are public bodies and are in principle subject to judicial review. These include ministers, departments of state, and local authorities. A body's duties, powers, and sanctions are public if they affect the general population and can be imposed without consent. Many other organizations perform public duties as well as regulatory functions. They may make decisions which directly or indirectly affect the public at large. They may also act judicially. Some of them may have government support and exercise compulsory jurisdiction. The jurisdiction of the court over such organizations was considered by the Court of Appeal in *Datafin* (1987).

R v Panel of Take-Overs & Mergers, ex p Datafin [1987] QB 815

The Court of Appeal considered, among other things, whether the High Court had jurisdiction to subject the decisions of the Panel to judicial review.

On this issue the key principle is that where there is a dispute concerning whether a defendant is a public body, the court must consider at least the source of power; the nature of the body's duties; and the consequences of the body's decisions. A body can be subject to judicial review if its source of power is not solely the consent of those over whom it exercises its powers provided it performs public law duties and it is supported by public law sanctions.

The Court of Appeal decided that the High Court did have jurisdiction to review the Panel's decision.

The Court of Appeal developed these principles further in the following case.

R v Disciplinary Committee of the Jockey Club, ex p Aga Khan [1993] 1 WLR 909

The Court of Appeal had to decide whether the Disciplinary Committee of the Jockey Club was subject to judicial review.

The key principle is that the court looks at the origin, history, constitution, and membership of an organization to determine if it is a public body. A body whose origin and constitution owe nothing to the exercise of governmental control may be subject to judicial review. The claimant must show that the body in question:

- has been woven into the fabric of public regulation or a system of governmental control; or
- has been integrated into a system of statutory regulation; or

---

- has been carrying out functions normally performed by an organ of government; or
- has been doing something which would be done by an organ of government if the body in question did not exist.

A body will not be subject to judicial review if its powers are based on agreement; and effective private law remedies are available.

The Court of Appeal decided that the Jockey Club was not a public body and not subject to judicial review.

These principles were applied in *R (on the application of Mullins) v Jockey Club Appeal Board* (2006) where it was decided that a newly appointed board, set up to hear appeals from the disciplinary committee, was not subject to judicial review.

LOOKING FOR EXTRA MARKS?

These issues have attracted a great deal of academic argument. You should consult your textbook and learning materials to explore these developments and the Key cases given later in this chapter.

Abuse of process: is the claim a public law matter?

REVISION TIP

Remember that public bodies are potentially subject to all forms of civil proceedings.

If the public body's decision is a public law matter it must be challenged by judicial review or the claimant might be accused of abuse of process. Lord Diplock in *O'Reilly v Mackman* (1983) said that it is contrary to public policy and an abuse of the process of the court for a claimant to bring a public law matter to court by way of ordinary civil procedure thereby avoiding the protection given to public authorities by judicial review procedure. **Abuse of process** means that the claimant seeks to gain unfair advantage. In this context unfair advantage means depriving a public body of the judicial protection given to it by judicial review procedure. The requirement that a claimant must seek permission to proceed with a claim for judicial review within three months of becoming aware of a public body's decision is one of the ways in which judicial review procedure aims to protect public bodies.

What should a claimant do to avoid an accusation of abuse of process?

The Court of Appeal in *Rye v Sheffield City Council* (1998) said that if it is unclear whether a case is a public law matter, the claimant should seek judicial review to avoid an accusation of abuse of process. If the claimant chooses private law civil procedure and it is unclear whether judicial review is more appropriate, the court should ask whether permission would have been granted had the claimant asked for judicial review. If so, this indicates that no harm has been done to the interests judicial review protects. The court should consider transferring the case to the appropriate list before striking it out.

In *Clark v University of Lincolnshire and Humberside* (2000) the Court of Appeal said that flouting the protection given to public authorities by judicial review procedure is contrary to the overriding objective in **Pt 1 Civil Procedure Rules** and that the claimant must help the court to fulfil the overriding objective by acting reasonably and by not using procedure to gain unfair advantage. If the court is asked to review something and grant a discretionary remedy, the use of ordinary civil procedure is inappropriate. If a claimant chooses private law proceedings, to make a claim normally made by judicial review, because of delay, the court must ask whether the delay was justified. Unjustified delay can be a ground for refusal to grant a discretionary remedy and can be taken into account in an application for summary judgment in normal civil proceedings. If the court is asked to review something and grant a discretionary remedy, the use of ordinary civil procedure is inappropriate.

Exceptions to the rule

Collateral challenge is an exception to the rule in *O'Reilly v Mackman* (1983) recognized by the House of Lords in *Wandsworth LBC v Winder* (1985). The key principle is that it is not an abuse of process for someone to raise a public law matter as a defence in civil proceedings. The defence is a collateral challenge in a private law matter.

In *Boddington v British Transport Police* (1998) the House of Lords had to consider whether a defendant to a criminal charge laid under subordinate legislation could argue by way of defence that the subordinate legislation, or an administrative act bringing that legislation into operation (such as, in this case, the posting of no smoking notices throughout all railway carriages), was itself ultra vires and unlawful. After a lengthy review of the relevant case law, the Lord Chancellor, Lord Irvine, decided that the right to collateral challenge is available in criminal cases and that Boddington was entitled to raise the legality of the decision to post no smoking notices throughout the train, as a possible defence to the criminal charge against him.

Does the claimant have the right to bring a claim for judicial review?

 REVISION TIP

This topic should be covered in detail in an answer to a problem question where the defendant is a representative organization.

According to the **Pre-Action Protocol for Judicial Review** a person can bring a claim if they have sufficient interest in the matter. It is also possible for someone other than the claimant or defendant to take part in the claim as an interested party. **Part 54 Civil Procedure Rules** defines 'interested party' as anyone other than the claimant or defendant who is directly affected by the decision. 'Sufficient interest' was considered by the House of Lords in the following case.

IRC v National Federation of the Self-Employed and Small Businesses [1982] AC 617

The House of Lords had to decide whether the National Federation of the Self-Employed and Small Businesses had the right to bring a claim for judicial review against the IRC after it had decided not to collect income tax from casual Fleet Street newspaper workers.

The key principle is that the question of whether a person has sufficient interest should not be treated as a preliminary issue, but must be considered in the legal and factual context of the whole case. The merits of the challenge are an important, if not dominant, factor when determining whether a claimant has sufficient interest. The real question is whether the claimant has a potentially good case and not whether their personal rights or interests are involved.

The House of Lords decided that the Federation had no claim because the IRC had acted within its powers.

In *R v Inspectorate of Pollution, ex p Greenpeace* (1994) and *R v Secretary of State for Foreign Affairs, ex p World Development Movement* (1995) the following key principles were formulated.

Where the claimant is a representative organization the court can take into account the reputation of the body; whether a significant number of its members are affected by a decision; and whether it is reasonable for the organization to claim on behalf of its members. Other significant factors include the importance of vindicating the rule of law; importance of the issue raised; likely absence of any other responsible challenger; nature of the breach of duty against which relief is sought; and the prominence of the organization in giving advice, guidance, and assistance.

Has judicial review been excluded by Parliament?

 REVISION TIP

In problem questions you may be asked to consider the effect of a provision in a statute which purports to limit or exclude the jurisdiction of the court to consider a case. Your understanding of judicial policy will be improved by considering the relevant case law.

By statute, Parliament may seek to exclude or limit judicial review. **Section 12 Tribunals and Inquiries Act 1992** provides that any provision in an Act of Parliament passed before 1 August 1958 that an order or determination shall not be called into question by a court, or any provision in any such Act which by similar words excludes any of the powers of the High Court, shall have no effect. Such provisions passed after 1 August 1958 are subject to the following rules.

Finality clauses

If a statute says that some decisions or orders 'shall be final' this means merely that there is no appeal. Judicial review remains unimpaired. This was determined by the Court of Appeal in *R v Medical Appeal Tribunal, ex p Gilmore* (1957). The key principle is that it would be contrary to the rule of law to give tribunals the power to determine their own jurisdiction and that the words used in a statute must be sufficiently clear to show that Parliament intended to exclude judicial review. The word final is not enough.

'Shall not be questioned' clauses

Some statutes say that an order or determination 'shall not be questioned in any legal proceedings whatsoever'. The effect of such provisions was considered by the House of Lords in *Anisminic v Foreign Compensation Commission* (1969). This case concerned a provision in the **Foreign Compensation Act 1950** which said that any 'determination by the Commission of any application made to them under this Act shall not be called in question in any court of law'.

The key principle is that a provision that a determination shall not be called in question in any court of law does not protect a determination which is made as a result of a mistake of law which is a nullity and can be quashed by the court. This includes anything amounting to grounds for judicial review.

This key principle was applied by the Court of Appeal in *R v Secretary of State for the Home Department, ex p Al-Fayed* (1997).

Section 44(2) British Nationality Act 1981 provided, among other things, that the decision of the Secretary of State concerning naturalization 'shall not be subject to appeal to, or review in, any court'. Lord Woolf MR held that there was an inference that Parliament did not intend to exclude judicial review in cases alleging unfairness or discrimination.

Time limit clauses: partial ousters

Under **Pt 54 Civil Procedure Rules** a claim for judicial review must be made promptly and in any event not later than three months after the grounds to make the claim first arose. The time limit may not be extended by agreement between the parties. This rule does not apply when any other enactment specifies a shorter time limit for making the claim for judicial review. Sometimes statutes impose a shorter time limit, for example six weeks. Statutes may also limit the grounds for judicial review. Such clauses are generally upheld by the courts. Parliament's intention to impose such restrictions is sufficiently clear. This was determined by the House of Lords in *Smith v East Elloe RDC* (1956). The House of Lords had to consider whether a compulsory purchase order could be challenged on the ground that it was made unfairly and in bad faith in spite of a six-week limitation period. Although the Law Lords expressed a variety of opinions, it was decided that the time limitation clause was effective to prevent judicial review. *Smith v Elloe RDC* was critically discussed by the Law Lords in *Anisminic v Foreign Compensation Commission*. After *Anisminic* it was suggested that time limitation clauses were no longer effective. This argument was rejected by the Court of Appeal in *R v Secretary of State for the Environment, ex p Ostler* (1977). Lord Denning stressed the point that such clauses were necessary to ensure efficient administration and economy. In subsequent cases like *R v Secretary of State for the Environment, ex p Kent* (1990) and *R v Cornwall CC, ex p Huntingdon* (1994) such clauses were upheld on the basis that Parliament's intention was sufficiently and clearly expressed. Strict six-week time limits are also imposed where Neighbourhood Development Orders, under **s 61N Town and Country Planning Act 1990**, and National Policy Statements and Orders Granting Development, under **ss 13** and **118 Planning Act 2008**, as amended by **s 92 Criminal Justice and Courts Act 2015**, are challenged by judicial review.

For a summary of all the matters which need to be considered when deciding whether judicial review is appropriate, see Fig 10.1.

Are there any other reasons why judicial review is not appropriate?

Judicial review is discretionary. The defendant may be a public body, the matter may be within public law, the claimant may have the right to claim, and Parliament may not have chosen to exclude judicial review. The High Court, however, may refuse to exercise the supervisory jurisdiction if it is thought inappropriate to do so.

R v Cambridge Health Authority, ex p B [1995] 1 WLR 898

The Court of Appeal considered whether it was appropriate to review and quash the decision of a health authority to refuse to fund treatment where it was revolutionary and the chances of success were limited or unknown. It was held that the health authority's decision was not unlawful. It would be inappropriate for the court to review the funding priorities of such bodies where resources are limited and budgeting necessary or to intervene where matters of medical judgement are concerned.

The requirement there must be a material difference to the outcome: the Criminal Justice and Courts Act 2015

The courts have long held that judges may refuse to provide a remedy where there would have inevitably been no difference to the outcome even if the reason for bringing the judicial review had not occurred. **Section 84 Criminal Justice and Courts Act 2015** modifies the existing approach by amending **s 31 Senior Courts Act 1981**. Neither permission to bring a claim for judicial

Figure 10.1 Is judicial review appropriate?

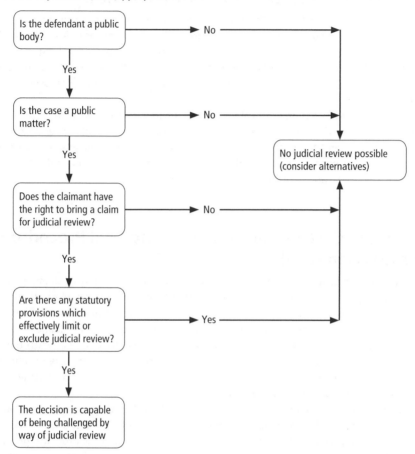

review nor relief will be granted where the court considers the conduct complained of would be highly likely not to have resulted in a substantially different outcome for the applicant.

What procedural steps must be taken by the claimant to commence a claim for judicial review?

The law is contained in **s 31 Senior Courts Act 1981** as amended by the **Civil Procedure Act 1997** and the **Civil Procedure (Modification of the Supreme Court Act) Order 2004**. The detailed procedure is contained in the **Pre-Action Protocol for Judicial Review** and **Pt 54, Section One Civil Procedural Rules**. Judicial review procedure begins with consideration of the **Pre-Action Protocol for Judicial Review** and goes on to follow the provisions of **Pt 54, Section One Civil Procedure Rules**.

The Pre-Action Protocol for Judicial Review

The **Pre-Action Protocol for Judicial Review** provides a code of good practice and contains the steps which parties should generally follow before making a claim for judicial review. There are some types of cases in which it is not necessary to follow the procedural requirements of the **Pre-Action Protocol** and the claimant is free to determine whether or not it is appropriate. However, if the claimant decides that it is not appropriate the reason for this must be stated in the claim form.

Assuming that the **Pre-Action Protocol for Judicial Review** is appropriate, the following procedural steps remain. The claimant writes and sends to the defendant a letter before claim. The defendant is given 14 days to write and send to the claimant a letter in response. If the claimant is acting through a solicitor, and is relying on public funding, this is the appropriate time for the solicitor to advise on and organize funding.

Initial procedure under Part 54 of the Civil Procedure Rules (Section One)

Part 54, Section One Civil Procedure Rules must be used where the claimant claims a quashing order, mandatory order, or prohibiting order. **Section One** may be used where the claimant seeks a declaration or an injunction. The claimant must ask for permission to proceed with a claim for judicial review. Among other things, the claim form requires the claimant to specify the decision being challenged; the date the decision was made; the date on which the claimant became aware of the decision; the factual background to the claim; the grounds upon which the claimant challenges the decision; the remedies being sought; and whether the case raises any issues under the **Human Rights Act 1998**.

The claimant, or their solicitor, makes a Statement of Truth and must prepare a bundle of supporting documents. The claim has to be made to the Administrative Court. The claim form must be filed promptly and in any event not later than three months after the grounds to make the claim first arose. Under current government proposals for planning cases the time limit will be six weeks and for immigration cases four weeks. The time limit may not be extended by agreement between the parties. This rule does not apply when any other enactment specifies a shorter time limit for making a claim for judicial review. The claimant must serve a copy of the claim form on the defendant and any other person the claimant considers to be an interested party within seven days after the date of issue.

Appeals

An appeal lies with permission from the decision of the Administrative Court to the Court of Appeal.

Remedies and judicial review

The following remedies may be claimed only by judicial review:

Quashing order

The court examines the defendant public authority's proceedings. If there is any illegality, irrationality, or procedural impropriety its decision is empty of legal effect.

Mandatory order

This is an order to do something as the law requires.

Prohibiting order

This is an order not to do something or to discontinue doing something which is unlawful.
The following remedies may be claimed by judicial review procedure:

An injunction

This may be mandatory or prohibitive.

A declaration

This is a statement declaring whether something the defendant public authority has done or is about to do is unlawful. **Section 4 Human Rights Act 1998** gives the High Court in England and Wales the jurisdiction to state whether a statute is compatible with Convention rights.

Damages in conjunction with any other remedy available by judicial review

Part 54 Civil Procedure Rules provides that a claim for judicial review may include a claim for damages, restitution, or the recovery of a sum due but a claimant may not seek such a remedy alone.

Figure 10.2 First-tier Tribunal and the Upper Tribunal

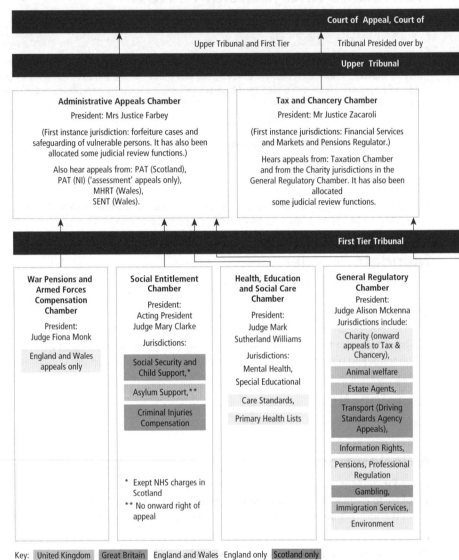

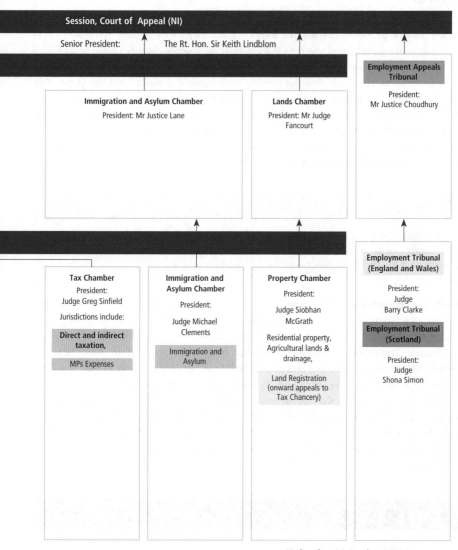

Session, Court of Appeal (NI)

Senior President: The Rt. Hon. Sir Keith Lindblom

Immigration and Asylum Chamber

President: Mr Justice Lane

Lands Chamber

President: Mr Judge Fancourt

Employment Appeals Tribunal

President:
Mr Justice Choudhury

Tax Chamber

President:
Judge Greg Sinfield

Jurisdictions include:

Direct and indirect taxation,

MPs Expenses

Immigration and Asylum Chamber

President:

Judge Michael Clements

Immigration and Asylum

Property Chamber

President:

Judge Siobhan McGrath

Residential property, Agricultural lands & drainage,

Land Registration (onward appeals to Tax Chancery)

Employment Tribunal (England and Wales)

President:
Judge
Barry Clarke

Employment Tribunal (Scotland)

President:
Judge
Shona Simon

Updated on 26 October 2020

Tribunals

A tribunal is a body established to settle certain types of dispute. In some contexts, 'tribunal' and 'court' are capable of meaning the same thing. A tribunal may be a court in the sense that it exercises compulsory jurisdiction given to it by statute to resolve disputes between private individuals, as well as between the citizen and the state, and to regulate the rights and obligations of citizens. Some tribunals, like the Employment Appeal Tribunal and the Upper Tier Tribunal, are courts of record. But arbitrators, committees of clubs, and professional and university disciplinary bodies are sometimes called domestic tribunals. Their functions are quasi-judicial. They affect the rights of citizens; however, they are not courts. As far as statutory tribunals are concerned there are important differences between tribunals and the courts. Their jurisdiction is specific. Their procedure is informal.

REVISION TIP

Develop an awareness and comprehensive knowledge of the present system of tribunals and the personnel responsible for them. Again, consider the separation of powers and rule of law implications especially with regard to judicial independence.

The **Tribunals, Courts and Enforcement Act 2007** established the First-tier Tribunal and the Upper Tribunal. See Fig 10.2. The First-tier Tribunal and the Upper Tribunal have judges assigned to them. The Senior President of Tribunals presides over both the First-tier Tribunal and the Upper Tribunal. The Upper Tribunal is a superior court of record and, in many respects, has the same rights, privileges, and powers as the High Court in England and Wales. The First-tier Tribunal is organized into the following chambers: the Social Entitlement Chamber; the War Pensions and Armed Forces Compensation Chamber; the Health, Education and Social Care Chamber; the Tax Chamber; the General Regulatory Chamber; and the Immigration and Asylum Chamber. The Upper Tribunal is organized into the Administrative Appeals Chamber; the Tax and Chancery Chamber; the Lands Chamber; and the Immigration and Asylum Chamber of the Upper Tribunal.

KEY CASES

CASE	FACTS	PRINCIPLE
Clark v University of Lincolnshire and Humberside [2000] 3 All ER 752	The Court of Appeal had to decide whether the claimant had abused the process of the court by claiming that the university was in breach of contract in the way it had applied its own student regulations.	It is not an abuse of process for a student at a university where there is no charter or appointed visitor to claim breach of contract by private law procedure.

CASE	FACTS	PRINCIPLE
O'Reilly v Mackman [1982] 3 All ER 1124	The House of Lords had to decide whether the claimants had abused the process of the court by bringing their claim under private law procedure.	As a general rule it would be contrary to public policy and an abuse of the process of the court for a claimant complaining of a public authority's infringement of their public law rights to seek redress by ordinary action.
R v Cambridge Health Authority, ex p B [1995] 2 All ER 129	The Court of Appeal had to decide whether it was appropriate to review the decision of a health authority which had refused to fund treatment.	Unless a public authority exceeds or abuses its powers, it is not appropriate for the court to intervene especially where matters of professional judgement are concerned. It is also not appropriate for the court to pass judgement on the way a public authority, acting within its powers, spends its allocated budget.
R v Disciplinary Committee of the Jockey Club, ex p Aga Khan [1993] 1 WLR 909	The Court of Appeal had to decide whether the disciplinary committee of the Jockey Club was amenable to judicial review.	Such a body will not be amenable to judicial review unless it is clear that its origin, history, constitution, and membership show that it has been woven into a system of governmental control.
R v Panel on Take-overs and Mergers, ex p Datafin [1987] QB 815	The Court of Appeal had to decide whether the Code of Practice Committee of the city panel on take-overs and mergers was susceptible to judicial review.	A non-statutory, self-regulatory body may be amenable to judicial review if there is a sufficient public element in its functions.

KEY DEBATES

Topic	'Ouster Clauses, Separation of Powers and the Intention of Parliament: From *Anisminic* to Privacy International'
Author/Academic	Robert Craig
Viewpoint	This article reflects on the constitutional implications of ouster clauses, especially regarding separation of powers. Discusses the approach adopted in *Anisminic Ltd v Foreign Compensation Commission* (HL), the case's subsequent application, and the impact of *R (on the application of Privacy International) v Investigatory Powers Tribunal* (CA). Robert Craig considers whether a distinction should be drawn between clauses addressed to judicial and administrative bodies.
Source	[2018] Public Law 570–584

Topic	'The Outer Limits of English Judicial Review'
Author/Academic	Neil Duxbury
Viewpoint	This article considers the reasons for restricting the Administrative Court's judicial review powers to public law concerns, and why a measure of uncertainty over the outer limits of judicial review's supervisory jurisdiction is likely to remain. It examines possible arguments to support the restriction based on issues of jurisdiction, the monopoly powers test, public interest, the operation of the rule of law, and the available remedies.
Source	[2017] Public Law 235–248

Topic	'Judicious Review: The Constitutional Practice of the UK Supreme Court'
Author/Academic	Jo Eric Khushal Murkens
Viewpoint	This article analyses the form of constitutional review exercised by the UK Supreme Court Justices, and assesses its democratic legitimacy. It goes on to discuss the conditions under which judicial review is legitimate. It identifies the principles that the Justices may balance against that of legislative intent.
Source	(2018) 77 Cambridge Law Journal 349–374

Topic	'Functions of a Public Nature under the Human Rights Act'
Author/Academic	Dawn Oliver
Viewpoint	Considers the scope of **s 6(3)(b) Human Rights Act 1998**, which allows judicial review of 'functions of a public nature' if exercised incompatibly with the **ECHR**.
Source	[2004] Public Law 329–351

Topic	'The Question of What Constitutes a Public Body for the Purposes of Judicial Review'
Author/Academic	Michael J Beloff
Viewpoint	Reviews the Jockey Club cases and addresses the debate concerning the reviewability of sports organizations. Examines the options open to the House of Lords if it ever has to decide whether such bodies should be open to judicial review.
Source	(2006) 1 (Feb) International Sports Law Review 1–3

EXAM QUESTIONS

Problem question

Antonio makes and sells ice-cream. The Food Standards Authority is a non-statutory body which lays down rules concerning the quality and safety of food. All manufacturers and retailers must comply with the rules laid down by the Food Standards Authority. It has power to discipline and ultimately ban any manufacturer or retailer which makes or sells food which does not comply with the rules.

Antonio is accused of making and selling poor quality ice-cream which is believed to have been responsible for an outbreak of food poisoning. Antonio is subsequently banned from making and selling ice-cream by the Food Standards Authority. Both he and the Society of Ice-Cream Manufacturers are unhappy about the decision and seek your advice.

Advise Antonio and the Society of Ice-Cream Manufacturers as to whether, and if so on what basis, the Food Standards Authority is a public body, capable of being subject to judicial review.

Advise Antonio and the Society of Ice-Cream Manufacturers as to whether the decision of the Food Standards Authority is a public law matter.

Advise the Society of Ice-Cream Manufacturers as to whether it would have the right to challenge the decision either on its own behalf or on Antonio's behalf.

Advise Antonio and the Society of Ice-Cream Manufacturers as to the procedure they would be expected to follow should they decide to apply for judicial review and the remedies they would seek.

See the Outline Answers section in the end matter for help with this question.

Essay question

Explain what is meant by public law and the extent to which, if at all, the distinction between public and private law is important when deciding if judicial review is appropriate.

Online Resources

For an outline answer to this essay question, as well as interactive key cases and multiple-choice questions, please visit the online resources.
www.oup.com/he/faragher-concentrate7e

Concentrate Q&As

For more questions and answers on public law, see the *Concentrate Q&A: Public Law* by Richard Clements.

Go to the end of this book to view **sample pages**.

Grounds for judicial review

Illegality

11

KEY FACTS

- Judicial review is based on technical grounds.

- These are classified as illegality, irrationality, and procedural impropriety.

- Illegality includes ultra vires, improper purpose, irrelevant considerations, lack of evidence, and unlawfully failing to exercise a discretionary power.

The classification of grounds for judicial review

REVISION TIP

In your answer to a problem question analyse the facts under these headings. This will ensure that your answer is well organized and complete.

In *Council of Civil Service Unions v Minister for the Civil Service* (1985) Lord Diplock classified the grounds for judicial review as illegality, irrationality, and procedural propriety. He also thought that proportionality might be adopted as an independent ground for judicial review following the example of other European countries.

Illegality

REVISION TIP

In some problem questions on judicial review you will have to consider whether the defendant had the power to make a decision. You may be expected to demonstrate understanding of the basic principles the court might apply to address this issue.

Ultra vires jurisdictional and non-jurisdictional error

A public body must not go beyond its powers. This is the ultra vires doctrine. In many cases the court has to decide whether a public body has the statutory power to do something. An example of this is the decision of Sargant J in *Attorney General v Fulham Corporation* (1921). The Attorney General applied for an injunction on behalf of local ratepayers in Fulham to stop Fulham Corporation operating a laundry at public expense. Fulham Corporation claimed to have the power to do this under the **Baths and Wash Houses Acts 1846** and **1847**. The judge held that these statutes empowered Fulham Corporation to provide baths and self-service washing facilities but not a laundry service.

REVISION TIP

In a problem question you should initially refer to the empowering statute to determine the nature and extent of the power which is conferred.

The ultra vires doctrine has evolved greatly. Today it applies where the court has to decide if a public body has misinterpreted or abused its statutory powers. The court may draw a distinction between jurisdictional and non-jurisdictional error. A jurisdictional error is a mistake of law which takes a public body outside the powers it has been given to inquire into matters and make decisions. The court can review all the vital findings on which the existence of a public body's jurisdiction depends, including findings of fact. Ministerial confirmation has no effect on the court's power to do this. This is the key principle in the Court of Appeal decision in **White and Collins v Minister of Health** (1939). In this case the court had to decide whether a compulsory purchase order for slum clearance made by a local authority and confirmed by the Minister of Health under the **Housing Act 1936** was valid. The claimant argued that his land was exempt because it was part of a park, garden, or pleasure ground. The Minister of Health argued that the court had no jurisdiction because the case concerned a finding of fact and the compulsory purchase order had been confirmed. It was held that the decision to make a compulsory purchase order was ultra vires because the land in question was part of a park and was, therefore, exempt under the provisions of the **Housing Act 1936**. A non-jurisdictional error does not take a public body outside its jurisdiction. It may be reversible on appeal but only if there is a right to do so. If there is no right of appeal the error may be unchallengeable.

 REVISION TIP

You should spend more time revising this topic. It illustrates how the ultra vires doctrine has been widened.

The meaning of jurisdictional error has been widened. Any misinterpretation or abuse of power made by a public body is capable of being a jurisdictional error. Practical examples of this include acting in bad faith; failing to comply with the rules of natural justice; taking into account irrelevant considerations or failing to take into account any relevant matters. This was determined by the House of Lords in **Anisminic v Foreign Compensation Commission** (1969).

The **Foreign Compensation Act 1950** empowered the Foreign Compensation Commission (the Commission) to hear claims for compensation agreed under international treaties. Its detailed powers, including the matters it was required to take into consideration when making a determination, were contained in regulations called Orders in Council. Following the Suez Crisis in 1956, in which British-owned property in Egypt was nationalized by the Egyptian Government, the British Government negotiated a treaty with the Egyptian Government under which funds were made available to compensate those who had lost their property. The Foreign Compensation Commission was empowered to hear and decide these claims. The matters the Commission had to take into consideration when deciding claims were contained in an Order in Council. A claimant had to have owned property in Egypt in 1956 or be a successor in title to such an owner. The claimant also had to be a British national. In this case the Commission had to decide whether Anisminic was entitled to compensation following the nationalization of its property in Egypt in 1956 even though it had come to a private agreement with the Egyptian Government to 'sell' its property to an Egyptian organization called TEDO. This agreement was without prejudice to further claims. The Foreign Compensation Commission determined that Anisminic was not entitled to compensation because Anisminic had sold its property to TEDO which was not a British national as required by the Order in Council.

LOOKING FOR EXTRA MARKS?

You should read the dissenting speeches, compare and contrast them, and then compare them with the majority speeches.

Anisminic asked a High Court judge for a declaration that the determination of the Foreign Compensation Commission (FCC) was null and void because there had been a jurisdictional error. Anisminic argued that the Commission had misinterpreted the Order in Council because having found that TEDO was Anisminic's successor in title it went on to ask itself whether TEDO was a British national. This was a question it did not have the jurisdiction to ask itself. Therefore the determination of the FCC was null and void because it was based on the nationality of TEDO which was an irrelevant consideration. Judicial opinion was divided.

In the High Court Browne J granted the declaration. The Court of Appeal, by majority, reversed his decision. The case went to the House of Lords. A majority of the Law Lords (Lords Reid, Wilberforce, and Pearce) thought that the word 'determination' in the **Foreign Compensation Act 1950** should not be construed as including everything which purported to be a determination because the FCC had misconstrued the statutory regulations defining their jurisdiction. The House of Lords granted the declaration. It was held that the FCC had made a jurisdictional error and had misunderstood the meaning of 'successor in title'. TEDO was not a successor in title so the FCC had no jurisdiction to consider TEDO's nationality.

REVISION TIP

Although **Anisminic** is primarily concerned with jurisdiction, it links up with all the technical bases for the grounds for judicial review considered in this chapter. When you revise grounds for judicial review, you should remember that the court is concerned as much with how a public body exercises the powers it has as it is with whether it had the power to do something.

In **R v Lord President of the Privy Council, ex p Page** (1993) Lord Browne-Wilkinson said that the decision in **Anisminic Ltd v Foreign Compensation Commission** rendered obsolete the distinction between non-jurisdictional errors and other errors of law by extending the doctrine of ultra vires. Lord Griffiths added that it is important to keep the purpose of judicial review clearly in mind. He went on to say that the purpose is to ensure that those bodies that are susceptible to judicial review have carried out their public duties in the way it was intended they should. In the case of bodies other than courts, insofar as they are required to apply the law they are required to apply the law correctly. If they apply the law incorrectly they have not performed their duty correctly and judicial review is available to correct their error of law so that they may make their decision upon a proper understanding of the law. In the case of inferior courts, that is, courts of a lower status than the High Court, such as the justices of the peace, Lord Griffiths said it was recognized that their learning and understanding of the law might sometimes be imperfect and require correction by the High Court and so the rule evolved that certiorari was available to correct an error of law of an inferior court. At first it was confined to an error on the face of the record but it is now available to correct any error of law made by an inferior court.

The Supreme Court in *R (on the application of Cart) v Upper Tribunal* (2012) had to decide whether the designation of the Upper Tribunal as a 'superior court of record' by **s 3 Tribunals, Courts and Enforcement Act 2007** meant that its decisions were not amenable to the supervisory jurisdiction of the High Court.

The key principle is that the words used by the 2007 Act are not clear enough to exclude judicial review of unappealable decisions of the Upper Tribunal. Parliament never intends to perpetuate errors of law. There should be the possibility that a second judge, who should always be someone with more experience or expertise than the judge who first heard the case, could check for errors in the case.

In order to keep important errors to a minimum and to provide the level of independent scrutiny outside the tribunal structure required by the rule of law, while recognizing that the enhanced tribunal set up under the 2007 Act deserved a restrained approach to judicial review and that the best use should be made of the courts' limited judicial resources, the criteria upon which permission to make a second-tier appeal to the Court of Appeal was granted should be adopted in relation to applications for permission to proceed with claims for judicial review.

The ultra vires doctrine and subjective discretionary powers

Statutes sometimes say that a public body *may* do something. This is a discretionary power. When a public body considers a claim, it may decide how it will exercise the power. It may act, with or without conditions, or refuse to act. Statutes sometimes provide that a power may be exercised as a public body sees fit or if the Secretary of State is satisfied or if they reasonably believe it is necessary. This is a subjective discretion. In times of war or emergency the courts often refuse to intervene on the basis that, subject to the requirement of good faith, the executive is better placed than the judiciary to make a decision. This was the case in the House of Lords' decisions in *Liversidge v Anderson* (1942) and *Secretary of State for the Home Department v Rehman* (2001). In other contexts, the court may be prepared to imply words into statutes and make a discretionary power subject to implied principles, undertakings, and duties. Examples of this are social policy, local government finance, and the relationship between local and central government. One implied duty the courts impose is that if a public body is given powers to spend public money it owes a duty to taxpayers to use the money in a businesslike manner with reasonable skill and caution. Political promises do not create legally binding obligations.

In *Bromley LBC v Greater London Council* (1983) the Greater London Council (GLC) resolved that the London Boroughs should contribute 6.1 pence in the pound towards reducing bus and Tube fares by 25 per cent. The GLC planned to finance the scheme by making grants to the London Transport Executive (LTE) to make good the loss. The London Borough of Bromley applied for judicial review. The House of Lords held that although the GLC's statutory power to make grants to the LTE 'for any purpose' included a large degree of discretion this was subject to three implied restrictions. The first, stated by Lords Wilberforce, Keith, Scarman, and Brandon was that LTE's discretion was impliedly limited by LTE's general duty as a statutory transport undertaking to run its operations on ordinary business principles. The LTE in submitting, and the GLC in approving, an arbitrary reduction of fares which had been fixed without regard to ordinary business principles had therefore acted ultra vires. The second implied restriction, supported by Lords Wilberforce, Scarman, and Brandon was that the GLC was under a duty to run its operations, so far as possible, on a break-even basis so that it balanced expenditure with self-generated income. This meant that the GLC was only entitled to make grants to LTE as a necessity to make good unavoidable losses and not to further social policy. The third implied restriction, supported by Lords Wilberforce, Diplock, Scarman, and Brandon, was that the GLC owed a fiduciary duty to ratepayers and was obliged to balance that duty against its duty to transport users when making a grant. In addition to identifying these implied restrictions, Lords Wilberforce, Diplock, and Brandon expressed the opinion that an election manifesto pledge does not create any legally binding obligations. For this reason, the GLC had not exercised its discretion lawfully in regarding itself as irrevocably bound by the majority group's commitment in their election manifesto to implement the reduction in fares regardless of the loss of rate support grant and the consequent additional cost to ratepayers which had not been foreseen when the commitment was made.

Improper purpose

A public body must exercise a discretionary power for the purpose for which it is granted. If a statute states the purposes for which discretion is to be exercised, the courts will treat the stated purposes as exhaustive. If the power is exercised for any other purpose the public body's action or decision will be ultra vires. In *Congreve v Home Office* (1976), for instance, the claimant renewed his television licence early to avoid an increase in the TV licence fee. His TV licence was revoked. The Home Secretary said that he was entitled to revoke TV licences under **s 1(4) Wireless Telegraphy Act 1949**. The claimant sought a declaration that the revocation of his TV licence was unlawful. The Court of Appeal held that a statutory power conferred on a minister for the purpose of granting and revoking licences cannot be used for the unauthorized purpose of raising money and granted the declaration.

If the statute does not specify the purpose for which discretion may be exercised, the court can impose implied restrictions. The first implied restriction is that statutory powers may not be used so as to defeat the policy and purpose of the Act. This was determined by the House of Lords in *Padfield v Minister of Agriculture* (1968). A statute established a scheme for the marketing of milk. Under the statute, aggrieved milk producers could complain to the minister. A committee of investigation could be set up to hear a complaint if the minister in any case so directed. The minister refused to intervene for political reasons. The House of Lords held that Parliament conferred discretion on the minister so that it could be used to promote the policy and objects of the Act which were to be determined by the construction of the Act; this was a matter of law for the court. Though there might be reasons which would justify the minister refusing to refer a complaint, their discretion was not unlimited and, if it appeared that the effect of their refusal to appoint a committee of investigation was to frustrate the policy of the Act, the court was entitled to interfere.

Statutory powers cannot be used to penalize conduct. This was determined in *R v Lewisham LBC, ex p Shell UK Ltd* (1988). Shell UK Ltd was part of a multinational group which had subsidiaries in South Africa. Eighteen per cent of the population of the Borough was black, and the council decided to boycott Shell UK Ltd's products, and to seek to persuade other councils to follow suit. Shell UK Ltd sought a declaration that the decision and the campaign was unlawful and ultra vires, and also unreasonable. It was held that in the light of the duty to promote good race relations imposed by **s 71 Race Relations Act 1976,** the decision was not unreasonable but that it had been influenced by an extraneous and improper purpose, namely to oblige Shell UK Ltd to sever links with South Africa when those links were not contrary to English law.

Statutory powers cannot be used to promote the political or moral views of the decision-maker. This is illustrated by two cases.

The first is *Wheeler v Leicester City Council* (1985). In this case Leicester City Council banned a leading rugby club from using a recreation ground for 12 months because several players accepted invitations to participate in tours of South Africa. Leicester City Council had a policy of withholding support for and discouraging sporting links with South Africa because of that country's practice of apartheid. The House of Lords held that the council had power under **s 71** of the 1976 Act to consider the best interests of race relations when exercising its statutory discretion in the management of the recreation ground, but that, in the absence of any infringement of the law or any improper conduct by the club, the resolution penalizing it for its failure to support the council's policy by complying with the insistence on a public condemnation of the tour, amounted to exercising a statutory power for an improper purpose.

The second is *R v Secretary of State for Foreign Affairs, ex p World Development Movement* (1995). **Section 1(1) Overseas Development and Co-operation Act 1980** empowered the British Government to grant aid to countries for the purpose of promoting development. The Foreign Secretary decided to grant aid to the Malaysian Government to build a dam. Many thought that the project was economically unsound and the World Development Movement sought judicial review of the Foreign Secretary's decision. One of their arguments was that the purposes behind the decision were political and not the promotion of the development of Malaysia. The judge held that the decision was unlawful. The project was so economically unsound that it did not fall within the purpose of the Act, namely 'promoting the development' of an overseas country.

Statutory powers cannot be exercised to gain an unauthorized financial advantage. This was determined by the Court of Appeal in *Hall v Shoreham UDC* (1964). The claimants were sand and gravel importers and the owners and occupiers of land in an area scheduled for industrial development. They applied for planning permission to develop part of their land for industrial purposes. The land adjoined a busy main road which was already overloaded and the highway authority intended to widen it at a future date and to acquire for that purpose a strip forming part of the claimants' land. The planning authority granted planning permission on condition that the claimants build an access road at their own expense which could be used by nearby residents. The Court of Appeal held that although the object sought to be attained by the defendants was a perfectly reasonable one, the terms of the conditions, requiring the plaintiffs to construct an ancillary road at their own expense for the use of persons proceeding to and from adjoining properties and amounting to a requirement that the plaintiffs should in effect dedicate the road to the public without any right to compensation, there being a more regular course available under the **Highways Act 1959**, were so unreasonable that they were ultra vires.

Mixed motives

A public body may do something for more than one reason. Some may be valid while others are not. The court adopts one of two approaches. It may look for the dominant or true purpose and if that is authorized the court will hold that the decision is lawful even though some secondary or incidental purposes are technically outside the public body's powers. This was determined by the House of Lords in **Westminster Corporation v London & North-western Railway Co** (1905). The other approach is that the court may distinguish between the primary and any secondary purposes and if the secondary purpose has significantly influenced the decision-making process the whole decision will be invalid. This was determined by Glidewell J in **R v ILEA, ex p Inner London Education Authority** (1986).

Relevant and irrelevant considerations

A public body must take into account relevant matters and discard anything irrelevant. Where the relevant considerations are expressly stated in a statute any deviation will make a decision invalid. This key principle was applied in **R v Secretary of State for the Home Department, ex p Venables and Thompson** (1998). Venables and Thompson were convicted of the murder of a young child, committed when they were both ten years old, and sentenced to be detained during Her Majesty's pleasure pursuant to **s 53(1) Children and Young Persons Act 1933**, as amended. Following sentence, the trial judge, in a report to the Secretary of State, stated that in his view the minimum period of detention necessary to satisfy the requirements of retribution and deterrence was, given their youth, eight years. The Lord Chief Justice agreeing that a shorter period was appropriate than that for an adult, recommended a tariff of ten years. The Secretary of State, in the exercise of their powers under **s 35 Criminal Justice Act 1991**, as applied by **ss 43** and **51** and in accordance with a policy statement made by him in July 1993, informed the applicants of the judicial recommendations and invited representations as to the appropriate length of the tariff. He informed them of extensive material that he had received from members of the public by way of petitions and correspondence, together with similar expressions of opinion supplied by a national newspaper, in support of a long or whole-life tariff. In July 1994, he informed each applicant that he had fixed a tariff of 15 years as appropriate to satisfy the requirements of retribution and deterrence.

In accordance with his policy, it followed that the first review date for each applicant would take place after 12 years' detention. In proceedings by way of judicial review the applicants sought to quash the decisions. The House of Lords decided to quash the Home Secretary's decision because he had taken into account public opinion and his own party political policies and had not considered the welfare of the applicants as required by **s 44(1) Children and Young Persons Act 1933**.

If the statute does not expressly specify the relevant considerations, the court adopts a similar approach to improper purpose. Improper purposes can also be classified as irrelevant considerations. This is illustrated by cases like *R v Lewisham LBC, ex p Shell UK Ltd* (1988); *Bromley London Borough Council v Greater London Council* (1983); and *Padfield v Minister of Agriculture* (1968). Another example is *R v Somerset County Council, ex p Fewings* (1995). In this case a decision to ban fox hunting on council-managed land was held to be ultra vires because it was partly based on the view that fox hunting involved unacceptable and unnecessary cruelty to deer. The political and moral views of the members of the council were irrelevant and should not have influenced the decision-making process.

Lack of evidence

A public body must base its conclusions of fact on the evidence before it. A public body's decision can be challenged by judicial review on the ground that it has ignored relevant evidence or has misinterpreted evidence or has unreasonably made a decision which is contrary to the weight of the evidence presented to it during the decision-making process. This was determined by Lord Denning MR in the Court of Appeal decision in *Coleen Properties v Minister of Housing and Local Government* (1971).

REVISION TIP

As grounds for judicial review, ultra vires, improper purpose, irrelevant considerations, and lack of evidence overlap and run into each other. For this reason you must revise these grounds comprehensively. It is not safe to leave anything out.

Unlawful failure to exercise a discretionary power

REVISION TIP

This ground for judicial review presupposes that a public body has refused to think about exercising its discretion. Read problem questions very carefully to determine whether or not a public body has considered whether to exercise its discretion. If it has done this, then look for other grounds for judicial review.

When a public body is given a discretionary power it is entitled to formulate and adopt a policy governing its decision-making process. But it cannot adopt a policy which prevents it exercising its discretion by shutting its ears to certain types of application. It must be prepared to consider every application on its merits. It must also be prepared to consider whether there are any special circumstances justifying departure from its usual policy. This is the key principle which forms the basis of the decision of the Court of Appeal in *R v Port of London Authority, ex p Kynoch Ltd* (1919), Kynoch challenged the decision of the Port of London Authority (PAL) not to grant a licence to build a deep-water wharf on the Thames. This was because the PAL had a policy to carry out such works itself under powers conferred by the **Port of London Act 1908** and the **Thames Conservancy Act 1894**. The court found that the PAL had properly heard and determined licensing applications in this case.

The law was developed further by the House of Lords in *British Oxygen Co Ltd v Minister of Technology* (1971). Lord Reid said that there are two general grounds on which the exercise of an unqualified discretion can be attacked. It must not be exercised in bad faith and it must not be so unreasonably exercised as to show that there cannot have been any real or genuine exercise of the discretion. But, apart from that, if the minister thinks that policy or good administration requires the operation of some limiting rule, there is nothing to stop him. Lord Reid went on to say that the general rule is that anyone who has to exercise a statutory discretion must not shut their ears to an application. There is no great difference between a policy and a rule. There may be cases where an officer or authority ought to listen to a substantial argument, reasonably presented, which urges a change of policy. What the authority must not do is to refuse to listen at all.

These principles were applied by the House of Lords in *R v Secretary of State for the Home Department, ex p Hindley* (2001). This case concerned the discretionary power of the Home Secretary to release mandatory life sentence prisoners under **s 27 Prison Act 1952**. The Home Secretary had adopted a policy that a review and reduction of a sentence would be considered only in exceptional circumstances including exceptional progress. It was alleged that he had unlawfully fettered his discretion. The House of Lords held that the Home Secretary had not unlawfully fettered his discretion because his policy did not rule out reconsideration from time to time.

The courts have subsequently determined that a public body cannot limit its discretion by:

1. estoppel based on a representation made by an official that the claimant had the right to do something—this was determined by the Court of Appeal in *Western Fish Products v Penrith DC* (1979);

2. agreement—this was determined in *Stringer v Minister of Housing* (1970);

3. wrongful delegation—this was determined by the Court of Appeal in *Barnard v National Dock Labour Board* (1953).

CASE	FACTS	PRINCIPLE
Bromley LBC v Greater London Council [1983] 1 AC 768	The House of Lords had to decide whether the Greater London Council was within its powers to require the London Boroughs to contribute financially to a scheme to reduce London Transport fares by 25 per cent.	The discretionary powers of the Greater London Council were limited by implied fiduciary duties and undertakings to run London Transport on business principles.
Congreve v Home Office [1976] QB 629	The claimant renewed his TV licence early to avoid an increase in the licence fee. His TV licence was revoked. The Home Secretary said that he was entitled to revoke TV licences under **s 1(4) Wireless Telegraphy Act 1949**. The claimant sought a declaration that the revocation of his TV licence was unlawful.	A public body must exercise a discretionary power for the purpose for which it is granted. If a statute states the purposes for which discretion is to be exercised, the courts will treat the stated purposes as exhaustive. If the power is exercised for any other purpose the public body's action or decision will be ultra vires.
R v Secretary of State for the Home Department, ex p Venables and Thompson [1998] AC 407	The Home Secretary took into account public opinion and his own policies and ignored the statutory requirement to consider the welfare of the child when setting tariffs of youth custody.	A public body must take into account relevant matters and discard anything irrelevant. Where the relevant considerations are expressly stated in a statute any deviation will make a decision invalid.
Coleen Properties v Minister of Housing and Local Government [1971] 1 WLR 433	The Court of Appeal had to consider whether it was lawful to confirm a slum clearance compulsory purchase order when one of the buildings was fit for human habitation according to an inspector's report.	A public body must base its conclusions of fact on the evidence before it. A public body's decision can be challenged by judicial review on the ground that it has ignored relevant evidence, or has misinterpreted evidence or has unreasonably made a decision which is contrary to the weight of the evidence presented to it during the decision-making process.
British Oxygen Co Ltd v Minister of Technology [1971] AC 610	The House of Lords had to decide whether the minister's policy concerning awarding grants of financial assistance was lawful.	When a public body is given a discretionary power it is entitled to formulate and adopt a policy governing its decision-making process. But it cannot adopt a policy which prevents it exercising its discretion by shutting its ears to certain types of application. It must be prepared to consider every application on its merits. Whether there are any special circumstances justifying departure from its usual policy.

KEY DEBATES

Topic	'The Relationship Between Judicial Review and the Upper Tribunal: What Have the Courts made of Cart?'
Author/Academic	Joanna Bell
Viewpoint	This article discusses how the courts have responded to *R (on the application of Cart) v Upper Tribunal* (2011) which gave guidance on the operation of judicial review in relation to decisions of the Upper Tribunal. It goes on to examines the justifications for the court finding such applications were restricted by the 'second-appeals criteria', whether subsequent cases have seen the criteria as a filter or set of restricted grounds, and the approach of the High Court.
Source	[2018] Public Law 394–412

Topic	'Ultra Vires Revisited'
Author/Academic	Thomas Adams
Viewpoint	Explains the importance of Trevor Allan's arguments that theories of judicial review were too focused on conceptual aspects of constitutionality instead of on its moral foundations. Examines the debate between supporters of the competing ultra vires and common law theories of judicial review, and suggests why it was conducted under the mistaken belief that a choice must be made between the two theories. Proposes an alternative approach.
Source	[2018] Public Law 31–43

Topic	'Outcomes Aren't All: Defending Process-Based Review of Public Authority Decisions under the Human Rights Act'
Author/Academic	David Mead
Viewpoint	Evaluates the approach adopted by the House of Lords in its judgments in *R (on the application of Begum) v Denbigh High School Governors, Belfast City Council v Miss Behavin' Ltd* and *R (on the application of Nasseri) v Secretary of State for the Home Department* that, where a public authority measure has been challenged under the **Human Rights Act 1998** for being disproportionate, it is sufficient for the authority to show that it had proportionate outcomes, known as the 'outcomes is all' approach, rather than that its proportionality was addressed during the decision-making process.
Source	[2012] Public Law 64–84

Topic	'The Flexibility Rule in Administrative Law'
Author/Academic	Adam Perry
Viewpoint	The author argues that the flexibility rule, relating to the ability for administrative officials to rely on policies enabling them to exercise discretionary powers, requires authorities to treat policies as rules of thumb. He asserts that the rule should apply equally to policies on the use of statutory, non-statutory, and prerogative powers.
Source	(2017) 76 Cambridge Law Journal 375–398

 ## EXAM QUESTIONS

Problem question

Assume that the Financial Institutions Act 2011 (the Act) sets up the Banking Commission (the Commission) and empowers it to nationalize any bank where it is satisfied that any bank is in financial difficulties and there is a danger that its customers will lose their money. The Act provides further that any decision of the Commission must be confirmed by the Secretary of State for Business, Innovation and Skills.

Justin is the managing director of Castlebar Bank plc (the Bank). He learns that the Commission intends to nationalize the Bank. Justin immediately sends a report compiled by the accountants responsible for auditing the Bank's accounts showing that the Bank has an excellent financial record. Justin has, in the past, been highly critical of government economic policy and had opposed the setting up of the Commission. He fears that this might be the real reason for the Commission's decision.

The Commission's decision to nationalize the Bank is confirmed by the Secretary of State for Business, Innovation and Skills following a meeting with the Chancellor of the Exchequer where he is reminded that tighter control of the availability of consumer credit is a fundamental principle of current economic policy.

Advise Justin as to the grounds upon which he might challenge the decision of the Commission and the Secretary of State successfully.

See the Outline Answers section in the end matter for help with this question.

Essay question

Explain the distinction between jurisdictional and non-jurisdictional error and the extent to which, if at all, this distinction is now effectively abolished.

Online Resources

For an outline answer to this essay question, as well as interactive key cases and multiple-choice questions, please visit the online resources.
www.oup.com/he/faragher-concentrate7e

Concentrate Q&As

For more questions and answers on public law, see the *Concentrate Q&A: Public Law* by Richard Clements.

Go to the end of this book to view **sample pages**.

Grounds for judicial review

12

Irrationality, proportionality, merits-based judicial review, and the Human Rights Act 1998

- Irrationality means unreasonableness which is now linked to the principle of proportionality.

- Unreasonableness is a comprehensively used term capable of meaning that a person given a discretionary power has, among other things, reached a conclusion which is so absurd that no reasonable authority could ever have come to it.

- Proportionality requires that there must be a reasonable relationship between the objective being sought and the means used to achieve it.

- Following the **Human Rights Act 1998** the court is concerned with whether the claimant's Convention rights have been infringed, not with whether the public authority has properly taken them into account.

- Where a public authority measure is challenged by way of judicial review under the **Human Rights Act 1998** for being disproportionate, it is sufficient for the authority to show that it had proportionate outcomes rather than that its proportionality was addressed during the decision-making process.

Irrationality and *Wednesbury* unreasonableness

In Lord Diplock's scheme, irrationality means unreasonableness.

REVISION TIP

In most problem-type questions focusing on grounds for judicial review, irrationality is examined in conjunction with other grounds for judicial review. Proportionality is inseparably linked to human rights. The material discussed should be revised in conjunction with the **Human Rights Act 1998**.

The House of Lords, in *Roberts v Hopwood* (1925) determined that discretionary powers must be exercised reasonably. Lord Greene MR in *Associated Provincial Picture Houses Ltd v Wednesbury Corporation* (1948) said that unreasonableness is a comprehensively used term capable of meaning that a person given a discretionary power has not directed themselves properly in law; has acted in bad faith; failed to pay attention to all the matters they are bound to consider; based their decision on irrelevant considerations; or reached a conclusion which is so absurd that no reasonable authority could ever have come to it. It is very difficult to prove that a decision is so absurd that no reasonable authority could ever have come to it. This requires something overwhelming.

In *Backhouse v Lambeth LBC* (1972) a housing authority passed a resolution under **s 111(1) Housing Act 1957** increasing the rent of an unoccupied and unfit house by £18,000 a week. It did this in order to be able to invoke the provisions of **s 63(1) Housing Finance Act 1972** exempting it from increasing rents of council houses under **s 62**. The resolution was one which no reasonable authority could have passed and was accordingly a nullity.

Irrationality in the context of human rights was considered by the Court of Appeal in *R v Ministry of Defence, ex p Smith* (1996). By a statement made in 1994 the Ministry of Defence reaffirmed its policy that homosexuality was incompatible with service in the armed forces and that personnel known to be homosexual or engaging in homosexual activity would be administratively discharged. The four applicants were serving members of the armed forces who had been administratively discharged between November 1994 and January 1995 on the sole ground that they were of homosexual orientation. In proceedings for judicial review each applicant challenged the decision. One of the grounds was irrationality.

The key principle is that where an administrative decision is made in the context of human rights the court will require a proportionately greater justification before being satisfied that the decision is within the range of responses open to a reasonable decision-maker, according to the seriousness of the interference with those rights. Applying the test of irrationality, which is sufficiently flexible to cover all situations, the court will show greater caution where the nature of the decision is esoteric, policy-laden, or security-based. The Court of Appeal decided that the policy was not irrational.

Proportionality

REVISION TIP

When revising this topic you should always be aware how the different parts of the subject link up and interact. In particular, the principle of proportionality should always be linked to situations where judicial review scenarios involve Convention rights or EU law issues.

In the context of human rights it applies where the state can limit rights for legitimate purposes. The state should do no more than is absolutely necessary to achieve the legitimate purpose of limiting the right. Proportionality requires that there must be a reasonable relationship between the objective being sought and the means used to achieve it. There is a close relationship between *Wednesbury* unreasonableness and proportionality. The possibility that proportionality might become an independent ground for judicial review was first discussed by Lord Diplock in *Council of Civil Service Unions v Minister for the Civil Service* (1985). There was also speculation about how the principle would develop by Lord Roskill and Lord Bridge in *R v Secretary of State for the Home Department, ex p Brind* (1991). But these cases were inconclusive. Lord Slynn, however, in *R (on the application of Alconbury Developments Ltd) v Secretary of State for the Environment, Transport and the Regions* (2003) said that it is time to recognize proportionality as a principle of English administrative law. This principle is applied in cases where the court is:

- asked to consider whether legislation is compatible with Convention rights;
- applying principles of EU law;
- deciding whether to quash a penalty or punishment; or
- asked to review the decision of a public body on the ground that it is unreasonable.

The distinction between merits-based and procedural review

REVISION TIP

Always revise judicial review in conjunction with the **Human Rights Act 1998**.

At least until the **Human Rights Act 1998** came into force it was generally asserted that judicial review meant procedural review. This means that judicial review is concerned primarily with the decision-making process as opposed to the correctness of the decision itself. In *Associated Provincial Picture Houses Ltd v Wednesbury Corporation* (1948) Lord Greene MR made it clear that the courts can interfere with executive decisions only if it is shown that a public body has contravened the law. The court, when exercising its supervisory jurisdiction, is not a court of appeal. It must not substitute its own opinion for that of the authority. When discretion is granted the law recognizes certain principles upon which that discretion must be exercised, but within those principles the discretion is absolute and cannot be questioned in any court.

Subsequently, Lord Hailsham, in the House of Lords' decision in *Chief Constable of North Wales Police v Evans* (1982) said that it is important to remember in every case that the purpose of judicial review is to ensure that the individual citizen is given fair treatment by public bodies and that it is no part of that purpose to substitute the opinion of the judiciary or of individual judges for that of the public body set up by law to decide the matters in question. In Lord Hailsham's opinion, the function of the court in the context of judicial review is to see that lawful authority is not abused by unfair treatment and not to attempt itself the task entrusted to that authority by the law.

Lord Ackner in *R v Secretary of State for the Home Department, ex p Brind* (1991) said that it would be wrong for the judiciary to quash an executive decision on its merits. It would invite an abuse of power by the judiciary. The test of *Wednesbury* unreasonableness was necessarily severe to confine the jurisdiction exercised by the judiciary to a supervisory, as opposed to an appellate, jurisdiction.

Following the **Human Rights Act 1998** proportionality, according to Lord Slynn in the *Alconbury* case, cannot exist in a separate compartment from *Wednesbury* unreasonableness. Moreover, Laws LJ in *R (on the application of Mahmood) v Secretary of State for the Home Department* (2001) said that it is a recognized common law principle that the intensity of review in a public law case will depend on the subject matter in hand. Any interference by the action of a public body with a fundamental right will require a substantial objective justification. This was accepted and discussed by Lord Steyn in the House of Lords' decision in *R (on the application of Daly) v Secretary of State for the Home Department* (2001). He said that the court must look at how the decision-maker strikes a balance with fundamental rights. Proportionality may go further than the traditional grounds of review. The intensity of the review, in similar cases, is guaranteed by the twin requirements that the limitation of the right was necessary in a democratic society, in the sense of meeting a pressing social need, and the question whether the interference was really proportionate to the legitimate aim being pursued. He would not go as far as to say that there had been a shift to merits-based review. Again, in the *Alconbury* case Lord Slynn said that there was nothing in Strasbourg jurisprudence to suggest a merits-based approach to judicial review.

 LOOKING FOR EXTRA MARKS?

Proportionality, irrationality, and the distinction between merits-based and procedural review have been the subjects of intense academic debate. You should look up and read the articles in the Key debates section at the end of this chapter. See also Professor David Feldman, 'Proportionality and the Human Rights Act 1998', essay in *The Principle of Proportionality in the Laws of Europe* edited by Evelyn Ellis (1999), 117, 127 *et seq.*

The 'outcomes is all' approach

When applying the normal principles of administrative law, judges hearing applications for judicial review usually look at the decision-making process rather than the merits of the decision. This is not the correct approach when the challenge is based on an alleged infringement of a Convention right under the **Human Rights Act 1998**. In accordance with Strasbourg jurisprudence, the court is concerned with whether the claimant's Convention rights have been infringed, not with whether the public authority has properly taken them into account. What is important is the practical outcome of the decision not the quality of the decision-making process itself. This means, for instance, that where a public authority measure is challenged by way of judicial review under the **Human Rights Act 1998** for being disproportionate, it is sufficient for the authority to show that it had proportionate outcomes rather than that its proportionality was addressed during the decision-making process.

This was determined by the House of Lords in three cases. The first was *R (on the application of Begum) v Denbigh High School Governors* (2007). In this case a school's refusal to allow a pupil to wear a jilbab at school did not interfere with her right under **Art 9 European Convention on Human Rights and Fundamental Freedoms (ECHR)** and therefore **Sch 1, Pt I Human Rights Act 1998** to manifest her religion and, even if it did, the school's decision was objectively justified under **Art 9(2) ECHR**. In the circumstances, the pupil had not been denied access to education in breach of **Art 2 ECHR** as incorporated by **Sch 1, Pt II** of the Act. The House of Lords emphasized that where a public authority measure is challenged by way of judicial review under the **Human Rights Act 1998** for being disproportionate, it is sufficient for the authority to show that it had proportionate outcomes rather than that its proportionality was addressed during the decision-making process.

The second case was *Belfast City Council v Miss Behavin' Ltd* (2007). The appellant local authority appealed against a decision to quash its refusal of an application by the respondent company (B) for a licence for a sex establishment in Belfast under the provisions of the **Local Government (Miscellaneous Provisions) (Northern Ireland) Order 1985**. B had applied to the local authority for a licence to run a sex shop at premises in Belfast, but that application was refused under **Sch 2, para 12** of the Order on the ground that the appropriate number of sex shops in the relevant locality was nil.

The Court of Appeal held that in exercising its statutory powers, the local authority had not sufficiently taken into account B's right to freedom of expression under **Art 10 ECHR**, and its right to peaceful enjoyment of its possessions under, **Art 1 First Protocol ECHR**. The local authority submitted that if the 1985 Order complied with **Art 10**, it was not open to a disappointed applicant, such as B, to raise an **Art 10** argument in relation to his own application.

The House of Lords held that the court was concerned with whether B's human rights had been infringed, not with whether the local authority had properly taken them into account, and what was important was the practical outcome of the decision not the quality of the decision-making process itself.

The third case was *R (on the application of Nasseri) v Secretary of State for the Home Department* (2010). The appellant asylum seeker (N) appealed against a decision that his removal to Greece did not breach **Art 3 ECHR**, and a decision to discharge a declaration of incompatibility. The claimant was an Afghan national who had entered the UK illegally after the rejection of his claim for asylum in Greece. The Secretary of State decided to remove the claimant to Greece. The claimant sought judicial review of the Secretary of State's decision on the grounds that his removal would be contrary to **Art 3 ECHR**, as the Greek authorities were likely to send him back to Afghanistan where he would be ill-treated.

The House of Lords dismissed the appeal. The judge at first instance had been wrong to find that **Art 3** created a procedural obligation to investigate whether there was a risk of a breach by the receiving state, independently of whether such a risk actually existed. The House of Lords decided that it is understandable that a judge hearing an application for judicial review might think that they are undertaking a review of the decision-making process, rather than the merits of the decision, in accordance with normal principles of administrative law. However, that is not the correct approach when the challenge is based upon an alleged infringement of a Convention right. The focus should be upon whether the individual's Convention rights have in fact been violated.

KEY CASES

CASE	FACTS	PRINCIPLE
Associated Provincial Picture Houses Ltd v Wednesbury Corporation [1948] 1 KB 223	The Court of Appeal had to decide whether conditions attached to the licensing of cinemas for Sunday opening were reasonable.	For a decision to be unreasonable it must be so absurd that no sensible person could ever contemplate that it would be within their decision-making powers.
R v Ministry of Defence, ex p Smith [1996] QB 517	By a statement made in 1994 the Ministry of Defence reaffirmed its policy that homosexuality was incompatible with service in the armed forces and that personnel known to be homosexual or engaging in homosexual activity would be administratively discharged. The four applicants were serving members of the armed forces who had been administratively discharged between November 1994 and January 1995 on the sole ground that they were of homosexual orientation. In proceedings for judicial review each applicant challenged the decision. One of the grounds was irrationality.	Where an administrative decision is made in the context of human rights the court will require a proportionately greater justification before being satisfied that the decision is within the range of responses open to a reasonable decision-maker, according to the seriousness of the interference with those rights.

CASE	FACTS	PRINCIPLE
R (on the application of Alconbury Developments Ltd) v Secretary of State for the Environment, Transport and the Regions [2003] 2 AC 295	The House of Lords had to decide whether the principle of proportionality applied in EU law is a recognized principle of English administrative law.	Lord Slynn said that it is time to recognize proportionality as a principle of English administrative law. This principle is applied in cases where the court is asked to consider whether legislation is compatible with Convention rights; applying principles of EU law; deciding whether to quash a penalty or punishment; asked to review the decision of a public body on the ground that it is unreasonable.
R (on the application of Nasseri) v Secretary of State for the Home Department [2010] 1 AC 1	The claimant was an Afghan national who had entered the UK illegally after the rejection of his claim for asylum in Greece. The Secretary of State decided to remove the claimant to Greece. The claimant sought judicial review of the Secretary of State's decision on the grounds that his removal would be contrary to **Art 3 ECHR**, as the Greek authorities were likely to send him back to Afghanistan where he would be ill-treated.	In accordance with Strasbourg jurisprudence, the court is concerned with whether the claimant's Convention rights have been infringed, not with whether the public authority has properly taken them into account. What is important is the practical outcome of the decision not the quality of the decision-making process itself.

KEY DEBATES

Topic	'Structuring Substantive Review'
Author/Academic	Rebecca Williams
Viewpoint	This article examines, with reference to cases such as the Supreme Court ruling in *R (on the application of Keyu) v Secretary of State for Foreign and Commonwealth Affairs*, the debate over whether *Wednesbury* grounds of review should be replaced by proportionality. Suggests why neither approach optimizes predictability of review, and argues for a focus on the substance of what is allegedly wrong in the decision, and how intensively it should be reviewed.
Source	[2017] Public Law 99–123

Topic	'From *Wednesbury* Unreasonableness to Accountability for Reasonableness'
Author/Academic	Daniel Wei L Wang
Viewpoint	This article highlights the role the courts have played in altering social policy on the rationing of NHS health care. It comments on the gradual transition from an approach based on *Wednesbury* unreasonableness to one incorporating the conditions for 'accountability for reasonableness'.

Topic	'Outcomes Aren't All: Defending Process-Based Review of Public Authority Decisions Under the Human Rights Act'
Author/Academic	David Mead
Viewpoint	Evaluates the approach adopted by the House of Lords in its judgments in *R (on the application of Begum) v Denbigh High School Governors, Belfast City Council v Miss Behavin' Ltd*, and *R (on the application of Nasseri) v Secretary of State for the Home Department* that, where a public authority measure has been challenged under the **Human Rights Act 1998** for being disproportionate, it is sufficient for the authority to show that it had proportionate outcomes, known as the 'outcomes is all' approach, rather than that its proportionality was addressed during the decision-making process.
Source	[2012] Public Law 64–84

 EXAM QUESTIONS

Problem question

Assume that the Sport and Fitness Act 2012 (the Act) sets up the Sports Commission and empowers it to give financial assistance in the form of grants to help anyone wishing to provide facilities to promote health and fitness. The Act provides that a decision of the Sports Commission shall not be challenged in any legal proceedings whatsoever.

SportAid is a national charity which promotes widening the participation of disabled people in sports. John, who runs a private school, wishes to build a gymnasium in association with SportAid, which is fully equipped to meet the needs of disabled people. He applies to the Sports Commission for a grant. His application is refused because he runs a private school. John wishes to challenge the decision of the Sports Commission. SportAid is very concerned about the impact this decision will have on its work.

Advise John and SportAid as to whether and if so on what basis judicial review is the appropriate way to challenge the decision of the Sports Commission, whether SportAid has the right to bring a claim for judicial review and as to the effect of the provision of the Sport and Fitness Act 2012 that a decision of the Sports Commission shall not be challenged in any legal proceedings whatsoever.

See the Outline Answers section in the end matter for help with this question.

Essay question

Referring to decided cases, critically assess how, if at all, the impact of the principle of proportionality on *Wednesbury* unreasonableness.

Online Resources

For an outline answer to this essay question, as well as interactive key cases and multiple-choice questions, please visit the online resources.
www.oup.com/he/faragher-concentrate7e

Concentrate Q&As

For more questions and answers on public law, see the *Concentrate Q&A: Public Law* by Richard Clements.

Go to the end of this book to view **sample pages**.

13

Grounds for judicial review

Procedural impropriety, natural justice, and legitimate expectation

KEY FACTS

- Procedural impropriety focuses on natural justice and failure to observe procedural rules.

- A fair hearing includes the right to be heard, adequate notice, and the right to answer the allegations made.

- Everyone is entitled to an unbiased hearing.

- Although there is no general duty to give reasons for a decision in English law there are significant exceptions to this rule.

- A person may have a legitimate expectation of being treated in a certain way by an administrative authority even though there is no other legal basis upon which they could claim such treatment.

Procedural impropriety and natural justice

Procedural impropriety means breach of the rules of natural justice and failure to comply with statutory procedural requirements.

REVISION TIP

When considering procedural impropriety, you should consider if the rules of natural justice apply in principle and then the extent to which they apply to the body concerned.

What are the rules of natural justice?

The rules of natural justice form a judicial code of procedural fairness. The rules are that no man is to be a judge in their own cause and that all the parties to a dispute shall be fairly heard. When looking at natural justice in the context of judicial review it is necessary to consider:

- whether or not the rules of natural justice apply in principle to a public body's decision-making process;
- the extent to which the rules of natural justice apply; and
- whether the rules of natural justice have been substantially breached.

REVISION TIP

It is important, when analysing the facts of a problem question in the examination to break down your answer into manageable stages. When answering a problem question involving natural justice you should identify and state the rules, determine whether they apply to the defendant in principle, and then assess the extent to which the rules apply.

Do the rules of natural justice apply in principle?

The rules of natural justice apply to all judicial proceedings in courts and tribunals. It is possible to raise matters concerning natural justice in civil and criminal appeals. In the context of judicial review there is a long-standing distinction between public bodies which make judicial decisions and public bodies which make administrative decisions. For a long time it was held that the rules of natural justice applied to judicial bodies. They did not apply to bodies exercising purely administrative functions. This meant that by the mid-twentieth century the protection of the rules of natural justice was held not to be available when challenging administrative public bodies which were required to act within their statutory powers and on reasonable grounds. Claimants would, instead, argue **ultra vires** or unreasonableness. The leading persuasive authority for this was the decision of the Privy Council in *Hadduka Ali v Jayaratne* (1951).

However, in *Ridge v Baldwin* (1964), the House of Lords refused to follow *Hadduka Ali* on the grounds that, according to Lord Reid, it was neither binding nor relevant and that it was based on a serious misapprehension of the effect of the older authorities. Lord Reid concluded that the true effect of the older cases was that the rules of natural justice are capable of applying in principle where an administrative body acts judicially.

Assuming they apply in principle, to what extent do the rules of natural justice apply?

One unique feature of procedural impropriety as a ground for judicial review is that the extent to which the rules of natural justice apply varies depending on the context of the case. Courts and tribunals feel the full force of the rules and are strictly bound by them along with all the rules of evidence. This is necessary and in the public interest to maintain public confidence in the administration of justice by the civil and criminal justice system.

In the context of judicial review the Administrative Court has to deal with a wide variety of bodies making different types of decision. This was recognized by Lord Lane CJ in *R v Commissioner for Racial Equality, ex p Cottrell & Rothon* (1980). He said that there are degrees of judicial hearing, ranging from the borders of pure administration to the borders of a full hearing in a criminal case in the Crown Court. They cannot be easily pigeon-holed into the judicial role. It is necessary to ask 'what is the basic nature of the proceeding which is going on here'.

Lord Bridge, in the House of Lords' decision in *Lloyd v McMahon* (1987), said that the requirements of natural justice depend, among other things, on the circumstances of the case; the nature of the inquiry; the rules under which the tribunal is acting; and the subject matter.

An example of these principles at work is *R v Army Board of the Defence Council, ex p Anderson* (1991). The claimant was a former soldier who alleged that he had been subjected to forms of racial abuse which caused him to go absent without leave. The papers relating to the complaint were seen separately by two members of the Army Board who reached individual conclusions that, although there was some truth in the applicant's claim, there was no basis for making an apology and awarding him compensation. His requests for disclosure of documents relating to investigations into his complaints were refused, as was his request for an oral hearing. He applied for judicial review of the Board's decision. The court took the view that the Army Board's functions were judicial because the Board was required to adjudicate an alleged breach of a soldier's statutory rights and award compensation. Its decisions were final apart from judicial review.

Examples of factors which can limit the extent to which the rules of natural justice may apply include:

- lack of legitimate expectation;
- national security; and
- the need to preserve confidentiality of sources of information or to keep certain kinds of matters secret in the public interest.

In *Schmidt v Secretary of State for Home Affairs* (1969), for instance, the Court of Appeal held that Schmidt could not challenge refusal of an extension of permission to remain in the UK on the basis that he had not been given the opportunity to make representations to the Home Secretary. He did not have any legitimate expectation of being allowed to remain.

An example of a case where national security was a limiting factor was the House of Lords' decision in *Council of Civil Service Unions v Minister for the Civil Service* (1985). Employees at GCHQ had their right to be members of a trade union taken away from them. The CCSU had not been consulted about this important change in the conditions of service. The House of Lords held that normally the unions had a legitimate expectation of being consulted, but because the reason for the removal of trade union membership was national security, the normal rules of natural justice did not apply.

Sometimes the normal rules of natural justice may be modified in view of the need to preserve confidentiality of sources of information or simply to keep certain kinds of matters secret in the public interest. An example of this is *R v Gaming Board, ex p Beniam and Khaida* (1970). The Court of Appeal said that the Board had a duty to act fairly, but this obligation had been discharged notwithstanding the refusal of the Board to disclose sources or details of information, which had been received by it in confidence.

The extent to which rules of natural justice apply generally to disciplinary hearings

 REVISION TIP

The next step when answering an examination problem question is to assess the extent to which the rules of natural justice apply.

One of the consequences of the House of Lords' decision in *Ridge v Baldwin* was a potential application of the rules of natural justice in disciplinary hearings. Disciplinary boards are not courts. They are not bound to comply with all the rules of evidence or the rules of natural justice to the same extent as a criminal court. Many of the rights which would be mandatory if the case were being heard in a criminal court are discretionary when they are applied to disciplinary hearings outside the criminal justice system. Nevertheless because disciplinary action can have extremely adverse consequences for the accused, involving loss of livelihood and reputation, a very high standard of impartiality and procedural fairness may be required. The rules of natural justice apply in principle to varying extents depending on the context. Two examples of this are university disciplinary and assessment boards and licensing cases.

The extent to which the rules of natural justice apply to university disciplinary and assessment boards

In *R v Aston University Senate, ex p Roffey* (1969) two students had failed examinations. They were required by the examiners to withdraw from the course. The examiners were bound by the rules of natural justice. The examiners had taken into account extraneous factors such as family background and personal problems. The students should have been able to give first-hand testimony of these matters. Natural justice demanded this. Although there had been breaches of natural justice, the court declined to grant relief because the students had delayed in applying to the court.

In *Glynn v Keele University* (1971) Glynn had breached university discipline by sunbathing naked on university premises. The university fined him £10 and excluded him from the university halls of residence for one year. The rules of natural justice had been ignored. The judge acknowledged that there had been a breach of the rules of natural justice but declined to grant an injunction; the student had only been deprived of a plea of mitigation, which the judge felt would not have affected the outcome of the case.

In *R v Manchester Metropolitan University, ex p Nolan* (1994) a student on the Common Professional Examination Course (CPE) was accused of committing a disciplinary offence. He had taken notes into the exam and was spotted by the invigilators. He was given the chance of being heard and represented by the Faculty Examinations Disciplinary Committee. He claimed that he had not referred to the notes and brought evidence in the form of testimonials and a psychiatrist's report. The Committee taking into account the mitigating circumstances found him guilty, not of cheating but of the lesser offence of attempting to secure an unfair advantage. It was left to the CPE Board to determine the penalty. The Board imposed its ultimate penalty—declaring that he had failed all six exams and denying him the chance to resit them. The Board did not have the mitigating evidence before it. It was held that the Board's decision would be quashed by certiorari—not having the evidence before it amounted to a breach of procedural justice.

The extent to which the rules of natural justice apply to licensing cases

A licence gives a person permission to do something, which might otherwise constitute a criminal offence. Statute empowers bodies to act as licensing authorities and enables them to issue, renew, and revoke licences. The statutes will also lay down rules, conditions, and procedural requirements which the licensing authority has to follow. As to whether, and to what extent, such bodies are bound by the rules of natural justice depends upon the type of matter being considered. There are three recognized categories of licensing case, namely application cases, expectation cases, and revocation cases.

- An application case concerns someone who merely seeks to obtain a licence when they do not already have one.

- In an expectation case the claimant says that they legitimately expect that a licence will be granted. Such an expectation is usually based on past experience. This may occur where the applicant applies for renewal of a licence.

- A revocation case is one in which the licensing authority seeks to take away some existing right or position.

In all three categories, the rules of natural justice apply in principle but to differing extents. In application cases, for instance, there is a basic duty to consider applications fairly and on their merits but nothing more. The rules apply more rigorously to expectation and revocation cases.

These rules were laid down by Megarry V-C in *McInnes v Onslow Fane* (1978). The claimant applied to the British Boxing Board of Control (the Board) for a boxers' manager's licence. He also asked for an oral hearing and prior information of anything that might militate against a favourable recommendation. The Board refused his application. He was given neither an oral hearing nor reasons for the refusal. The claimant applied for a declaration that the Board was in breach of the rules of natural justice.

It was held that although the Board was subject to the rules of natural justice, as an applicant the claimant was only entitled to expect that the Board would reach an honest conclusion without bias or caprice. The Board was not under any obligation to provide an oral hearing. The declaration was refused.

Examples of the different kinds of cases include:

- An application case. In *R v Gaming Board, ex p Beniam and Khaida* (1970), the Court of Appeal said that although the Gaming Board must act fairly it is not obliged to disclose sources or details of information or their reasons when refusing a certificate of consent.

- An expectation case. In *R v Liverpool CC, ex p Liverpool Taxi Fleet Operators' Association* (1970) a taxicab licensing authority gave a public undertaking not to increase the number of licences. This created a legitimate expectation and gave the court grounds to intervene.

- A revocation case. In *R v Barnsley MBC, ex p Hook* (1976) the key principle is that a local authority reviewing a decision to revoke the licence of a market trader to operate from a stall on a market controlled by the authority has a duty to act judicially and in accordance with the rules of natural justice.

Have the rules of natural justice been breached?

 REVISION TIP

Now focus on the substance of the rules, apply it to the facts of the problem and assess whether the rules of natural justice have been breached.

Once the court has considered fully the questions of applicability in principle and the extent of applicability, it will go on to look at the substance of the rules of natural justice and consider whether or not they have been breached.

REVISION TIP

When you come to this part of your answer you need to break it down to consider, first, whether there is a real possibility or danger of bias and, second, whether all the parties to the dispute have been given a fair hearing.

Is there a real danger or possibility of bias?

No man shall be a judge in their own cause. Both sides in a dispute have the right to expect that the matter will be impartially adjudicated. There are two types of bias. The first is pecuniary bias. The second is personal bias.

Pecuniary bias arises where the adjudicator may have a financial interest in the outcome of a decision. In *Dimes v Grand Junction Canal* (1852) the Lord Chancellor was held to be disqualified from hearing a case because he was a shareholder in the company which was a party to the action.

Personal bias is anything which might cause an adjudicator to view one side in a dispute more or less favourably than the other. In *Bradford v McLeod* (1986) a Scottish judge said, at a social function during a miners' strike, that he would not grant legal aid to miners. Subsequently a miner represented by a solicitor who had heard the sheriff's remarks appeared for trial before the same sheriff on a summary complaint alleging breach of the peace at a picket line. The solicitor asked the sheriff to disqualify himself. The sheriff refused. It was held that the sheriff should have disqualified himself because a reasonable person would see a danger of personal bias.

The rule that it is not enough that justice should be done but that justice must also be seen to be done goes back to Lord Hewart CJ's decision in *R v Sussex Justices, ex p McCarthy* (1924). This means that the party alleging bias does not have to prove that the adjudicator *was* biased. In the House of Lords' decision in *R v Gough* (1993) Lord Goff held that the party alleging bias had to prove that there was a real danger of bias. The test was modified by the House of Lords in *Porter v Magill* (2002). This case involved many issues including the question of whether the test concerning bias formulated by Lord Goff in *R v Gough* (1993) and subsequent cases needed to be modified.

The key principle is that when considering bias the court will ascertain all the circumstances which have a bearing on the suggestion that the judge was biased and ask whether those circumstances would lead a fair-minded and informed observer to conclude that there was a real possibility or a real danger that the tribunal was biased. There is no difference in meaning between real possibility and real danger. On this issue, the law was modified.

Has a fair hearing taken place?

REVISION TIP

This is the heart of the subject. Revise it thoroughly. This also has important human rights implications. You should link this up with your revision of the material contained in Chapter 14.

Both sides in a dispute have the right to be heard. Lord Hodson in *Ridge v Baldwin* (1964) said that there were three outstanding features of a fair hearing:

- the right to be heard by an unbiased tribunal;
- the right to have notice of charges of misconduct; and
- the right to be heard in answer to those charges.

In *Ridge v Baldwin* (1964) a chief constable was dismissed for being negligent in the discharge of his duty under **s 191 Municipal Corporations Act 1882**. The committee which dismissed him did not say how he was negligent and the initial decision was taken in his absence. The appellant then brought an action against members of the committee for a declaration that his dismissal was illegal, ultra vires, and void, and for payment of salary from 7 March 1958 or, alternatively, payment of pension from that date and damages. The declaration was granted by the House of Lords.

These principles were applied by the Court of Appeal in *R (on the application of Shoesmith) v Ofsted* (2011). One of the key principles in this case is that although a Director of Children's Services is ultimately responsible and accountable for the way those services are provided, they are entitled to be given a proper opportunity to explain the state of affairs for which they are being held accountable.

A party to the proceedings must be given the opportunity to state their case and to challenge and correct anything that is presented to a decision-maker that might be prejudicial to their case. This rule was applied in *Errington v Minister of Health* (1935). The key principle is that when a minister conducts an inquiry they are performing a judicial function and must invite objectors to the meeting and hear their objections before making a final decision.

In *R v Thames Magistrates' Court, ex p Polemis* (1974) the claimant was the master of a ship who was convicted by magistrates of an offence in his absence because the summons was issued on the day his ship was due to sail and an adjournment was refused. It was held that the applicant had been deprived of the opportunity to present his case in that he had been given no reasonable opportunity to prepare his case before the hearing, and in those circumstances there had been a denial of natural justice.

The right to legal representation is mandatory in any court or tribunal. In other contexts the right is discretionary and depends upon the seriousness of the charge and of the penalty; the likelihood of points of law arising; the ability of the party to conduct their case; and the need for speed in making an adjudication. This was determined in *R v Secretary of State for the Home Department, ex p Tarrant* (1985).

The right to be given reasons for a decision

 REVISION TIP

This is an issue which links up with rights under **Art 6 European Convention on Human Rights and Fundamental Freedoms**. You should revise this issue in conjunction with the **Human Rights Act 1998.**

Courts and tribunals give reasons for their decisions. It is part of a group of rights collectively known as 'due process'. The existence of reasons supports the principle that justice is done on a rational basis. As far as public bodies other than courts and tribunals are concerned there is no general common law obligation to give reasons for a decision. There are, however, significant exceptions. Lord Bingham CJ in *R v Ministry of Defence, ex p Murray* (1998) gave detailed guidance on the principles to be applied when deciding whether or not to give reasons for a decision in the context of judicial review of the decision of a public body which is not a court or tribunal.

Lord Bingham CJ deduced a number of principles from earlier cases which should guide the court when deciding whether or not to give reasons. The law does not, at present, recognize a general duty to give reasons. Where, however, a statute confers a power to make decisions affecting individuals, the court will readily apply necessary procedural safeguards so as to ensure the attainment of fairness. If there is no express requirement to give reasons, the burden is on the person seeking to argue that reasons should have been given to show that the procedure was unfair. There is a perceptible trend towards an insistence on greater openness.

In determining whether reasons should be given, relevant considerations will include (1) the absence of any right of appeal and (2) the importance of detecting the kind of error which would entitle the court to intervene. It is also relevant whether the body in question is exercising a judicial function. Reasons should also be given where either (a) a decision without reasons is insufficient to achieve justice or (b) the decision appears aberrant.

A factor in favour of the giving of reasons is that such a duty concentrates the mind of the decision-maker and shows that the issues have been conscientiously addressed so as to demonstrate how the result has been reached or—if it be so—that there is a justiciable flaw in the process. There may be factors which militate against the duty to give reasons. It may place an undue burden on decision-makers or demand an appearance of unanimity where there is diversity or call for articulation of sometimes inexpressible value judgements and offer an invitation to the captious to comb the reasons for previously unsuspected grounds of challenge.

Even if fairness does favour a requirement of giving reasons, there may be considerations of public interest, which outweigh the advantages of requiring reasons. The giving of reasons will not be required if the procedures of the particular decision-maker would be frustrated by a requirement to give reasons, even short reasons.

Lord Mustill in *R v Secretary of State for the Home Department, ex p Doody* (1994) said that the principles of fairness are not to be applied by rote identically in every situation. What fairness demands is dependent on the context of the decision. Lord Mustill went on to say that the giving of reasons may be inconvenient, but he could see no ground at all why it should be against the public interest.

These principles were applied with a negative result in *R v Higher Education Funding Council, ex p Institute of Dental Surgery* (1994). Following its assessment of the Institute by the HEFC, its research grant had been cut. The institute was seeking to challenge the decision, in particular the fact that no reasons had been given. It was held that academic judgements of this kind were not of a class which required reasons to be given.

Legitimate expectation

REVISION TIP

This will apply where you see something which looks like a promise, representation, or a consistent past practice which, for instance, creates the impression that the renewal of a licence is a mere formality. Consider also whether the person you are advising has acted to their detriment or would suffer severe hardship if the promise were not kept.

A person may have a legitimate expectation of being treated in a certain way by an administrative authority even though there is no other legal basis upon which he could claim such treatment. A legitimate expectation may arise from a representation or promise; a consistent past practice, and the conduct of the decision-maker. The basic principle is that the principles of fairness, predictability, and certainty should not be disregarded, provided there are no overriding policy considerations like national security.

In *Council of Civil Service Unions v Minister for the Civil Service* (1985) the claimants sought judicial review of a decision of the Minister for the Civil Service (the Prime Minister) to ban trade union membership at a defence establishment on national security grounds. The key principle here is that a legitimate expectation may arise based on consistent past practice. It was held that the applicants would, apart from considerations of national security, have had a legitimate expectation that unions and employees would be consulted before the minister issued her instruction of 22 December 1983 and, accordingly, the decision-making process would have been unfair by reason of her failure to consult them and would have been amenable to judicial review.

An example of legitimate expectation based on promises can be seen in the Court of Appeal decision in *R v North and East Devon Health Body, ex p Coughlan* (2001). The key principle is that if a public body exercising a statutory function makes a promise as to how it will behave in the future which induces a legitimate expectation of a benefit which is substantive, rather than merely procedural, to frustrate that expectation can be so unfair that it will amount to an abuse of power. In such circumstances, the court had to determine whether there was a sufficient overriding interest to justify a departure from what had previously been promised.

These principles were reviewed by the House of Lords in *R (Bancoult) v Secretary of State for Foreign and Commonwealth Affairs (No 2)* (2009). The House of Lords had to decide whether a statement made by the Secretary of State revoking immigration controls in 2000 created a legitimate expectation that the Chagos Islanders would be allowed to return and settle permanently on the outer islands. The key principle applied here is that legitimate expectation has to be based on a promise which is both clear and unambiguous. The House of Lords decided that no legitimate expectation had been created on which the islanders could rely.

KEY CASES

CASE	FACTS	PRINCIPLE
Council of Civil Service Unions v Minister for the Civil Service [1985] AC 374	The claimants sought judicial review of a decision of the Minister for the Civil Service (the Prime Minister) to ban trade union membership at a defence establishment on national security grounds.	A legitimate expectation may arise based on consistent past practice.
R (on the application of Bancoult) v Secretary of State for Foreign and Commonwealth Affairs (No 2) [2009] 1 AC 453	The House of Lords had to decide whether a statement made by the Secretary of State revoking immigration controls in 2000 created a legitimate expectation that the Chagos Islanders would be allowed to return and settle permanently on the outer islands.	Legitimate expectation has to be based on a promise which is both clear and unambiguous.
R v North and East Devon Health Body, ex p Coughlan [2001] QB 213	C was severely disabled. In 1993, she and number of other disabled patients were moved from hospital to Mardon House. The Health Authority (HA) had promised that this would be their home for life. The HA decided to close Mardon House and transfer C to the local authority for long-term nursing care.	If a public body exercising a statutory function makes a promise as to how it will behave in the future which induces a legitimate expectation of a benefit which is substantive, rather than merely procedural, to frustrate that expectation can be so unfair that it will amount to an abuse of power. In such circumstances, the court had to determine whether there was a sufficient overriding interest to justify a departure from what had previously been promised.

CASE	FACTS	PRINCIPLE
R v Secretary of State for the Home Department, ex p Doody [1994] 1 AC 531	This case concerned a group of prisoners sentenced to mandatory terms of life imprisonment. The actual sentence is divided between a penal component, consisting of the period that the trial judge considers necessary, and an additional risk component, which is the period after the penal element has been served that is considered necessary before the risk to the public is sufficiently reduced to justify release. This is decided by the Home Office. The trial judge will make a recommendation (which does not have to be followed) after which the Home Secretary and senior officials at the Home Office exercise a wide discretion. Mandatory lifers were not informed about the tariff or told of the original judicial recommendation, nor were they made aware whether the Home Office had departed from the sentence that had been set by the trial judge.	The principles of fairness are not to be applied by rote identically in every situation. What fairness demands is dependent on the context of the decision. Lord Mustill went on to say that the giving of reasons may be inconvenient, but he could see no ground at all why it should be against the public interest.
Porter v Magill [2002] 2 AC 357	The House of Lords had to decide whether or not to modify the rules regarding the test for bias.	When considering bias the court will ascertain all the circumstances which have a bearing on the suggestion that the judge was biased and ask whether those circumstances would lead a fair-minded and informed observer to conclude that there was a real possibility or a real danger that the tribunal was biased. There is no difference in meaning between real possibility and real danger.
Ridge v Baldwin [1964] AC 40	Under **s 191 Municipal Corporations Act 1882** the watch committee had power to 'at any time suspend and dismiss any borough constable whom they think is negligent in the discharge of his duty or otherwise unfit for the same'. The appellant was dismissed by the committee. No specific charge had been formulated against him. He sought a declaration from the court that his dismissal was illegal and ultra vires.	The claimant had the right to a hearing before an unbiased tribunal, the right to know the accusations made against him, and the opportunity to answer those allegations.

KEY DEBATE

Topic	'The Scope of Judicial Review'
Author/Academic	Louis Blom-Cooper
Viewpoint	This article reflects on the development of procedural impropriety as a ground of judicial review. Discusses its operation with reference to the House of Lords ruling in **Kennedy v Spratt** (1972), which illustrates how contemporary courts may interpret legislation relevant to sentencing. Details the facts of **Kennedy** and how Wilberforce LJ's approach reveals how fairness must prevail both at trial and during the administrative process of setting an appropriate penalty.
Source	[2017] Public Law 183–185

EXAM QUESTIONS

Problem question

Assume that the Estate Agents' Licensing Bureau has been set up by estate agents to curb criticism of the practices of the more unscrupulous elements in the business and to ensure that proper standards are maintained. The Code of Conduct under which the profession operates provides that those who wish to set up in business as estate agents must be licensed by the Bureau.

Andrew has been employed as an estate agent for many years. He has been very successful and now wants to set up in business on his own. He applies to the Bureau for a licence. He is given 24 hours' notice of the hearing which will decide on his application but, since he assumes that this is a mere formality, he does not object.

When Andrew attends the hearing, however, he is dismayed to see that it is being chaired by Gary, a disgruntled former client of his. Gary has refused to pay Andrew his commission on the sale of Gary's house and Andrew has started legal proceedings against him. Gary asks Andrew why he thinks he is fit to hold a licence as, 'It is agents like you who bring the profession into disrepute.' When Andrew tries to speak, Gary says, 'I don't think anything you say is likely to sway us.' Realizing that the hearing is going badly for him, Andrew asks if it might be adjourned so that he can have his lawyer present. Gary refuses to allow this. Andrew's application for a licence is turned down.

Advise Andrew as to his chances of a successful challenge to the refusal of the licence.

See the Outline Answers section in the end matter for help with this question.

Essay question

Explain what is meant by legitimate expectation and when it is most likely to succeed as a ground for judicial review.

Online Resources

For an outline answer to this essay question, as well as interactive key cases and multiple-choice questions, please visit the online resources.
www.oup.com/he/faragher-concentrate7e

Concentrate Q&As

For more questions and answers on public law, see the *Concentrate Q&A: Public Law* by Richard Clements.

Go to the end of this book to view **sample pages**.

14 Introduction to human rights in UK law

KEY FACTS

- Before the **Human Rights Act (HRA) 1998**, civil and political rights were recognized and enforced in the UK solely within the established framework of statutory and common law principles.

- During the twentieth century, human rights principles were developed in international law by the law of treaties and by international organizations.

- The Council of Europe drafted the **European Convention on Human Rights and Fundamental Freedoms (ECHR)** to guarantee basic civil and political rights, which have been expanded by a series of supplementary treaties called protocols, and provide a judicial system for their enforcement.

- The **ECHR** is a treaty and, as such, could not give individual citizens directly enforceable rights until the 'Convention rights' were incorporated by the **HRA 1998**.

- A poor record in the European Court of Human Rights, human rights problems in the English courts, and worries about the relationship between the executive and Parliament provide the background to the Act.

- The **HRA 1998** incorporates 'Convention rights' into UK law.

- The **HRA 1998** creates new rules of statutory interpretation, enables citizens to test the compatibility of legislation with Convention rights, and obliges the courts to take 'Strasbourg principles' into account when considering human rights issues in litigation.

- The **HRA 1998** makes it unlawful for a public authority to act in any way which is incompatible with Convention rights, allows individuals to rely on breach of Convention rights in any proceedings brought against public authorities, and provides some extra remedies.

Human rights and English law

REVISION TIP

You should begin looking at this subject by reviewing how human rights principles are embedded into English common law and statute.

Before the **HRA 1998** came into force, human rights protection in the UK was based on remedies contained in specific causes of action or penalties available through the criminal justice system. International law has had a considerable influence on the development of human rights law. The twentieth century saw the formation of international organizations, committed to the promotion of human rights, and a growing number of treaties which dealt with human rights.

The European Convention on Human Rights and Fundamental Freedoms

REVISION TIP

You should have a working knowledge of the content of the **ECHR** and link it to your revision of **s 1** and **Sch 1 HRA 1998**.

The **ECHR** guarantees civil and political rights. These are the right to life; the prohibition of torture, inhuman, and degrading treatment or punishment; the prohibition of slavery and forced labour; the right to liberty; the right to a fair and unbiased hearing; the prohibition of retrospective legislation; the right to respect for private and family life; freedom of conscience and religion; freedom of expression; freedom of association; and the right to marry and found a family.

The **ECHR** has been supplemented and amended by a series of additional treaties called protocols. The **First** and **Sixth Protocols** give individuals additional rights which were incorporated into British law by the **HRA 1998**.

The **First Protocol** covers the protection of property; the right to education; and the right to free elections. The **Sixth** and **Twelfth Protocols** cover the abolition of the death penalty.

LOOKING FOR EXTRA MARKS?

The reasons for the decision to incorporate the **ECHR** into British law include problems with the UK human rights record both in the British courts and the European Court of Human Rights. You should refer to your recommended standard textbook and read some of the cases contributing to this debate.

Human Rights Act 1998

REVISION TIP

This topic links up with Chapters 3, 4, 6, 9, 12, and 15. If you choose to revise this topic you are strongly advised to read these chapters and consider how the **HRA 1998** has affected the development of constitutional and administrative law.

The Convention rights

The first thing the Act does is create **'Convention rights'**. These are defined in **s 1** and set out in **Sch 1** to the Act. They are the substantive rights guaranteed under those parts of the **ECHR** which the UK has signed and ratified. They are contained in **Arts 2–12**, **Art 14**, and the **First** and **Sixth Protocols**. The most controversial omission was **Art 13** which provides that everyone whose rights and freedoms set forth in the Convention are violated shall have an effective remedy before a national authority. The reason for this omission is that the later portions of the Act, in particular **ss 7–9** are intended to lay down a remedial structure. There was a concern that inclusion of **Art 13** among the Convention rights might confuse or undermine the interpretation of the Act.

The interpretation of Convention rights

Under **s 2(1)** a court or tribunal determining a question which has arisen in connection with a Convention right must take into account any judgment, decision, declaration, or advisory opinion of the European Court of Human Rights; opinion of the Commission in a report adopted under **Art 31 ECHR**; decision of the Commission in connection with **Art 26** or **27(2) ECHR**; or decision of the Committee of Ministers under **Art 46 ECHR** whenever made or given, so far as, in the opinion of the court or tribunal, it is relevant to the proceedings in which that question has arisen.

Proportionality

In the context of judicial review, this principle has had a significant effect on the development of the law. This, and the relevant case law, was discussed in Chapter 12. The court considers what is necessary to achieve the legitimate aims of a particular policy or legislation. This was the case in the House of Lords' decision in the following case.

R (on the application of Daly) v Secretary of State for the Home Department [2001] 2 AC 532

The applicant was a prisoner. He kept correspondence with his solicitor in his cell. Every day his cell was searched. In accordance with rules made under **s 47(1) Prison Act 1952**, he was excluded from his cell while the search was conducted. Officers could examine, but not read, any legally privileged correspondence

---

to check that nothing had been written on it by the prisoner, or stored between its pages, likely to endanger prison security. The applicant sought judicial review of the decision to require examination of prisoners' legally privileged correspondence in their absence. The principle from this case was that a person sentenced to a custodial order retains the right to communicate confidentially with a legal adviser under the seal of legal professional privilege. Such rights can be curtailed only by clear and express words and then only to the extent reasonably necessary to meet the ends which justify the curtailment. It was held that the policy was an unlawful intrusion into personal privacy protected by **Art 8(1) ECHR** and amounted to a breach of legal professional privilege. The reasons for the policy went beyond what was necessary to achieve the legitimate aims of **s 47(1)**. It was also beyond what was necessary to satisfy **Art 8(2) ECHR**.

In addition to this, proportionality often involves striking a balance between the benefits to be achieved by doing something and the harm that may be done by interfering with a person's Convention rights in the process. This was considered by the House of Lords, in the context of **Art 8 ECHR**, in *Campbell v MGN Ltd* (2004).

Campbell v MGN [2004] 2 AC 457

The claimant was a model who brought an action against the owners of the *Daily Mirror* for breach of confidence and breach of the **Data Protection Act 1998**, because they had published material which revealed that she was a drug addict who was receiving treatment. It also revealed precise details of where, when, and how often she was receiving treatment and included a photograph of her leaving a clinic.

The House of Lords held that the publication of the material which revealed that she was a drug addict receiving treatment was justified in the public interest because it corrected untrue statements which were circulating about the claimant. The publication of material revealing precisely where, when, and how often she was receiving treatment, together with the photograph of her leaving a clinic, was not justified and amounted to a wrongful disclosure of private information.

In reaching its decision the House of Lords stated and applied the key principle that although there is no all-embracing action for 'invasion of privacy' in English law, the tort of breach of confidence has developed to provide a remedy where there has been a 'wrongful disclosure of private information'.

The House of Lords also had to consider the claimant's right to privacy set against the right to freedom of expression. The House of Lords laid down the following principles. The exercise of balancing **Art 8** and **Art 10** may begin when the person publishing the information knows or ought to know that there is a reasonable expectation that the information in question will be kept confidential. Once the information is identified as 'private' in this way, the court must balance the claimant's interest in keeping the information private against the countervailing interest of the recipient in publishing it. When two Convention rights are in play, the proportionality of interfering with one has to be balanced against the proportionality of restricting the other. The court looks at the comparative importance of the actual rights being claimed in the individual case; the justifications for interfering with or restricting each of those rights; and applies the proportionality test to each.

It was held by the House of Lords that in the circumstances the claimant's right to privacy protected by **Art 8** was violated because the publications amounted to a breach of confidence.

Section 3(1) requires the courts to interpret primary and secondary legislation in a manner which is compatible with Convention rights so far as it is possible to do so.

The **s 3** requirement was interpreted and applied by the House of Lords in *R v A* (2002).

R v A [2002] 1 AC 45

The House of Lords was asked to interpret **s 41 Youth Justice and Criminal Evidence Act 1999** in a manner which is consistent with **Art 6 ECHR**. The section concerns the admissibility of evidence in rape cases relating to consent. The House of Lords laid down the following principle. The evidential material had to be so relevant to the issue of consent that to exclude it would violate the fairness requirement in **Art 6**. Where that test is satisfied, the evidence should not be excluded. The appeal was dismissed.

The judicial use of **s 3** is illustrated by the House of Lords' decision in **Ghaidan v Godin-Mendoza** (2004) (see Chapter 6). It is also illustrated, in relation to **s 23 Anti-terrorism, Crime and Security Act 2001** in **A and Others v Secretary of State for the Home Department** (2005).

With regard to legislation which post-dates the Act, the minister introducing the bill has to issue a 'statement of compatibility', that is, that the bill is compatible with the Convention rights.

Using the Convention against public authorities

 REVISION TIP

When answering problem questions you will have to determine whether the defendant is a public authority within the meaning of **s 6(3)**. This is a tricky issue and you should revise the relevant case law carefully.

It is unlawful for a public authority to act in a way which is incompatible with a Convention right. This provision is contained in **s 6(1)** of the 1998 Act. Under **s 6(3) HRA 1998** 'public authority' includes a court or tribunal, and any person certain of whose functions are functions of a public nature, but does not include either House of Parliament or a person exercising functions in connection with proceedings in Parliament. There are two types of public authority. The first type is made up of core public authorities. The second type is made up of hybrid public authorities. Core public authorities are clearly public in the sense that they are governmental in nature and serve and regulate the general population, as in the public at large. These include government ministers and departments, local authorities, the police, and statutory regulatory bodies. Hybrid public authorities come from **s 6(3)(b)**. They primarily exercise private functions but some of their functions are of a public nature. In this context 'public' means that their functions are governmental or regulatory and are not dependent on consent or agreement. Their decisions affect the rights and obligations of the public at large.

The following are examples of bodies which are not public authorities for the purposes of **s 6(3) HRA 1998**:

- an adjudicator (**Austin Hall Building Ltd v Buckland Securities Ltd** (2001));
- a charitable foundation which provides accommodation, on behalf of a local authority, to persons to whom the authority owes a duty to provide accommodation (**R (on the application of Heather) v Leonard Cheshire Foundation** (2002));

- a parochial church council (*Aston Cantlow and Wilmcote with Billesley Parochial Church, v Wallbank* (2004));

- Lloyd's of London (*R (on the application of West) v Lloyd's of London* (2004));

- a company responsible for the maintenance of rail infrastructure (*Cameron v Network Rail Infrastructure Ltd* (2007));

- a private body providing accommodation to persons in need of care and assistance pursuant to arrangements made with a local authority in the exercise of that authority's functions under **ss 21** and **26 National Assistance Act 1948** (*R (on the application of Johnson) v Havering LBC* (2007) and *YL v Birmingham City Council* (2008)); and

- a priest celebrating communion (*Re All Saints', Sanderstead* (2011)).

The following are examples of public authorities for the purposes of **s 6(1) HRA 1998**:

- a registered social landlord (*R (on the application of Weaver) v London and Quadrant Housing Trust (Equality and Human Rights Commission intervening)* (2010)); and

- embassy and consular staff working abroad (*R (on the application of B) v Secretary of State for Foreign and Commonwealth Affairs* (2005)).

The meaning of '**public authority**' was also discussed by the House of Lords in *L v Birmingham City Council* (2008) (see Key cases).

Proceedings against public authorities under the Human Rights Act 1998

Under **s 7(1)** any **victim** (or 'would be' victim) of an unlawful act under **s 6(1)** may bring proceedings against the authority in any appropriate court or tribunal, or rely on the Convention right or rights concerned in any legal proceedings.

Proceedings must, under **s 7(5)**, be brought within one year beginning with the date on which the act complained of took place; or such longer period as the court or tribunal considers equitable in all the circumstances. Shorter time limits apply as in judicial review.

'Victim' means anyone who is directly affected by the act or the omission that is the subject of the complaint. The extent of a person's right to rely on a breach of a Convention right was discussed by the House of Lords in the following case.

Matthews v Ministry of Defence [2003] 1 AC 1163

The claimant claimed damages in the tort of negligence. The defendant sought to escape liability by relying on **s 10 Crown Proceedings Act 1947**. The case raised a preliminary issue as to whether **s 10** of the Act was compatible with the right to a fair trial contained in **Art 6 ECHR**.

The key principle is that although the meaning of 'civil rights' in **Art 6 ECHR** is an autonomous concept, it cannot be interpreted solely by reference to domestic law. A litigant's right of access to the court under **Art 6(1)** applies only to civil rights which could, on arguable grounds, be recognized under domestic law and where the restriction on the right of access was procedural in nature.

The House of Lords decided that **s 10** meant that the claimant had no civil right to which **Art 6** might apply.

Remedies

If a public authority has breached a Convention right, the remedy which the court can grant to the victim is covered by s 8. The remedies available under s 8(1) are familiar: damages, declarations, injunctions, quashing orders, mandatory orders, and prohibiting orders.

Damages

The availability of damages under s 8 was discussed by the House of Lords in the following case.

Marcic v Thames Water Utility [2004] 2 AC 42

The defendant is a statutory sewerage undertaker under the **Water Industry Act 1991** and, as such, is a public authority under **s 6(3) HRA 1998**. The claimant was a householder whose premises were regularly flooded with sewage. He claimed damages in nuisance and under the **HRA 1998**. The principle from this case was that where a public authority is subject to an elaborate statutory scheme of regulation, which includes an independent regulator with powers of enforcement whose decisions are subject to judicial review, there is no claim for damages under **s 6(1) HRA 1998**.

It was held that the claimant had no claim for damages against Thames Water.

The approach to awarding damages in human rights cases was determined in the following case.

Anufrijeva v Southwark [2004] 2 WLR 603

This appeal arose out of three cases each of which was a claim for damages for breach of privacy under **Art 8 ECHR**. The Court of Appeal had to consider the rules determining awards of damages in England and Wales where **s 8** Convention rights are engaged.

The principle from this case was that the approach to awarding damages in this jurisdiction should be no less liberal than those applied by the European Court of Human Rights or one of the purposes of the 1998 Act will be defeated and claimants will still be put to the expense of having to go to Strasbourg to obtain just satisfaction.

Under **s 8 HRA 1998**, damages can be awarded on the basis of what is necessary and appropriate to give just satisfaction. Such awards should be modest. Where there is a claim for damages under **s 8 HRA 1998** involving maladministration, appropriate procedures should be followed to ensure that the cost of obtaining relief is proportionate to the amount of compensation being claimed.

It was held that on the facts in each case there had been no breach of the claimants' right to privacy.

The House of Lords considered the level of awards of damages and the effect of the jurisprudence of the European Court of Human Rights in *R v Secretary of State for the Home Department, ex p Greenfield* (2005). The House of Lords stated the following principles concerning awards of damages under s 8 HRA 1998.

- In deciding, under **s 8 HRA 1998**, whether an award of damages is necessary to give just satisfaction for violations of **Art 6**, and if so how much, the British courts had to look to the jurisprudence of the European Court of Human Rights for guidance.

- The focus of the **ECHR** is the protection of human rights rather than awards of compensation.

This is reflected in the approach of the European Court of Human Rights, which is to treat the finding that **Art 6** has been violated as in itself giving just satisfaction to the injured party, and not to speculate on what the outcome of the particular proceedings would have been if the violation had not occurred.

The House of Lords also laid down the following principles:

- The European Court will award damages only where it is satisfied that the loss or damage complained of is actually caused by the violation, although it has on occasions been willing in appropriate cases to make an award where it is deprived of a real chance of a better outcome.

- Awards of compensation for anxiety and frustration attributable to the **Art 6** violation suffered are made very sparingly and for modest sums. Awards are not precisely calculated but are such as were judged by the court to be fair and equitable in particular cases.

- Although judges in England and Wales are not inflexibly bound by awards of the European Court of Human Rights, they should not aim to be significantly more or less generous than that court might be expected to be if it were willing to make an award at all.

Injunctions

It is necessary to consider the effect of **s 12(3)** and **(4) HRA 1998** where an injunction is sought to restrain publication of any material and the issue is whether this would violate **Art 10 ECHR** which guarantees freedom of speech. The court may also have to consider **Art 8** where the claimant says that publication of material amounts to breach of privacy. This was discussed in *Douglas v Hello! Ltd* (2001). The Court of Appeal applied the following principles. Where a court has to decide whether to grant an injunction which might affect the exercise of the right to freedom of expression protected by **Art 10 ECHR**, it must, in accordance with **s 12(4) HRA 1998**, look at the importance of that right. Moreover, the qualifications set out in **Art 10(2)** are as relevant as, and entitled to no less regard than, the right set out in **Art 10(1)**. When determining, in accordance with **s 12(3)**, whether it is likely to be established at trial that publication should not be allowed, the court should take into account the full range of relevant Convention rights, including the right to respect for private and family life protected by **Art 8**. **Section 12(3)** requires the court, before it grants an injunction to restrain publication, to consider the merits of the case and seek to balance the merits of one right against another without giving undue weight to either of them. The principles of legality and proportionality must be used to articulate the rights involved and to determine whether it is possible to strike a balance in favour of restraint of publication.

LOOKING FOR EXTRA MARKS?

The judges in *Douglas v Hello! Ltd* (2001) made some significant comments concerning **Art 8** and its effect on English law. You should look this case up and read their judgments.

Declarations of incompatibility

REVISION TIP

You will find that **s 4 HRA 1998** has implications for parliamentary sovereignty and judicial review. You should revise this topic in conjunction with Chapters 6 and 12. This will help you to understand it in greater depth.

Section 4 of the Act creates the 'declaration of incompatibility'. The most important effect of making a declaration is that it puts pressure on the government to change the law. The courts which have power to make such declarations are the UK Supreme Court, the Judicial Committee of the Privy Council, the Courts-Martial Appeal Court, the High Court of Justiciary, the Court of Session, the High Court, and the Court of Appeal. It is important to note that declarations of incompatibility are not available in county courts, tribunals, the Crown Court, or magistrates' courts. Principles governing declarations of incompatibility were discussed by the Court of Appeal in the following case.

Wilson v First Country Trust Limited (No 2) [2001] 3 WLR 42
The Court of Appeal ordered a hearing in order to determine whether to make a declaration of incompatibility under **s 4(2) HRA 1998** that **s 127 Consumer Credit Act 1974** was incompatible with **Art 6 ECHR** and **Art 1 First Protocol** in that it barred a creditor from enforcing a loan agreement.
Ever since 1 October 2000, the court is required by the provisions of the **HRA 1998** to avoid acting in a way which is incompatible with a Convention right. The court must consider: (1) the facts as they were at the time when it made the order; and whether that obligation is affected by **s 22(4) HRA 1998**, which prevents a claimant from relying on the 1998 Act where a public authority has acted incompatibly with a Convention rights prior to 1 October 1998; and (2) the relevant date for deciding whether **s 22(4)** applies is the date the court made the order. The court had power to make a declaration of incompatibility pursuant to **s 4 HRA 1998**.

The principles governing declarations of incompatibility were developed further in *R (on the application of Alconbury Developments Ltd) v Secretary of State for the Environment, Transport and the Regions* (2001). The House of Lords laid down the following principles.

- To determine whether civil rights under **Art 6(1) ECHR** are involved in a claim, the court must look at the relevant jurisprudence of the European Court of Human Rights.
- A Secretary of State is not an independent and impartial tribunal.
- Decisions taken by a Secretary of State are compatible with **Art 6(1)** provided they are reviewable by an independent and impartial tribunal which has full jurisdiction to deal with the case as the nature of the decision requires.
- If the decision is one of administrative policy the reviewing body is not required to have full power to re-determine the merits of the decision and any review by a court of the merits of such a policy decision, taken by a minister answerable to Parliament and ultimately to the electorate, would be profoundly undemocratic.

- The power of the High Court in judicial review proceedings to review the legality of the decision and the procedures followed is sufficient to ensure compatibility with **Art 6(1)**. **Section 10** provides for a so-called 'fast track' procedure for the amendment of legislation, which has been declared to be incompatible with a Convention right. The minister can amend legislation.

What are the consequences of a declaration of incompatibility?

Such a declaration may be thought to carry some moral pressure and could not be ignored; but perhaps a government could ignore it on reflection. But such a declaration is most likely to be followed by a Remedial Order.

Remedial Orders

Remedial Orders are made under **s 10 HRA 1998**. These provisions apply if a provision of legislation has been declared to be incompatible with a Convention right or the European Court of Human Rights has determined that a provision of a UK statute is incompatible with Convention rights. If a Minister of the Crown considers that there are compelling reasons for proceeding, they may by order make such amendments to the legislation as they consider necessary to remove the incompatibility.

Statements of compatibility

Under **s 19 HRA 1998** a minister in charge of a bill in either House must, before second reading of the bill, make a statement that the bill is compatible with Convention rights or that although they are unable to make a statement of compatibility the government nevertheless wishes the House to proceed with the bill.

The Independent Human Rights Act Review 2021

The impact of the Human Rights Act 1998 on the relationship between the judiciary, the executive, and the legislature

The Independent Human Rights Act Review 2021 will consider the way the **HRA 1998** balances the roles of the judiciary, the executive, and the legislature. It will examine whether the current approach risks 'over-judicializing' the executive while requiring the judiciary to consider matters of policy best left to the executive.

The Review will also consider the following questions:

- Should any change be made to the framework established by **ss 3** and **4 HRA 1998**?

- Are there instances where, as a consequence of domestic courts and tribunals seeking to read and give effect to legislation compatibly with the Convention rights (as required by **s 3**), legislation has been interpreted in a manner inconsistent with the intention of the UK Parliament in enacting it? If yes, should **s 3** be amended (or repealed)?

- If **s 3** should be amended or repealed, should that change be applied to interpretation of legislation enacted before the amendment/repeal takes effect? If yes, what should be done about previous **s 3** interpretations adopted by the courts?

- Should declarations of incompatibility (under **s 4**) be considered as part of the initial process of interpretation rather than as a matter of last resort, so as to enhance the role of Parliament in determining how any incompatibility should be addressed?

- What remedies should be available to domestic courts when considering challenges to designated derogation orders made under **s 14(1)**?

- Under the current framework, how have courts and tribunals dealt with provisions of subordinate legislation that are incompatible with the Convention rights? Is any change required?

- In what circumstances does the **HRA 1998** apply to acts of public authorities taking place outside the territory of the UK? What are the implications of the current position? Is there a case for change?

- Should the remedial order process, as set out in **s 10** and **Sch 2 HRA 1998**, be modified, for example by enhancing the role of Parliament?

KEY CASES

CASE	FACTS	PRINCIPLE
Douglas v Hello! Ltd [2001] 2 WLR 992	This was an application for an injunction to restrain publication of unauthorized wedding photographs.	The Court of Appeal laid down principles relating to **s 12 HRA 1998**.
L v Birmingham City Council [2008] 1 AC 95	The question was whether the owners and proprietors of a care home who took people on behalf of a local authority was a public authority for the purposes of **s 6 HRA 1998**.	The provision of care and accommodation by a private company, as opposed to its regulation and supervision under statutory rules, is not an inherently public function and falls outside the ambit of **s 6(3)(b)**.
R v A [2002] 1 AC 45	The House of Lords was asked to interpret **s 41 Youth Justice and Criminal Evidence Act 1999** in a manner which is consistent with **Art 6 ECHR**. The section concerns the admissibility of evidence in rape cases relating to consent.	The test when applying the interpretative obligation under **s 3 HRA 1998**, is whether the evidential material was nevertheless so relevant to the issue of consent that to exclude it would endanger the fairness of the trial under **Art 6**. Where that test is satisfied the evidence should not be excluded.
R v Secretary of State for the Home Department, ex p Greenfield [2005] 1 WLR 673	The claimant was a prisoner who applied for judicial review of the deputy controller's decisions, contending that they infringed his right to a fair trial under **Art 6 ECHR**, as scheduled to the **HRA 1998**. He sought damages for violations of **Art 6**.	The House of Lords laid down significant principles concerning awards of damages under **s 8 HRA 1998**.

CASE	FACTS	PRINCIPLE
R (on the application of Alconbury Developments Ltd) v Secretary of State for the Environment, Transport and the Regions [2001] 2 WLR 1389	This case concerned several powers granted to the Secretary of State by the **Transport and Works Act 1992**, the **Town and Country Planning Act 1990**, the **Highways Act 1980**, and the **Acquisition of Land Act 1981**. The claimants sought declarations of incompatibility under **s 4 HRA 1998** on the ground that they were incompatible with **Art 6 ECHR**.	The impugned powers of the Secretary of State were not incompatible with Art 6(1).

KEY DEBATES

Topic	'Taking the Next Step? Achieving Another Bill of Rights'
Author/Academic	Colin Harvey
Viewpoint	Examines the debate over the potential implementation of a new UK constitutional Bill of Rights in terms of what it may mean in practice.
Source	(2011) 1 European Human Rights Law Review 24–42

Topic	'The Right to a Fair Trial and the Arbitration Act 1996: Apparent Conflicts Leave the English Courts Unmoved'
Author/Academic	Paul Stothard
Viewpoint	Assesses the approach of the courts to the application of **Art 6 ECHR** to commercial arbitration proceedings in England and Wales, falling under the courts supervision by virtue of the **Arbitration Act 1996**. Considers the **HRA 1998** and the right of access to a court under **Art 6**, commercial arbitration, and civil rights, the waiver of **Art 6**, case law guidance on the impact of **Art 6** on arbitration, and **Art 6** and the court's supervisory procedure. Argues that it is unlikely that **Art 6** can be regarded as a basis to challenge an arbitration agreement.
Source	(2008) 29(1) Business Law Review 2–6

Topic	'The Executive, the Parole Board and Article 5 ECHR: Progress within "An Unhappy State of Affairs"?'
Author/Academic	Patricia Londono
Viewpoint	Discusses the Court of Appeal decisions in: (1) *R (on the application of Brooke) v Parole Board* (2008) on whether the Parole Board was sufficiently independent to meet the requirements of **Art 5(4)** and **(2) ECHR**; and (2) *R (on the application of Walker) v Secretary of State for the Home Department* (2008) on whether failure to provide offenders imprisoned for public protection with rehabilitation programmes to assist them to demonstrate that their detention was no longer necessary was unlawful and their continued detention after expiry of their minimum term infringed Art 5.
Source	(2008) 67 Cambridge Law Journal 230–233

Topic	'Negligence Liability for Failing to Prevent Crime: The Human Rights Dimension'
Author/Academic	Iain Steele
Viewpoint	Comments on the Court of Appeal decision in *Smith v Chief Constable of Sussex* (2008) on whether a man who allegedly told police of threats made against him by a former partner could sue them in negligence after he was attacked by that person on the grounds that they did nothing to protect him. Reviews the court's approach to the principles set out by the House of Lords in *Hill v Chief Constable of West Yorkshire* (1989) and its analysis of the subsequent impact of the **HRA 1998** on common law negligence actions against the police. Notes the forthcoming appeal to the House of Lords (as it was at that time).
Source	(2008) 67 Cambridge Law Journal 239–241

Topic	May Day, May Day: Policing Protest
Author/Academic	ATH Smith
Viewpoint	Discusses the Court of Appeal decision in *Austin v Commissioner of Police of the Metropolis* (2007) on whether the police had been justified in depriving the claimants of their liberty, by cordoning them within an area for seven hours along with over 1,000 protestors, on the ground that it was necessary to prevent a breach of the peace. Considers whether the defendant was required to prove that the claimants had behaved unlawfully or had threatened to breach the peace. Assesses whether the deprivation of liberty was such that it breached the claimants' rights under **Art 5 ECHR**.
Source	(2008) 67 Cambridge Law Journal 10–12

EXAM QUESTIONS

Essay question 1

Explain what is meant by 'Convention right' and how the **Human Rights Act 1998** incorporates such rights into British law.

Essay question 2

Critically assess the roles of Parliament, the executive, and the judiciary in the enforcement of human rights.

 Online Resources

For outline answers to these essay questions, as well as interactive key cases and multiple-choice questions, please visit the online resources.
www.oup.com/he/faragher-concentrate7e

 Concentrate Q&As

 For more questions and answers on public law, see the *Concentrate Q&A: Public Law* by Richard Clements.

Go to the end of this book to view **sample pages**.

15 Police powers, public order, and terrorism

KEY FACTS

- Police officers detect and prevent crime, bring offenders to justice, keep the peace, and protect people and their property from injury and damage.

- The **Police and Criminal Evidence Act 1984**, as amended, and its Codes of Practice, contain rules concerning police powers of stop, search, entry, seizure of property, arrest, detention, and treatment of suspects.

- The **Public Order Act 1986** concerns the control of protests and assemblies.

- Police powers contained in the 1986 Act were extended by the **Criminal Justice and Public Order Act 1994** and the **Anti-social Behaviour Act 2003**.

- The **Serious Organised Crime and Police Act 2005** made important changes to the rules governing powers of arrest and introduced further restrictions to the right to protest in parts of Central London.

- The **Terrorism Act 2000** introduced comprehensive counter-terrorist measures throughout the UK.

- The **Anti-terrorism Crime and Security Act 2001** focuses on terrorist funding, intelligence gathering, immigration, and the elimination of organized crime.

- The **Terrorism Act 2006** extends the law further.

Police powers

The role of the police was explained by Lord Steyn in the House of Lords' decision in *Brooks v Commissioner of Police of the Metropolis* (2005) at 1509. He said that the prime function of the police is the preservation of the Queen's peace. The police must concentrate on preventing the commission of crime; protecting life and property; and apprehending criminals and preserving evidence. The organization of the police in England and Wales is contained in the **Police Act 1996** as amended by the **Police Reform Act 2002** and the **Police Reform and Social Responsibility Act 2011**. Under current statutory provisions a police force is maintained within each police area. The **Police Reform and Social Responsibility Act 2011** provides that police areas outside London will have a directly elected Police and Crime Commissioner and local policing bodies or panels. In London this role is carried out by the Mayor of London supported by the Mayor's Office for Policing and Crime. **Chapter 3 Police Reform and Social Responsibility Act 2011** sets out the functions of elected local policing bodies. The Police and Crime Commissioner for a police area and, in London, the Mayor's Office for Policing and Crime, must publish and have regard to an annual police and crime plan which sets out the body's police and crime objectives and how policing will be carried out in their area. The elected local policing body for a police area may also make a crime and disorder reduction grant to any person. The 2011 Act also obliges local policing bodies to publish progress reports on what they are doing and obtain the views of the community on policing. Police forces outside London are organized under the direction of a chief constable and a deputy or assistant chief constable. The other ranks, which may be held in a police force, are superintendent, inspector, sergeant, and constable. The creation of additional ranks may be made by regulation. A police force may employ civilians to assist the police force to discharge its functions. London is composed of the Metropolitan Police District and the City of London Police Area. The Metropolitan Police is headed by the Commissioner of Police of the Metropolis. **Section 56 London Police Act 1839** empowers the Common Council of the City of London to set up a police committee for the purpose of exercising such powers in connection with the police as the Common Council delegates to it. The City of London Police is led by the Commissioner of Police of the City of London.

The **Police and Criminal Evidence Act 1984 (PACE)**, as amended, and the Codes of Practice made under it contain rules concerning stop and search (**ss 1–7**); entry, search, and seizure of property (**ss 8–23**); arrest (**ss 24–33**); detention (**ss 34–51**); and treatment of suspects (**ss 53–65**).

The Codes of Practice

Code A deals with stop and search powers prior to making an arrest. Code B deals with the power to enter and search premises and seize property. Code C concerns detention, treatment, and questioning of non-terrorist suspects. Code D deals with identification of wanted persons and the keeping of accurate and reliable criminal records. Code E deals with the tape recording of interviews with suspects in the police station. Code F deals with the visual recording with sound of interviews with suspects. Code G deals with powers of arrest. Code H sets out the requirements for the detention, treatment, and questioning of suspects related to terrorism in police custody.

REVISION TIP

When learning police powers under **PACE** you should adopt a chronological approach starting with the point of first contact and ending with the decision of the police either to charge or release a suspect.

Stop and search

Acting on reasonable suspicion a police officer may stop and search anyone in order find stolen goods, drugs, an offensive weapon, any article made or adapted for use in certain offences, for example a burglary or theft, knives, or any items which could damage or destroy property. This includes spray-paint cans. A police officer may use reasonable force if the person being searched will not cooperate. Force, however, should be used only as a last resort.

In *R v Bristol (Christopher)* (2007) the Court of Appeal had to decide whether a drug search was unlawful because the police officer failed, before commencing the search, to take the reasonable steps required by **s 2 PACE**. This section requires a police constable to give their name and the name of the police station to which they are attached. The Court of Appeal held that the search was unlawful and the conviction was quashed.

The power to enter and search premises

Police officers may enter and search premises if they have obtained a search warrant, or have a statutory right to enter and search, or have obtained the permission of the owner or occupier.

If they have a search warrant, the police must search the premises at a reasonable hour and, if the owner is in occupation, with their cooperation. When they seek entry to any private premises, the police officers must identify themselves (and, if they are not in uniform, show their warrant card) and explain why they want to search, the rights of the occupier, and whether the search is made with a search warrant or not. Having obtained a search warrant the police may force entry if: the occupier has refused entry, it is impossible to communicate with the occupier, the occupier is absent, the premises are unoccupied, or they have reasonable grounds for believing that if they do not force entry it would hinder the search or someone would be placed in danger.

Police officers have statutory authority to enter private premises without a warrant in order to deal with a breach of the peace or prevent it, enforce an arrest warrant, arrest a person in connection with certain offences, recapture someone who has escaped from custody, or save life or prevent serious damage to property. Unless entering premises to save life or protect property, a police officer must have reasonable grounds to believe that the person for whom they are searching is there. Police officers may search premises occupied by an arrested person or visited by an arrested person during or immediately prior to their arrest. The police must reasonably believe that they might find evidence connected with the crime an arrested person is accused of committing.

Seizure of property

Police officers should seize goods only if they have reasonable grounds to believe that the goods have been obtained illegally or are evidence in relation to an offence. The police must also have reasonable grounds to believe that it is necessary to seize the goods to prevent them being lost, stolen, or destroyed.

Arrest

If a private citizen arrests anyone, they must inform the arrested person of the charge or the crime they are suspected of having committed. A police officer arresting someone without warrant must tell the arrested person the charge upon which the arrest is being made or the facts which are said to constitute the crime they are alleged to have committed.

This information must be given to the person being arrested at the time of their arrest or at the first reasonable opportunity after the arrest. This was determined by the House of Lords in *Christie v Leachinsky* (1947).

Police officers can arrest a person if they have a warrant. They may arrest a person without warrant if they have reasonable grounds to suspect that the person being arrested has committed certain offences; is committing certain offences; is about to commit certain offences.

The **Serious Organised Crime and Police Act 2005** gives police officers the power to arrest a person to find out the person's name and address. A person may also be arrested to prevent them causing physical injury to themselves or any other person; suffering physical injury; causing loss of or damage to property; committing an offence against public decency; or causing an unlawful obstruction of the highway. Police officers may also make an arrest in order to protect a child or other vulnerable person; allow the prompt and effective investigation of the offence the arrested person is suspected of committing or the conduct which has prompted their arrest; and prevent any prosecution for the offence from being hindered by the disappearance of the person being arrested.

Detention

At the police station, the arrested person has the right to: inform someone of their arrest, seek legal advice, and examine and read the Codes of Practice.

Limits to detention

Nobody should be detained for longer than 24 hours without charge. A police officer with the rank of superintendent (or above) can authorize detention for a further 12 hours. Magistrates can authorize further detentions up to a maximum of 96 hours. Once charged, if a person is still in detention they should be brought before the magistrates the next day (but not on Christmas Day, Good Friday, or any Sunday). At the time of writing, if a person is arrested as a suspected terrorist, different rules apply. A judge can authorize continued detention, in stages, for up to 28 days.

R (on the application of G) v Chief Constable of West Yorkshire [2008] 1 WLR 550

The question was whether a custody officer was entitled to detain an arrested person whilst they sought guidance from the Crown Prosecution Service under **s 37A PACE** on how to proceed with the charges.

The Court of Appeal held that **s 37(7) PACE** deals comprehensively with the alternatives available to a custody officer. These do not include a power to postpone the charging decision for the purpose of obtaining advice from the Crown Prosecution Service without admitting the suspect to bail. Such a power cannot be inferred by reference to guidance issued by the Director of Public Prosecutions. G's detention without charge was illegal.

Public order

 REVISION TIP

At this stage in your revision you should link police powers and public order with the human rights principles discussed in Chapter 14. There are also 'rule of law' implications to this topic which link up with material discussed in Chapter 3. You should now take time to consider the material you revised in these chapters. Doing this will help you when answering essay questions in the examination.

The relevant statutes are the **Public Order Act 1986**, the **Criminal Justice and Public Order Act 1994**, the **Anti-social Behaviour Act 2003**, and the **Serious Organised Crime and Police Act 2005**.

Public Order Act 1986 as amended

Section 11 requires at least six clear days' written notice to be given to the police before most public processions, including details of the intended time and route, and giving the name and address of at least one person proposing to organize it. **Sections 12–14** give police power to impose conditions on processions 'to prevent serious public disorder, serious criminal damage or serious disruption to the life of the community'; ban public processions for up to three months by applying to the local authority for a banning order which needs subsequent confirmation from the Home Secretary; impose conditions on assemblies 'to prevent serious public disorder, serious criminal damage or serious disruption to the life of the community'. The conditions are limited to specifying the number of people who may take part, the location of the assembly, and its maximum duration.

Criminal Justice and Public Order Act 1994

Sections 34–39 substantially changed the right to silence of an accused person, allowing for inferences to be drawn from their silence. Sections 54–59 gave the police greater rights to take and retain intimate body samples. Section 60 increased police powers of unsupervised 'stop and search'. Section 70 prohibited trespassory assemblies.

Anti-social Behaviour Act 2003

Section 57 amends the definition of public assembly in s 16 Public Order Act 1986 from '20 or more persons' to '2 or more persons'. Section 58 amends s 63 Criminal Justice and Public Order Act 1994 to extend it to cover raves where 20 or more persons are present. Section 59 amends ss 68 and 69 Criminal Justice and Public Order Act 1994. Aggravated trespass covers trespass in buildings, as well as in the open air. Section 60 inserts a new s 62A into the Criminal Justice and Public Order Act 1994. A senior police officer may direct a person to leave land and remove any vehicle or other property with him.

Serious Organised Crime and Police Act 2005

Apart from changing the rules governing arrest this Act created an exclusion zone of one kilometre from any point in Parliament Square within which the right to demonstrate is restricted. Trafalgar Square is not included. Demonstrators must apply to the Metropolitan Police Commissioner six days in advance, or if this is not reasonably practicable then no less than 24 hours in advance.

Austin v Commissioner of Police of the Metropolis [2007] Ewca Civ 989

The Court of Appeal had to decide whether the police had been justified in depriving the claimants of their liberty, by cordoning them within an area for seven hours along with over 1,000 protestors, on the ground that it was necessary to prevent a breach of the peace.

In extreme and exceptional circumstances it is lawful for the police to contain demonstrators and members of the public caught up in that demonstration, even though they themselves do not appear to be about to commit a breach of the peace, where it is necessary to prevent an imminent breach of the peace by others, and no other means would achieve that.

LOOKING FOR EXTRA MARKS?

Police powers and public order are highly controversial subjects which have given rise to a great deal of academic argument. Some of these arguments are contained in articles referred to in the Key debates section at the end of this chapter. As essay questions, in particular, require you to demonstrate evidence of wider reading, you should read these articles, as well as those recommended in your course materials, and your recommended standard textbook.

Terrorism

REVISION TIP

This topic not only links up with human rights and the rule of law, as do police powers and public order, but also with separation of powers considered in Chapter 4. You should now reconsider the issues discussed in Chapter 3. This will help you to answer any essay question which focuses on the relationship between the executive and the judiciary or the nature and extent of judicial independence.

According to **s 1 Terrorism Act 2000** as amended by the **Terrorism Act 2006**, terrorism means the use or threat of action involving serious violence against a person; or serious damage to property; or danger to life; or a serious risk to the health and safety of the public; or interference with an electronic system.

The use or threat of action must be designed to influence the government or an international governmental organization or to intimidate the public or a section of the public. The use or threat of action must be made for the purpose of advancing a political, religious, or ideological cause.

The **Terrorism Act 2000** made it illegal for certain terrorist groups to operate in the UK. The groups listed are called proscribed organizations and include international terrorist groups. The police were given greater powers to help prevent and investigate terrorism, including wider stop and search powers; and the power to detain suspects after arrest for up to 28 days (periods of more than two days must be approved by a magistrate). This period was extended to 28 days under the **Terrorism Act 2006**. A number of new offences were introduced allowing the police to arrest people suspected of inciting terrorist acts or seeking or providing training for terrorist purposes at home or overseas and providing instruction or training in the use of firearms, explosives, or chemical, biological, or nuclear weapons.

The **Anti-terrorism, Crime and Security Act 2001** aimed to cut off terrorist funding; ensure that government departments and agencies can collect and share information required for countering the terrorist threat; streamline relevant immigration procedures; ensure the security of the nuclear and aviation industries; improve security of dangerous substances that may be targeted/used by terrorists; extend police powers available to relevant forces; and ensure that we can meet our European obligations in the area of police and judicial cooperation and our international obligations to counter bribery and corruption.

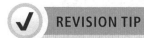

REVISION TIP

The measures enacted by the 2001 Act were considered by the House of Lords in *A v Secretary of State for the Home Department* (2005).

The **Prevention of Terrorism Act 2005** introduced control orders, which impose conditions on where a person can go and what they can do. These must be signed by the Home Secretary and confirmed by a judge within seven days. A control order may impose conditions banning possession or use of specified articles or substances; prohibiting the use of certain services, such as the internet or phones; restricting work or business; restricting association or communication with certain individuals, or other people generally; restricting the person's place of residence or who is allowed into the premises; requiring the person to be at specified places or in a particular area at certain times or days; and restricting movements within the UK or international travel.

A control order may also contain a specific 24-hour ban on movements and requirements to surrender a passport; give access to specified people to their home; allow officials to search their home; let officials remove items from premises for tests; be monitored by electronic tagging or other means; provide information to an official on demand; and report at a specified time and place.

Secretary of State for the Home Department v JJ [2007] UKHL 45, Secretary of State for the Home Department v MB [2007] UKHL 46, Secretary of State for the Home Department v E [2007] UKHL 47

In all three cases, the House of Lords had to consider whether the obligations placed upon the appellants breached their rights under **Art 5 European Convention on Human Rights (ECHR)**; compliance with the Secretary of State's duty under **s 8(2) HRA 1998** was a condition precedent to the making of an order; and, a control order constituted a criminal charge for the purposes of **Art 6 ECHR**; and procedures which allowed reliance on undisclosed material breached **Art 6**. The House of Lords determined, in these cases, that control orders must be subject to 'civil fair trial procedure', which has been breached in some cases by the 'special advocate procedure'. This procedure allows the government to release sensitive information to terror suspects' security-screened lawyers, on the condition that this information is not passed on to the suspect. Moreover, the Law Lords ruled that control orders do not constitute a criminal penalty and hence do not engage the much stricter requirements of 'criminal fair trial procedure'. The cases were referred back to the High Court.

The **Terrorism Act 2006** creates new offences including the following: acts preparatory to terrorism; incitement or encouragement to terrorism; dissemination of terrorist publications; terrorist training offences. The **Terrorism Act 2006** also makes amendments to existing legislation, including introducing warrants to enable the police to search any property owned or controlled by a terrorist suspect; extending terrorism stop and search powers to cover bays and estuaries; extending police powers to detain suspects after arrest for up to 28 days (though periods of more than two days must be approved by a judicial authority); improved search powers at ports; and increased flexibility of the proscription regime, including the power to proscribe groups that glorify terrorism.

The Counter-Terrorism Act 2008

The **Counter-Terrorism Act 2008** amends the law on terrorism in a number of ways. Its provisions affect the gathering and sharing of information for, among other things, counterterrorist purposes. This includes the disclosure and sharing of information by and with the security services. It also makes provisions relating to the post-charge questioning of terrorism suspects, the prosecution and sentencing of those charged with terrorism offences, the financial aspects of terrorism, sensitive information, and the creation of new powers and offences relating to terrorism.

The Counter-Terrorism and Security Act 2015

This Act:

- strengthens the legal powers and capabilities of law enforcement and intelligence agencies to disrupt terrorism and prevent individuals from being radicalized;
- ensures that the law enforcement and intelligence agencies can disrupt the ability of people to travel abroad to fight, and control their return to the UK;
- enhances operational capabilities to monitor and control the actions of those in the UK who pose a threat, and helps to combat the underlying ideology that supports terrorism.

This Act forms part of the CONTEST strategy, the aims of which are to:

- pursue: the investigation and disruption of terrorist attacks;
- prevent: work to stop people becoming terrorists or supporting terrorism and extremism;
- protect: improving our protective security to stop a terrorist attack; and
- prepare: working to minimize the impact of an attack and to recover from it as quickly as possible.

In addition the Act strengthens the independent oversight arrangements for UK counter-terrorism legislation by extending the statutory remit of the Independent Reviewer of Terrorism Legislation and enabling a more flexible reporting schedule, and by providing for the creation of a Privacy and Civil Liberties Board which will support the Independent Reviewer to discharge their statutory functions.

LOOKING FOR EXTRA MARKS?

This is a topic which has generated a huge debate, specific aspects of which may be examined as essay questions. As with other aspects of this topic, you should follow up your reading of this chapter with accounts of this debate in your recommended standard textbook and other materials recommended in the Key debates section.

Table 15.1 The measures introduced by the Act

TRAVEL	TPIMS	COMMUNICATION	BORDER CONTROL	IDEOLOGY	INSURANCE
The Act places temporary restrictions on travel where a person is suspected of involvement in terrorism.	The Act enhances existing Terrorism Prevention and Investigation Measures.	The Act enhances law enforcement agencies' ability to investigate terrorism and serious crime by extending the retention of relevant communications data to include data that will help to identify who is responsible for sending a communication on the internet or accessing an internet communications service.	The Act strengthens security arrangements in relation to the border and to aviation, maritime, and rail transport.	The Act reduces the risk of people being drawn into terrorism, by enhancing the programmes that combat the underlying ideology which supports terrorism through improved engagement from partner organizations and consistency of delivery.	The Act amends existing terrorism legislation to clarify the law in relation to both insurance payments made in response to terrorist demands and the power to examine goods under the **Terrorism Act 2000**.

 KEY CASES

CASE	FACTS	PRINCIPLE
A v Secretary of State for the Home Department [2005] 2 AC 68	The House of Lords had to decide whether s 23 **Anti-terrorism, Crime and Security Act 2001** was compatible with Convention rights incorporated by the **Human Rights Act 1998**.	The House of Lords stated and applied the following principles: 1. personal liberty is among the most fundamental of rights; 2. although national security is a matter of political judgement for the executive and Parliament, a court is required, when Convention rights are in issue, to give effective protection by adopting an intensive review of whether such a right has been impugned; and 3. the courts are not precluded by any doctrine of deference from examining the proportionality of a measure taken to restrict such a right.
Austin v Commissioner of Police of the Metropolis [2007] EWCA Civ 989	The Court of Appeal had to decide whether the police had been justified in depriving the claimants of their liberty, by cordoning them within an area for seven hours along with over 1,000 protestors, on the ground that it was necessary to prevent a breach of the peace.	In extreme and exceptional circumstances it is lawful for the police to contain demonstrators and members of the public caught up in a demonstration even though they themselves do not appear to be about to commit a breach of the peace, where it is necessary to prevent an imminent breach of the peace by others, and no other means would achieve that.

CASE	FACTS	PRINCIPLE
R (on the application of G) v Chief Constable of West Yorkshire [2008] 1 WLR 550	The question was whether a custody officer was entitled to detain an arrestee whilst he sought guidance from the Crown Prosecution Service under **s 37A PACE** on how to proceed with the charges.	**Section 37(7) PACE** dealt comprehensively with the alternatives available to a custody officer who had determined that he had before him sufficient evidence to charge an arrested person; that those alternatives did not include a power to postpone the charging decision for the purpose of obtaining advice from the Crown Prosecution Service without admitting the suspect to bail; that such a power could not be inferred by reference to guidance issued by the Director of Public Prosecutions under **s 37A**, which was not referred to in **s 37(7)** which was required to be consistent with and limited by the alternatives found in that subsection.

KEY DEBATES

Topic	'Terrorism: Prevention of Terrorism Act 2005 ss. 2 and 3—Non-derogating Control Order—Whether "Deprivation of Liberty" under Article 5 European Convention on Human Rights'
Author/Academic	Clive Walker
Viewpoint	Comments on three House of Lords' decisions on issues raised about non-derogating control orders made under **ss 2** and **3 Prevention of Terrorism Act 2005**.
Source	[2008] Criminal Law Review 486–503

Topic	'The Widening Gyre: Counter-terrorism, Human Rights and the Rule of Law'
Author/Academic	Arthur Chaskalson
Viewpoint	Examines the parallels between some counter-terrorism measures introduced around the world in the wake of the US attacks of September 11, 2001 and the legal regime introduced in South Africa to support the policy of apartheid.
Source	(2008) 67 Cambridge Law Journal 69–91

Topic	'Evidence and Procedure: Pre-charge Detention'
Author/Academic	Case comment
Viewpoint	Notes the Court of Appeal decision in *R (on the application of G) v Chief Constable of West Yorkshire* (2008).
Source	(2008) 8 Criminal Law Week 1–3

Topic	'Evidence and Procedure: Stop and Search'
Author/Academic	Case comment
Viewpoint	Reports of the Court of Appeal decision in *R v Bristol (Christopher)* (2007).
Source	(2008) 3 Criminal Law Week 1–2

Topic	'May Day, May Day: Policing Protest'
Author/Academic	ATH Smith
Viewpoint	Discusses the Court of Appeal decision in *Austin v Commissioner of Police of the Metropolis* (2007).
Source	(2008) 67 Cambridge Law Journal 10–12

 Q EXAM QUESTIONS

Essay question 1

Explain the nature and extent of police powers to detain suspects and indicate how these powers are limited.

Essay question 2

Critically assess the effectiveness of the **Serious Organised Crime and Police Act 2005** as a means of controlling protest in Central London.

 Online Resources

For outline answers to these essay questions, as well as interactive key cases and multiple-choice questions, please visit the online resources.
www.oup.com/he/faragher-concentrate7e

 C Concentrate Q&As

For more questions and answers on public law, see the *Concentrate Q&A: Public Law* by Richard Clements.

Go to the end of this book to view **sample pages**.

Exam essentials

Tips on linking the topics together

You need to acquire a thorough knowledge of the whole subject in order to achieve first-class marks in the examination. Nothing less than a complete answer will do. This requires awareness of how topics are related to each other. In Public Law the topics link together in a number of ways.

Revision exercise: note down areas of Public Law which you can draw links between and ways in which they are related.

Some examples of topics which are linked appear at the end of this guide.

Additionally, you should, by now, have acquired a set of past examination papers as part of your course materials. Read through them and note how the topics are combined.

Pointers for key topics/questions often tested

The key topics, which are unavoidably tested each year in Public Law examinations, will have been thoroughly covered by your subject lecturers and tutors in lectures and seminars. Review your Study Guide/Learning Materials together with your lecture and seminar notes. Record how much time was spent on each topic and the amount of detail and advice on further reading that was given to you by your lecturers and tutors. Read and analyse the past examination papers provided by your college or university. This analysis should cover between three to five years depending on what is available to you. Read all the questions and identify the topics tested in each question. List the topics in order from the most tested to the least tested topic.

Material to read and reference

At this point you should read and reference the key principles by reviewing your lecture notes, the relevant sections in your textbook, and this revision guide.

Common mistakes to avoid

Before the examination

Don't:

- leave revision to the last minute;
- restrict your revision topics to the number of questions you are required to answer in the examination in the hope that your questions come up; or
- adopt an unstructured and untimetabled approach to revision.

Above all don't panic!

During the examination

The most common mistakes students make during the examination could be avoided if they did the following:

- read through the whole of the examination paper during reading time and write out an outline answer giving essential details including cases and statutes to each question;

- answer every question in the examination paper that they are expected to answer; and

- organize their time effectively by dividing up their time as equally as may be between all the questions.

Ideas for revision activities

Find out about your exam

Find out about the examination. Obtain past examination papers and read them thoroughly. How long is the examination? Do you have reading time? How many questions do you have to answer? How many of the questions are problem-based or essay type?

Work out what you need to know

Review your notes and materials looking for gaps in your knowledge of key topics which are often tested. Make a list of things you need to know to top up your knowledge. Locate, read, and extract the information you need to fill the gaps.

Make a revision timetable

Set aside time each day for your revision and stick to it. It is better to do an hour each day of the week than seven hours on a Friday!

Have a programme of activities

Your lecturers and tutors may have organized a programme of revision activities as part of your course. If so you should follow their guidance and participate fully in the programme. In addition, the following may help:

- active reading in which you choose a past examination question on the topic you are re-vising and as you read use the material you are reading to answer the question;

- plan and answer past exam questions under timed conditions. Review your answers and look for ways to improve them;

- review your assignments; and

- review, reorganize, and refine your notes.

Commonly linked topics in Public Law

The following list is not exhaustive:

- constitutional conventions link up with the monarchy and Royal Prerogative, the executive, the nature and functions of Parliament, and the legislative process;
- rule of law links up with separation of powers, tribunals, judicial review, and human rights;
- separation of powers may be linked to human rights, judicial review, tribunals, and the rule of law;
- sovereignty of Parliament may be linked to separation of powers, the monarchy as part of the legislative process, constitutional conventions, and the Royal Prerogative in relation to Parliament and the legislative process and human rights; and
- EU law may be linked up with sovereignty of Parliament.

Outline answers

CHAPTER 2

Problem answer

Parties and causes of action

In any prospective legal proceedings the Leader of the Opposition would be the claimant, claiming a mandatory injunction to compel the incumbent Prime Minister and the other members of the government to resign. The application would be defended by the Attorney General on behalf of the government.

Cause of action: application for a mandatory injunction

The relevant constitutional conventions must first be explained.

Reference re Amendment to the Constitution of Canada (1982):

- Are there precedents?
- Do the actors consider themselves bound?
- Is there a good reason for the rule?

Define relevant conventions:

- government must have the confidence of the House of Commons;
- if the government loses the confidence of the House of Commons the Prime Minister should offer the Queen their resignation and ask for dissolution of Parliament and a General Election;
- the Queen is bound to accept the government's resignation; and
- in the event of a general election the Queen must ask the leader of the party with a majority in the House of Commons to form a government.

Apply *Attorney General v Jonathan Cape Ltd* (1975) grounds: it is against the public interest for the government to remain in office without the confidence of the House of Commons; that there is no other facet of the public interest in conflict with and more compelling than that relied upon; and that the Prime Minister's course of action is unconstitutional.

Relevant counter arguments

The court has no jurisdiction to grant the injunction because constitutional conventions are not enforceable in the courts: *Madzimbamuto v Larder Burke* (1969).

That because he has really 'won' the election by polling more votes than the Opposition his continuance in office will not prejudice the constitutional convention that the government must have the confidence of the House of Commons; and that his continuance in office is not contrary to the public interest.

This is based on *Attorney General v Jonathan Cape Ltd* (1975).

Conclusion—the court would probably decline jurisdiction.

The constitutional position of the Queen

You should break this stage down into two parts.

Part one: the Queen's legal powers

The Queen is the only person authorized to:

- dissolve (prorogue) and call Parliaments;
- appoint ministers; and
- appoint a prime minister and ask him or her to form a government.

The source of these powers is common law under the Royal Prerogative.

Part two: constitutional conventions

Whether the Queen is obliged to accept the Prime Minister's resignation; and whom she may ask to form the next government.

The relevant conventions are:

- the Queen acts on the advice of ministers; and
- Her Majesty's Government must have the confidence of the House of Commons.

You should explain the consequences:

- she may wait to see if the Prime Minister can form a coalition government;
- if not she is obliged to accept the Prime Minister's resignation; and
- ask the leader of the party with a majority in the House of Commons to form a government.

CHAPTER 6

Problem answer

Introduction

In this part of your answer you should identify: the parties, the causes of action, and the issues.

The jurisdictional issue

The relevant case law is:

- *Stockdale v Hansard* (1839);
- *Edinburgh & Dalkeith Railway v Wauchope* (1842);
- *Lee v Bude & Torrington Junction Railway* (1871);
- *Pickin v British Rail Board* (1974).

The effect of ss 2 and 3 of the 2020 Act

In this part of your answer you should: define express and implied repeal; define 'entrenchment'; apply the rule that Parliament cannot bind its successors.

Elizabeth could rely on:

- *Vauxhall Estates Ltd v Liverpool Corporation* (1932);
- *Ellen Street Estates v Minister of Health* (1934).

The doctor could rely on:

- *R v Military Governor of NDU Internment Camp* (1924);
- *AG of New South Wales v Trethowan* (1932);
- *Harris v Minister of the Interior* (1952).

Conclusion: entrenchment clauses are not effective against express or implied repeal.

Prospective formula

Here, you should define prospective formula and explain its effect on express and implied repeal. If the 2021 Act expressly repeals the 2020 Act, the 2021 Act prevails.

CHAPTER 7

Problem answer

This type of problem question asks you to write an opinion on selected issues, from a lawyer's point of view, to a specified audience, in this case

the Queen's Private Secretary. In the introductory section you need to identify all the issues upon which you are required to advise the Queen's Private Secretary. You can also use this section to define basic concepts. This question asks you to advise the Queen's Private Secretary on the role of the monarchy in the conduct and exercise of personal prerogatives. It also requires you to look at the interrelationship between the Royal Prerogative and constitutional conventions that are relevant to the role and duties of the monarch, including government formation, the appointment of the Prime Minister and the summoning and dissolution of Parliament.

Starting with the role and duties of the monarch you should begin this section by defining the Royal Prerogative quoting Blackstone and Dicey.

After this you should go on to give relevant examples of the personal prerogatives of the monarch acting as head of state. Of particular relevance is government formation and the appointment of the Prime Minister.

In the next part of your answer you have to concentrate on the relevant constitutional conventions. You should define constitutional conventions so that your advice clearly states what constitutional conventions are. You should use Dicey's definition of constitutional conventions and then refer to all the relevant constitutional conventions which inform the monarch as to how to exercise their powers in relation to the appointment of the Prime Minister.

In the concluding part of your answer you should concentrate on presenting the outcomes of your analysis and application of the rules. You may agree with Rodney Brazier in *Constitutional Practice*, 3rd edn (1999) where he says that the monarch's legal power to appoint a Prime Minister must be used to enhance the democratic process rather than to pre-empt it.

CHAPTER 8

Problem answer

Introduction

In this part of your answer it is important to emphasize that the Home Secretary's position is governed by constitutional conventions which cannot be enforced in the courts. Distinguish between law and convention (Dicey).

Collective Cabinet responsibility

You should begin by defining collective Cabinet responsibility in the way that Lord Widgery CJ did in *Attorney General v Jonathan Cape* (1975).

You should stress that the obligation is a political rather than a legal one.

The political and legal accountability of the Home Secretary

According to the *Crichel Down Principle* based on the Crichel Down Affair (1954) accountability arises when a civil servant:

- has carried out the minister's explicit order;
- acts in accordance with policy laid down by the minister; or
- makes a mistake or causes a delay.

As to whether the Home Secretary is politically bound to resign, you should consider:

- the Scott Report findings;
- the Report of the Public Service Committee.

The legal accountability of the Home Secretary

The relevant principle is that ministers have legal responsibility for whatever happens in their departments. It is the minister who is sued, not the civil servant. The courts accept and recognize the convention that a civil servant often acts in the name of ministers. The relevant case law is:

- *Carltona v Commissioners of Works* (1943);
- *R v Skinner* (1968);
- *R v Secretary of State for the Home Department, ex p Oladehinde* (1991);
- *M v Home Office* (1993).

CHAPTER 10

Problem answer

Introduction: parties and causes of action

Claimants = Antonio and the Society of Ice Cream Manufacturers.

Defendant = the Food Standards Authority.

Cause of action = for judicial review. He will ask a judge to review the lawfulness of the decision of the Food Standards Authority.

Is the Food Standards Authority amenable to judicial review?

First consider *Datafin* criteria, bearing in mind that all the criteria have to be considered (*R v Panel on Take-overs and Mergers, ex p Datafin* (1987)).

Consider whether: the functions of the Food Standards Authority are governmental; it is an integral part of a government-supported scheme of regulation; and would the government introduce legislation through Parliament to set up a regulatory body if the Food Standards Authority did not exist.

Key case: *R v Disciplinary Committee of the Jockey Club, ex p Aga Khan* (1993).

Is the decision of the Food Standards Authority a public law matter?

Consider whether the context of the decision is the exercise of a public function and whether the claimant would be accused of abuse of process if he brought a claim using private law procedure.

Key cases: *O'Reilly v Mackman* (1982); *Clark v University of Lincolnshire and Humberside* (2000).

Does the Society of Ice Cream Manufacturers have the right to bring a claim for judicial review?

You should consider whether, in your opinion, the organization has sufficient interest taking into account all the relevant criteria set out in the cases above.

Key cases: *IRC v National Federation of the Self-Employed and Small Businesses* (1981); *R v Inspectorate of Pollution, ex p Greenpeace* (1994); *R v Secretary for State for Foreign Affairs, ex p World Development Movement* (1995).

Remedies and procedure

You should choose a remedy or combination of remedies and explain its effect. Then you should outline the initial procedural steps.

CHAPTER 11

Problem answer

Parties and causes of action

Claimant = Justin.

Defendants = the Commission and the Secretary of State.

Cause of Action = Judicial Review. The defendants are public authorities and the decisions being challenged are public law matters (*O'Reilly v Mackman* (1983)).

Basic procedural steps

Pre-action Protocol:

- alternative dispute resolution;
- letter before claim;
- letter in response.

Commencement of proceedings under **Pt 54, s 1 Civil Procedure Rules**:

- application for permission;
- to Administrative Court;
- within three months of the decision;
- using appropriate claim form; and
- supporting documents.

Grounds for judicial review

Has the defendant acted ultra vires? Define ultra vires. Relevant case law includes:

- *AG v Fulham Corporation* (1921);
- *Bromley LBC v GLC* (1983).

In this question, the following grounds, with reference to relevant cases, are to be considered:

Improper purpose

The relevant case law to which you should refer includes:

- *Congreve v Home Office* (1976);
- *R v Lewisham LBC, ex p Shell* (1988);
- *Wheeler v Leicester City Council* (1985).

Relevant considerations

R v Secretary of State for the Home Department, ex p Venables and Thompson (1998).

Lack of evidence

Coleen Properties v Minister of Housing and Local Government (1971).

Fettering discretion by policy

British Oxygen Co Ltd v Minster of Technology (1971).

Remedies

Choose the remedy you think is most appropriate. In this case it would be a quashing order to nullify the decision.

CHAPTER 12

Problem answer

Parties and causes of action

You should begin your answer by identifying the prospective claimant and the defendant.

Cause of Action = Judicial Review. The defendants are public authorities and the decisions being challenged are public law matters (*O'Reilly v Mackman* (1983)).

Basic procedural steps

Pre-action Protocol:

- alternative dispute resolution;
- letter before claim;
- letter in response.

Commencement of proceedings under **Pt 54, s 1 Civil Procedure Rules**:

- application for permission;
- to Administrative Court;
- within three months of the decision;
- using appropriate claim form; and
- supporting documents.

Grounds for judicial review

You should be aware that the grounds of illegality and irrationality run together and that there is usually a mixture of such issues in examination questions.

The starting point for considering the notion of unreasonableness is:

- *Roberts v Hopwood* (1925);
- *Associated Provincial Picture Houses Ltd v Wednesbury Corporation* (1948);
- *Backhouse v Lambeth LBC* (1972);
- *R v Ministry of Defence, ex p Smith* (1996).

Then consider proportionality:

- *Council of Civil Service Unions v Minister for the Civil Service* (1985);
- *R v Secretary of State for the Home Department, ex p Brind* (1991);
- *R (on the application of Alconbury Developments Ltd) v Secretary of State for the Environment, Transport and the Regions* (2003).

CHAPTER 13

Problem answer

Parties and causes of action

Claimant = Andrew.

Defendants = Estate Agents Licensing Bureau.

Cause of Action = Judicial Review. The defendants are public authorities and the decisions being challenged are public law matters (*O'Reilly v Mackman* (1983)).

Basic procedural steps

Pre-action Protocol:

- alternative dispute resolution;
- letter before claim;
- letter in response.

Commencement of proceedings under **Pt 54, s 1 Civil Procedure Rules**:

- application for permission;
- to Administrative Court;
- within three months of the decision;
- using appropriate claim form; and
- supporting documents.

In the breakdown of a judicial review problem the first step is to determine:

- whether the dispute concerns 'public law';
- who can bring a challenge; and
- who can be challenged.

The second step is to set out the basic procedure.

The third step is to consider whether and, if so to what extent, the rules of natural justice apply.

The fourth step is to determine whether the rules of natural justice have been breached. This can be broken down into a number of stages. The first stage involves consideration of whether the trial has been fair. Consider, in particular:

- notice;
- opportunity to present a case;
- evidence;
- the right to cross-examine;
- legal representation.

The next stage concerns whether there is a real likelihood of bias.

You should back up all your points with relevant case law.

Glossary

Abuse of process In the context of judicial review, this means the unreasonable use of civil procedure for the purpose of gaining unfair advantage over an opponent in a legal dispute.

Ad hoc committees 'Ad hoc' means 'for this purpose'. An ad hoc committee is set up by Parliament for a specific reason and ceases to exist when its task is finished.

Collective Cabinet responsibility Any policy decision reached by the Cabinet has to be supported thereafter by all members of the Cabinet whether they approve of it or not, unless they feel compelled to resign.

Common law The common law is made up of judge-made rules applied in decided cases which apply throughout England and Wales.

Constitutional practices or conventions Informal political rules adopted by those who participate in the process of government, which are considered binding to a varying extent but which are not enforceable in the courts.

Control orders These impose conditions on where a person can go and what they can do.

Convention right In the **Human Rights Act 1998**, 'Convention right' means:

1. The rights contained in **Arts 2–12** and **14 ECHR;**

2. **Arts 1–3 First Protocol;** and

3. **Arts 1** and **2 Sixth Protocol.**

Delegated legislation Regulations and other laws made by government ministers empowered to do so by statute. The empowering statute may require such regulations to be scrutinized and approved by Parliament before they come into effect.

Directive A Directive is a legislative act of the European Union which requires member states to achieve a particular result without dictating the means of achieving that result. It can be distinguished from European Union regulations which are self-executing and do not require any implementing measures. Directives can be adopted by means of a variety of legislative procedures depending on the subject matter.

His/Her Majesty's Principal Secretaries of State Senior ministers who lead most, but not all central government departments. They are members of the Privy Council and the Cabinet.

Illegality In Lord Diplock's words, this ground means that the decision-maker must understand correctly the law that regulates his decision-making power and must give effect to it.

Injunction This is a discretionary court order which can be used to stop something being done or require something to be discontinued. It can also be used to order something to be done.

Judicial review According to the **Pre-Action Protocol on Judicial Review,** judicial review allows people with a sufficient interest in a decision or action of a public body to ask a judge to review the lawfulness of:

- an enactment; or

- a decision, action, or failure to act in relation to the exercise of a public function.

Jurisdictional error At common law, jurisdictional error developed as a ground of review which was available where a tribunal or inferior court (as opposed to an administrator such as a minister or public servant) purported to exercise jurisdiction in excess of that which had been conferred upon it, or failed to exercise jurisdiction which it properly had.

Justiciability This means that a matter is capable of being decided by a court.

Ministers of the Crown A Minister of the Crown is the formal constitutional term used to describe a member of His/Her Majesty's Government. Secretaries of State are Ministers of the Crown. The term indicates that the person appointed serves in theory at His/Her Majesty's Pleasure, and advises the monarch. In practice, all Ministers of the Crown are members of and are accountable to Parliament.

Non-jurisdictional error Under the traditional doctrine, non-jurisdictional (ie non-judicially reviewable unless on the face of the record) errors, are errors of law made by a tribunal or inferior court in the course of exercising jurisdiction which it properly has.

Ouster clause Any provision of an Act of Parliament which purports to limit or exclude the supervisory jurisdiction of the High Court.

Preliminary ruling To ensure the effective and uniform application of EU legislation and to prevent divergent interpretations, national courts may, and sometimes must, turn to the Court of Justice and ask that it clarify a point concerning the interpretation of Community law, in order, for example, to ascertain whether their national legislation complies with that law.

Private members' bills Private members' bills are Public Bills introduced by MPs and Lords who are not government ministers. As with other Public Bills their purpose is to change the law as it applies to the general population.

Procedural impropriety A decision of a public body suffers from procedural impropriety if, in the process of its making a decision, the procedures prescribed by statute have not been followed or if the 'rules of natural justice' have not been adhered to.

Proportionality Proportionality is a requirement that a decision is proportionate to the aim that it seeks to achieve.

Public Accounts Committee The Committee of Public Accounts is appointed by the House of Commons to examine the accounts showing the appropriation of the sums granted by Parliament to meet the public expenditure, and of such other accounts laid before Parliament as the Committee may think fit.

Public authority According to **s 6(3) Human Rights Act 1998** 'public authority' includes:

1. a court or tribunal, and

2. any person certain of whose functions are functions of a public nature

but does not include either House of Parliament or a person exercising functions in connection with proceedings in Parliament.

Public body Any organization whose functions are of a governmental nature whose powers are not wholly based on agreement.

Public interest This is a wide subjective principle usually referring to the safety and welfare of the state.

Public interest immunity This is a principle of English common law under which the English courts can grant a court order allowing one litigant to refrain from disclosing evidence to the other litigants where disclosure would be damaging to the public interest. This is an exception to the usual rule that all parties in litigation must disclose any evidence that is relevant to the proceedings. In making a PII order, the court has to balance the public interest in the administration of justice (which demands that relevant material is available to the parties to litigation) and the public interest in maintaining the confidentiality of certain documents whose disclosure would be damaging.

Regulation A Regulation is a legislative act of the European Union which becomes immediately enforceable as law in all member states simultaneously. Regulations can be distinguished from Directives which, at least in principle, need to be transposed into national law.

Republic A country which has an executive or non-executive president as head of state.

Royal Assent The monarch's acceptance of a parliamentary bill which has either received the necessary assents of the House of Lords and the House of Commons or has received the assent of the House of Commons under the **Parliament Acts 1911** and **1949**.

Royal Commissions A Royal Commission is a major government public inquiry into an issue.

Royal Prerogative The judicially accepted definition of Royal Prerogative is that it represents the residue of arbitrary and discretionary power possessed by the Crown.

Rule of law The rule of law implies the equal subordination of governmental bodies to the substantive and procedural requirements of the law so as to prevent them exercising purely arbitrary and discretionary power. It also embodies the idea that everyone is equally subject to the law and that the rights of citizens are protected by the legal system.

Separation of powers The separation of powers is capable of meaning that:

- the same persons should not form part of more than one of the three organs of government;
- one organ of government should not control or interfere with the work of another; and
- one organ of government should not exercise the functions of another.

Standing committees These are established by an official and binding vote providing for their scope and powers. 'Standing' in this context means that they are permanent. Standing committees meet on a regular or irregular basis dependent upon their enabling Act, and retain any power or oversight claims originally given them until subsequent official actions of the committee of the whole (changes to law or by-laws) disband the committee or change their duties and powers.

Supremacy of law In this context it means that governmental power is based on law rather than arbitrary force exercisable with absolute discretion.

Ultra vires This is a Latin phrase that literally means 'beyond the powers'.

Unreasonableness Under Lord Diplock's classification, a decision is irrational if it is so outrageous in its defiance of logic or of accepted moral standards that no sensible person who had applied his mind to the question could have arrived at it.

Victim Under **s 7(7) Human Rights Act 1998** a person is a victim of an unlawful act only if he would be a victim for the purposes of **Art 34 ECHR** if proceedings were brought in the European Court of Human Rights in respect of that act.

Whip system The aim of the whip system is to maintain party discipline within Parliament. Whips are MPs or peers appointed by each party to maintain party discipline. In a sense they are personnel managers who convey information between party leaders and backbench members. Part of their role, however, is to encourage members of their party to vote in the way that their party would like.

Index

Concentrate QUESTIONS & ANSWERS

Revision & study guides
from the **No. 1** legal education publisher

Q&A
PUBLIC LAW

Third Edition

Richard Clements

practise technique   boost your confidence   achieve success

OXFORD

→
LOOK
INSIDE

8 Freedom to protest and police powers

ARE YOU READY?

The questions in this chapter concern the law relating to public order and police powers of arrest, entry, and search and seizure. In order to attempt these questions, you need to have covered all of these topics in your work and your revision:

- the **Public Order Act 1986** and the case law interpreting the provisions of this Act;
- obstruction of the highway;
- breach of the peace;
- the **Criminal Justice and Public Order Act 1994** and the case law interpreting the provisions of this Act;
- the **Police and Criminal Evidence Act 1984** and the case law interpreting the provisions of this Act;
- the **European Convention on Human Rights**, particularly **Articles 11** and **10**.

KEY DEBATES

Debate: The Complexity of the Law

The **Public Order Act 1986** and the **Criminal Justice and Public Order Act 1994** are two major Acts of Parliament governing this area of law. There are also offences such as obstruction of the highway, the concept of breach of the peace, and the **European Convention on Human Rights**. Many of these provisions overlap, making the law complex enough for a law lecturer to interpret, let alone a police officer or protester.

⊙

Debate: Public Order or Freedom to Protest

The **Public Order Act 1986** increased police powers to deal with public protest, which has been the general tendency of most modern legislation. The **Criminal Justice and Public Order Act 1994** was targeted at the activities of certain groups of whom Parliament disapproved. It criminalized some types of trespass and increased police powers to deal with public assemblies. Is there an increased danger to the public from processions or demonstrations or are we just less tolerant of disruptions to our daily lives?

Debate: The Police and Criminal Evidence Act 1984

The **Police and Criminal Evidence Act 1984** was generally seen as a good modernization of the law, bringing together different statutes, case law, and codes of practice into one place. Is it, however, unnecessarily complex and bureaucratic, making it difficult to understand for both police and suspect?

Q QUESTION 1

Twelve members of the 'No Abortion Campaign' are protesting on the pavement outside an abortion clinic on Eastby High Street. They are displaying placards with the words 'No to abortion' and speaking to each woman who enters the clinic, asking her to consider whether she is 'doing the right thing'.

The owner of the abortion clinic summons the police and PC Kent arrives. She stands on the pavement observing the 'No Abortion Campaign' members, but takes no action.

Then twelve members of a group in favour of abortion, 'Women's Choice', arrive and start shouting at the 'No Abortion Campaign' members, using insulting words. Three of the members of 'Women's Choice' throw stones, breaking the windows of the clinic.

PC Kent asks the 'No Abortion Campaign' members to leave, which they unwillingly do. They slowly walk the half a mile down the High Street to the railway station.

PC Kent, together with other police officers who have joined her, follow them to the railway station where they arrest them.

Advise the 'No Abortion Campaign' on whether they have committed any public order offences and whether the police actions are legal.

! CAUTION!

- There are a lot of public order offences; concentrate on those actually raised by the facts of the question.
- In a problem like this there may also be breaches of the ordinary criminal law; concentrate on public order law.
- There are statutes that regulate this area, but do not forget to use case law as well.

practise technique > boost your confidence > achieve success

Concentrate QUESTIONS & ANSWERS

DIAGRAM ANSWER PLAN

Identify the issues	■ Identify the legal issues: Is the 'No Abortion Campaign' committing any public order offences? Is 'Women's Choice' committing any public order offences? What powers do the police have to maintain public order?
Relevant law	■ Outline the relevant law: statutory, general principles, and case law, in particular: the **Public Order Act 1986**; the **European Convention on Human Rights**, in particular **Article 11**; breach of the peace; and obstruction of the highway
Apply the law	■ Have the 'No Abortion Campaign' obstructed the highway or used threatening, abusive, or insulting words? ■ Have 'Women's Choice' committed riot or violent disorder? ■ From the police point of view, is this a breach of the peace, public assembly, or procession?
Conclude	■ Have public order offences been committed? ■ What does this allow the police to do? ■ What should the police do?

SUGGESTED ANSWER

¹ A brief introduction, setting out what the answer is going to look at, can be enough.

There are a number of public order offences that could have been committed by both the 'No Abortion Campaign' and 'Women's Choice' and also a number of powers that PC Kent could have used to control the developing situation, which can be found in both public order legislation and common law.¹

A gathering on the pavement has been held to be obstruction of the highway in *Arrowsmith v Jenkins* **[1963] 2 QB 561**. It is still the offence of wilful obstruction, even if there was no intention to obstruct and even if no one was actually obstructed. The highway can only be used for passage and repassage and purposes incidental to that movement. However, the European Court of Human Rights has ruled, in *Plattform Ärzte für das Leben* **(1988) 13 EHRR 204**, that there is a right to hold meetings in a public place. Another case more favourable to the 'No Abortion Campaign' is *DPP v Jones (Margaret)*

[1999] 2 AC 240, where the House of Lords held that a small protest on a roadside verge near Stonehenge was not an obstruction of the highway, as there is a right of peaceful assembly. The protest by the 'No Abortion Campaign' is certainly peaceful and quite small in number, so it is probably not obstruction of the highway.[2]

They also do not seem to be committing any offences under the **Public Order Act 1986**. They are not using 'threatening, abusive or insulting words or behaviour', nor are their signs 'threatening, abusive or insulting', and there are no threats of violence, so there is no offence under **s. 4** of the Act. Even the lesser offence in **s. 5**, where it is enough for 'disorderly behaviour' to be likely to cause 'harassment, alarm or distress', is not committed. *DPP v Clarke, Lewis, O'Connell & O'Keefe* [1992] **Crim LR 60** also involved a protest outside an abortion clinic,[3] but the protesters had no intent to be threatening, abusive, or insulting. All that the defendants did in that case was to show pictures of an aborted foetus to police officers and one passerby. To commit an offence under **s. 5** the protest needs to be more vigorous, as in *DPP v Fidler and Moran* [1992] **1 WLR 91**, where there were also shouts and threats against those attending the clinic, in addition to the display of photographs and models of dead foetuses. *Percy v DPP* (2002) **166 JP 93** confirms that the 'No Abortion Campaign' is unlikely to have committed an offence. Even if behaviour is held to be insulting, this must be balanced against the right to freedom of expression under **Article 10 of the European Convention on Human Rights**.[4]

'Women's Choice' appears to have committed criminal offences.[5] Unlike the 'No Abortion Campaign', they are using insulting words, which seem intended or likely to cause their opponents to fear immediate personal violence: *R v Horseferry Road Magistrate ex parte Siadatan* [1991] **1 All ER 324**.

There is also a lesser offence under **s. 5 of the Public Order Act 1986**. It seems likely that the 'No Abortion Campaign' would experience harassment, alarm, or distress, unless the courts decide that by their frequent protesting they will have become used to insulting, threatening, and abusive words or behaviour, rather like the police officers in *DPP v Orum* [1988] **3 All ER 449**.

It is possible that more serious offences have been committed. **Section 1 of the Public Order Act 1986** defines riot as '12 or more persons who are present together use or threaten violence for a common purpose . . . as would cause a person of reasonable firmness present at the scene to fear for his personal safety'. There are over twelve members of 'Women's Choice' and according to **s. 7** 'violence' can include violence towards property, not just people, and would include the throwing of missiles: *Mitsui Sumitomo Insurance v*

[2] The preceding paragraph compares different cases, from the English courts and the **ECHR**, applies them to the facts, and comes to a conclusion.

[3] There are many cases on the meaning of **s. 5**. I happened to know of some about abortion clinics, which feature in this problem, but you could easily use other **s. 5** cases instead.

[4] Under the **Human Rights Act 1998** we must attempt to interpret English law to conform to the **ECHR**.

[5] Remember, there are two opposing groups in this problem, doing different things and committing different offences.